D1029193

# FURY BEACH

# FURY BEACH

THE
FOUR-YEAR ODYSSEY
OF CAPTAIN JOHN ROSS
AND THE *Victory*

## RAY EDINGER

HARRISON COUNTY
PUBLIC LIBRARY

**B**
BERKLEY BOOKS, NEW YORK

Most Berkley Books are available at special quantity discounts for bulk purchases for sales promotions, premiums, fund-raising, or educational use. Special books, or book excerpts, can also be created to fit specific needs.

For details, write: Special Markets, The Berkley Publishing Group, 375 Hudson Street, New York, New York 10014.

A Berkley Book
Published by The Berkley Publishing Group
A division of Penguin Putnam Inc.
375 Hudson Street
New York, New York 10014

Lyrics to "The Sea" SC-259, a song by Barry Cornwall and Sigismond Neukomn, courtesy of Dartmouth College Library.

Copyright © 2003 by Ray Edinger
Book design by Tiffany Kukec

All rights reserved.
This book, or parts thereof, may not be reproduced in any form without permission. The scanning, uploading, and distribution of this book via the Internet or via any other means without the permission of the publisher is illegal and punishable by law. Please purchase only authorized electronic editions, and do not participate in or encourage electronic piracy of copyrighted materials. Your support of the author's rights is appreciated.
BERKLEY and the "B" design are trademarks belonging to Penguin Putnam Inc.

First edition: April 2003

Library of Congress Cataloging-in-Publication Data

Edinger, Ray.
Fury Beach : the four-year odyssey of Captain John Ross and the Victory /
Ray Edinger.—Berkley hardcover ed.
p. cm.
Includes bibliographical references and index.
ISBN 0-425-18845-0
I. Ross, John, Sir, 1777–1856. 2. Victory (Ship) 3. Arctic regions—Discovery and exploration—British. 4. Northwest Passage—Discovery and exploration—British. 5. Canada, Northern—Discovery and exploration—British. I. Title.

G635.R6 E45 2003
910'.9163'27—dc21
2002034263

PRINTED IN THE UNITED STATES OF AMERICA

10   9   8   7   6   5   4   3   2   1

*To Yvonne*

3-03  03-1330  mount  1

The winter went, the summer went,
The winter came around;
But the hard, green ice was strong as death,
And the voice of hope sank to a breath,
Yet caught at every sound.

George H. Boker,
from "A Ballad of Sir John Franklin"

# Contents

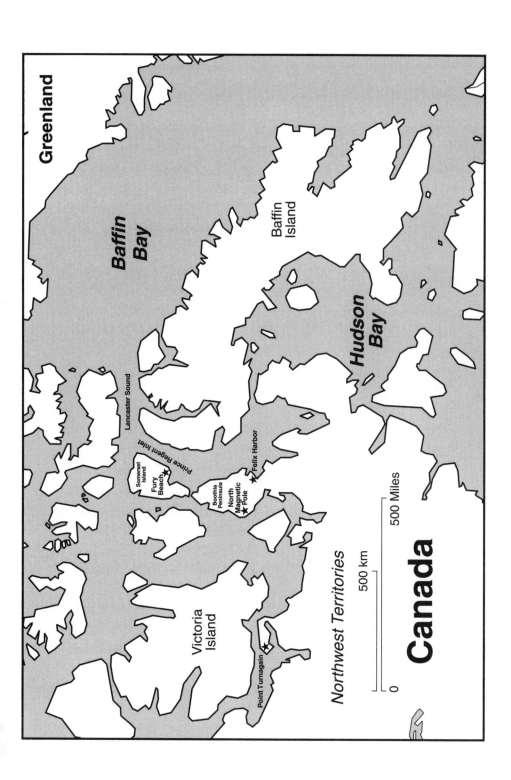

# Preface

I admit to a morbid curiosity about adventures in cold, icy regions—the more tragic, the better. I can't recall exactly when I first discovered my fascination. Yet, I remember as a young boy fifty years ago reading Maurice Herzog's tale of his disastrous experience climbing Mount Annapurna. Lying on the living room floor, warm and dry, I was mesmerized by the pictures and narrative. There he was, his gloves skittering down the mountainside, forever lost to him, and his horribly frostbitten hands, their frozen flesh hanging in ribbons!

Over the years Herzog became just a dim memory. Then one depressing wintry afternoon I visited the local bookstore for a little pick-me-up. Little? I came home with Pierre Berton's 672-page *Arctic Grail*. Not only did the tales fascinate me and feed my latent and forgotten curiosity, but the book unearthed a quirk that I had not known dwelt within me—bibliomania. Would it be possible, I wondered, to read the narratives of these nineteenth-century Arctic explorers in their original published form?

When I inquired at my local library, the librarian advised that although the book I sought had been out of print for eons she had a copy in the stacks—that tantalizing, forbidden place. In a few minutes she returned and handed me a musty, stained, and frayed two-volume set, its loosened leather covers held in place by neatly tied satin ribbons. Could I actually borrow these? Yes, she nodded with a hesitant smile. Clutching my find, I trudged home through the deepening snow. Over the next week or so, I read the wonderful narrative and began to dream and scheme of having my very own copy. And I knew it just *had* to be an edition that was printed and published while the long-forgotten explorer was still alive.

Since that snowy day, I've learned much about book collecting as one Arctic book inexorably led to another, and this succession of purchases in the polar genre continued to define the primary parameters of my collection. Yet, no mere collector was I. I *read* the books. I devoured the books. I assimilated the books. I digested the books. I lived with the books and the books lived with me. With passion, I perused each page and memorized whole passages. I loved the heroes and despised the villains. I shuddered at the explorers' incompetence and marveled at their ingenuity. And as I collected and read and studied, I learned about the tragedy of Sir John Franklin, the heroics of Sir James Ross, the obsession of Sir John Barrow, the accomplishments of Sir William Edward Parry, and the shame of Sir John Ross.

The shame? Indeed, John Ross had not fared well with historians. His reputation, it seemed, was destined to be eternally darkened by his "infamous" 1818 voyage to Baffin Bay. But why? How could this man, who brought most of his men safely through four Arctic winters, charted miles of new coastline, lived peacefully among the Inuit, and oversaw the discovery of the North Magnetic Pole, be given such short shrift? Surely, there was more to the story. Perhaps *Fury Beach* will uncover glints of sunlight within the cloudy reputation of Captain Sir John Ross. You decide.

I extend a special, heartfelt "thank you" to Colleen Sell for her encouragement, her advice on my proposal package and initial chapters, and her warm friendship as I traveled toward the fulfillment of this dream. And where would I be without the guidance and enthusiasm of my literary agent? Thank you, thank you, Elizabeth Frost-Knappman of New England Publishing Associates, not only for your faith in this project, but also for your suggestions, which greatly improved the telling of the tale of Barrow, Ross and *Victory*. To my editor at Berkley Books, Natalee Rosenstein, I extend my genuine appreciation and gratitude.

I offer sincere thanks to all those persons and institutions who responded so ably and graciously to my requests for information: Ali Grandey, Sibley Music School, Eastman School of Music, Rochester, New York; Sarah I. Hartwell and Stanley Brown, Dartmouth College Library, Hanover, New Hampshire; Stephen Z. Nonack, Boston Athenaeum; Laura Pereira, New Bedford Whaling Museum, New Bedford, Massachusetts; Martin Ruddy, National Library of Canada, Ottawa; Robert Sandford, Canmore, Alberta, Canada; and Elizabeth Verity, National Maritime Museum, London. I also give thanks to the

British Library, the New York Public Library, the Buffalo and Erie County Public Libraries, and the Rochester Public Library for the use of their priceless archives and holdings.

Lastly, I reserve a flaming "thank you" for my dear wife, Yvonne Morris-Edinger, to whom this book is dedicated. Without her unfailing belief in me, her beautiful expressions of encouragement, and the creation of an atmosphere that was delightfully conducive to writing, this book would not be.

# *Introduction*

THE year 1829 brought the eleventh consecutive year that Captain John Ross of the Royal Navy was denied command of a ship. Although he had been at sea since the unusually young age of nine, had served on thirty-six ships in His Majesty's Royal Navy—five of which he commanded—had been promoted through the ranks to Captain, and had been honored and awarded for his services in the Napoleonic Wars, his navy career came to a sudden halt in the winter of 1818–19 at the actions and opinions of one man—John Barrow.

As Second Secretary of the Admiralty, John Barrow was Great Britain's strongest advocate for polar exploration in the first half of the nineteenth century. More expeditions were conducted to the Arctic under his direction than during any other period. Barrow's parade of polar campaigns began in the spring of 1818, when he launched a two-pronged expedition to search for a shortcut to the Orient: one arm to seek the Northwest Passage; the other to sail over the North Pole. The Admiralty awarded command of the Northwest Passage contingent to John Ross.

The North Pole team returned in just four months after ice severely damaged one of its two ships, having accomplished literally nothing. John Ross's search for the Northwest Passage, on the other hand, accomplished much, although it, too, failed to achieve its primary goal of finding a shortcut to the Orient. Among Ross's achievements were discovery of an Inuit tribe who had never had contact with outsiders, discovery of the phenomenal red snow of Greenland, confirmation of the existence of Baffin Bay and mapping the coastline, disproval of the existence of the Sunken Land of Buss, and even establishment of a depth record (1,000 fathoms) for collecting specimens of marine life using Ross's own invention, the deep-sea clam.

Yet, unfortunately for Ross, he had missed his opportunity to discover the Northwest Passage. Although he had sailed about eighty miles down its length, Ross concluded that Lancaster Sound, extending from the west side of Baffin Bay, was not an opening to the passage and, thus, ordered his ships home—a decision that would haunt him the rest of his life.

Although disappointed with the failure of the North Pole venture, Barrow accepted the outcome with professional resignation. But when he heard that Ross might have missed an opportunity to sail through the Northwest Passage, Barrow was livid. He vented his rage with sarcasm and facetious acrimony through both a book and also a fifty-page article in the *Quarterly Review*. In the *Review*, he all but called Ross a coward... although Barrow, himself, hid behind the anonymity of the article. Barrow scoffed that Ross's mind was "impenetrably dull or intentionally perverse" and that he had spent too much time with the natives "pulling of noses" (an Inuit gesture of friendship). Of Ross's published narrative, he mocked that it was "of that kind of manufacture not worth the paper on which it is printed." To Ross's taking possession of what is today's Baffin Island, Barrow quipped, "the object is worthless . . . a barren, uninhabited country, covered with ice and snow, the only subjects of His Majesty . . . of his newly acquired dominions, consisting of half-starved bears, deer, foxes, white hares, and such other creatures. . . ."

Barrow's widely read venom moved sentiment against Ross. In the public's eye, his voyage began to look like sheer folly. A satirical cartoon published by George Cruikshank depicted Ross strutting at the head of a long procession that carried a bucket of red snow, a dead polar bear, and other voyage artifacts to the British Museum. Although the *Times* wrote in Ross's favor and most of his fellow officers rallied behind him, including the Lords of the Admiralty, Captain John Ross's career was stalled. John Barrow, the powerful Second Secretary of the Admiralty, held the reins to all exploratory expeditions to the Arctic, a position he would hold for the next twenty-six years.

Barrow sent six more expeditions to the Arctic from 1819 through 1827. None involved John Ross, despite his appeals and proposals to the Admiralty, including a proposal in 1827 to use a steam-propelled vessel. Obviously blackballed, yet determined to prove himself and continue his exploration in the Arctic, Captain John Ross sought and obtained private funding to conduct his own expedition.

At last, having found a sponsor, Ross, his crew, and his paddle-steamship *Victory* were ready in May 1829—more than ten years after the Baffin Bay setback—to embark for the Northwest Passage . . . and Captain John Ross's vindication?

# Characters

THOMAS ABERNETHY, *Victory's second mate*

ADLURAK, *a lively, attractive Inuk and wife of Tiagashu*

AJOUA, *an old woman and mother of Tulluahiu*

ALICTU, *feeble father of Tiagashu and first Inuk to communicate with the crew of* Victory

APELLAGLIU, *the doting, chubby wife of Ikmallik and a sister to Tulluahiu*

AWACK, *a nephew of Ikmallik and Inuk guide to Commander James Ross*

JOHN BARROW, *Second Secretary of the Admiralty and Captain John Ross's nemesis*

THOMAS BLANKY, *Victory's first mate; a highly competent sailor*

FELIX BOOTH, *a distiller of gin, philanthropist, sheriff of London, and Captain Ross's sponsor*

ALEXANDER BRUNTON, *Victory's first engineer*

ANTHONY BUCK, *an epileptic seaman aboard* Victory

HENRY EYRE, *an old sailor and Victory's cook*

WILLIAM HARDY, *Victory's principal stoker*

IKMALLIK, *an Inuk whose mapping skills earned him the appellation the "Hydrographer"*

WILLIAM LIGHT, *Victory's steward; he despised Captain Ross and sought to tarnish his reputation*

## Characters

GEORGE MACDIARMID, Victory's surgeon

JAMES MARSLIN, Victory's armorer; a sickly man

OOBLOORIA, son of Ikmallik and Apellagliu and Inuk guide for Commander Ross

OTOOGIU, Inuk Angekok and friend of Tulluahiu

WILLIAM EDWARD PARRY, a highly successful Arctic explorer and a favorite of John Barrow

POYETTAK, an Inuk guide for Commander Ross

COMMANDER JAMES CLARK ROSS, a tireless Arctic explorer and nephew to Captain Ross

CAPTAIN JOHN ROSS, Victory's captain and leader of the expedition

GEORGE TAYLOR, Victory's third mate

WILLIAM THOM, Victory's purser

CHIMHAM THOMAS, Victory's carpenter; a compassionate man, he kept Tulluahiu supplied with wooden legs

TIAGASHU, a frail but hard-working Inuk and good friend of Captain Ross

TIRIKSHIU, wife of Tulluahiu, sister of Ikmallik, and an excellent cartographer

TULLUAHIU, a one-legged Inuk for whom Chimham Thomas made wooden legs

# CHAPTER ONE

# A Desperate *Victory* Makes Fury Beach

### (August 1829–October 1829)

*P*RINCE *Regent Inlet, August 12, 1829, 2 A.M.* "Let fly the storm trysail sheet," shouted First Mate Thomas Blanky. "Put up the helm and hoist the storm jib. Reef the boom-foresail." *Victory* reeled about but still received a violent shock on the port side bow as she glanced off the thick ice, which had been hidden from view by a heavy fog. Blanky's only warning that something lay ahead was breakers booming against the edge of the ice pack. As *Victory* rebounded, the crew set all sail the ship could carry and drove her through a lead to the lee side of the pack. There she remained secure for the night, sheltered from the ice boulders dashed about by the gale. The next morning, the storm abated, and Captain Ross ordered the mainsail set. To everyone's great mortification, however, a strong current pushed *Victory* right by their destination, Fury Beach, site of the wreck of the HMS *Fury*. *Victory's* crew grew anxious. Would their ship fall to the same forces that wrecked HMS *Fury?* Would they freeze to death on the barren, stony shore?

Rapidly coalescing ice, a swift current, hidden rocks, no wind, fog, and too close to the North Magnetic Pole for compasses to function reliably, all worked against Ross and the *Victory*. But unlike HMS *Fury*, Captain Ross's *Victory* was equipped with the latest marvel of the blossoming Industrial Revolution: a steam engine. Surely, the engine would halt *Victory*'s out-of-control drift that carried her beyond the life-saving stores at Fury Beach. Ross ordered the steam up. Down in the hold, the stoker shoveled coal while the engineer worked the control valves. Boiling seawater soon turned to steam, and the pistons slid back and forth with earsplitting blasts. The paddle wheels turned, slowly at first; then more rapidly as the pressure built. Fifteen pounds of steam. Twenty pounds. Thirty. Suddenly, steam screamed from every pipe and fitting. Leaking water doused the coals. The engine hissed and fell silent. The paddle wheels stopped. *Victory* again drifted at the mercy of the current.

Her crew looked at one another in the silence. Their stomachs reminded them that provisions were running low. Could they still make landfall at Fury Beach? And if not, how would they survive without the wrecked *Fury*'s abandoned provisions?

Four years prior to the voyage of the *Victory*, two other British ships of discovery, HMSs *Hecla* and *Fury*, were the first ships to travel down the ice-choked Prince Regent Inlet. These ships, like the *Victory*, were also in quest of the fabled Northwest Passage.

That expedition was under command of thirty-five-year-old Captain William Edward Parry (later Sir Edward). Parry was born in Bath in

1790, the eighth child of a fashionable doctor who counted Jane Austen among his patients. At the age of twelve, Parry signed onboard the flagship of the Royal Navy Channel Fleet, *Ville de Paris*. His father had been attending to the fleet admiral's favorite niece, who had become ill, and this connection surely helped Parry obtain the position aboard the ship. Young Parry carried himself well and excelled in his naval career so that by the age of nineteen he was already a lieutenant. The competent, charismatic, six-foot-tall young officer with wavy chestnut hair was soon the darling of John Barrow, Second Secretary of the Admiralty. Under Barrow's tutelage, Captain William Edward Parry grew to be perhaps the most successful British explorer of the Arctic in the early nineteenth century.

Then, on the third Arctic expedition under Parry's command, the *Hecla* and *Fury* ran into trouble when, about ninety miles down Prince Regent Inlet, a sudden shift in wind direction rapidly closed the ice channel through which the ships sailed. The *Hecla* escaped to open water, but the *Fury* was caught. Squeezed in the ice's grasp, *Fury*'s timbers moaned and her beams cracked like gunshots. Water poured in. For forty-eight nonstop hours, a third of *Fury*'s crew manned her four pumps. Their hands, already stiff from the icy water, turned raw with the constant friction of the pump ropes. Unlaying the ropes to soften them was little help. Outside, their fellow mates slipped and fell on the icy deck as they hauled on hawsers fastened to the ice ahead, trying to work the ship into open water. But the exhausted men soon lost control. The unrelenting ice forced *Fury* onto a stony beach. Driven almost completely up on the shore, she heeled over, her keel and stern post broken and nine feet of water in her hold.

The crew carried her provisions ashore, still hoping to heave her down to make repairs. Perhaps they could save her by foddering—stuffing the holes with cordage and passing a sail underneath to wrap the hull in a waterproof blanket. To the officers inspecting the broken ship, however, it was obvious the damage was fatal.

Abandoning her on the beach named for her, *Fury*'s crew and officers aborted their quest for the Northwest Passage and returned home to England in the still seaworthy *Hecla*.


Now, four years later, Captain John Ross took up the quest for the Northwest Passage where Edward Parry's *Hecla* and *Fury* had left off.

Explorations along the northern coast of Canada by Samuel Hearne in 1771, Alexander Mackenzie in 1789, and John Franklin in 1819–22 and 1825–27 had proved that a polar sea bounds North America at about the 69th parallel. These explorations, combined with discoveries by Parry in 1821–25, left only about 500 miles unexplored between Prince Regent Inlet and Franklin's farthest point east where he turned back: Point Turnagain at 68° 33' N, 109° 10' W. Bridging this gap would complete the discovery of the Northwest Passage. Captain Ross's plan was to determine if there were any channels through the western shore of Prince Regent Inlet to Point Turnagain. If such an opening existed, Ross would sail through it, make his way west along the Canadian north coast to Bering Strait, and sail out into the Pacific Ocean.

Captain John Ross, a somewhat overweight, bluff Scotsman, had already been at sea for forty-three of his fifty-one years when *Victory* set sail in 1829. Clearly destined for a life at sea, legend has it that when Ross was three years old, his father found him one day paddling around the garden pond in a tub. Yet Ross was a homebody. Having indentured himself to the navy at the unusually young age of nine, he returned to his family's home in Stranraer, Scotland, at every opportunity. Always drawn back to his roots, Ross was delighted when, in 1815, he received command of HMS *Driver*, which patrolled the Scottish coast and his childhood haunt, Loch Ryan.

John Ross's love for the sea touched every aspect of his life. North West Castle, his charming home overlooking Loch Ryan, was appointed throughout with a nautical theme. A camera obscura in the roof projected scenes of the surrounding countryside and seascape onto the walls of the castle. He had the front windows fitted with ports through which he could aim his telescope to view ships in the loch below. And when he returned home after the voyage to Fury Beach, Ross added a room to North West Castle that was a perfect replica of *Victory*'s cabin.

Ross's sea adventures kept him well occupied, and he did not marry until he was thirty-nine, when he took the hand of Christian Adair, a daughter of his second cousin. Christy, as Ross called her, bore him a daughter, who died in infancy, and a son, whom they named Andrew after Ross's father. Tragically, after just six years of marriage, Christy died.

In his early years in the navy, Ross saw considerable action during the Napoleonic Wars and was gravely wounded in 1806 while boarding a Spanish vessel. In hand-to-hand combat he suffered three saber slashes to his head, had both legs and one arm broken, and was pierced through the side by a bayonet. These new injuries were added to battle scars from 1801 and 1803 that already marred both his legs. Rugged, scarred, and toughened by navy combat, John Ross was, nonetheless, always the proper gentleman with the ladies. When Jane Griffin, later Lady

Franklin—husband to Sir John Franklin, one of the best known and most tragic of British Arctic explorers—was introduced to Ross at a dinner party, she described the disfigured, hardy sea captain, who seemed to take pleasure in talking with her, as

> *short, stout, sailor-looking & not very gentlemanly in his person, but his man-ners & his language are perfectly so; his features are coarse & thick, his eyes grey, his complexion ruddy, & his hair reddish sandy hue.—Yet notwith-standing his lack of beauty, he has a great deal of intelligence, benevolence, & good humour in his countenance.*

Ross was an accomplished, thorough sailor and a tough disciplinarian. Brought up under the strict rules of a man-of-war, in which instant obedience to a commander's orders were crucial, Ross was never able to gain the more easy-going demeanor appropriate for command of a scientific or exploratory ship. To *Victory's* crew, he often came across as stubborn and irascible. Ship's steward William Light wrote,

> *Capt. Ross himself was not a sociable character, but in extenuation of his reserve and haughtiness, it must be admitted that the school in which he had been bred, namely, the quarter deck of a British man-of-war, is not the one best adapted to teach a man urbanity and civility toward his inferior.*

Although well liked by his fellow officers, Ross's hot temper and refusal to admit wrong eventually resulted in his ill treatment by some of his colleagues and, most notably, by Second Secretary of the Admiralty, Sir John Barrow. Even Edward Parry, who served under Ross on his voyage to the Arctic in 1818, came to wonder about his former commander. When he first met Ross in 1818, Parry remarked, "He is a good-tempered, affable man in his manners . . . Ross is clever in the surveying way and is a good seaman. I like his appearance and manner very much." However, by 1835, after running up against Ross's intransigence, Parry expressed a different opinion. In a letter to John Franklin, Parry wrote, "That foolish man, Ross, is determined *always* to get himself in a hobble."

Ross was almost boyishly naive about the irritation he caused in others with his bull-headedness. Yet in spite of his obstinate ways, Ross's good sense of humor, coupled with a genuinely friendly and likeable manner, was a strong redeeming trait. That, along with his roughened countenance and his exploits in the Arctic Sea, made the square-shouldered, stocky captain a regular invitee to the fashionable drawing rooms of London.

Ross had chosen *Victory* for the expedition, in part, because she drew only seven and a half feet of water. Although this gave her an advantage in uncharted waters, the 150-ton *Victory* was too small to carry sufficient provisions for the planned fifteen-month voyage. To meet the needs, a second ship, the whaler *John,* was to accompany *Victory* as far as Fury Beach. At Fury Beach, the extra provisions in the *John* were to be transferred to the *Victory* to replace those already consumed. The *John,* loaded with the wrecked *Fury's* stores, would then head back to England, where the goods would be sold to help defray the expedition's expenses. Any whaling the *John* might do along the way would be an added bonus. At least, that was the plan.

John Ross was an early advocate of steam power and a recognized expert in the field. In 1828, he published his critically acclaimed *A Treatise on Navigation by Steam.* His attempts to sell the Admiralty on steam propulsion, however, were met with stalwart resistance. Nevertheless, Ross believed that steam was the answer to a chronic problem in navigating the ice-strewn waters of the Arctic. As he wrote in his journal,

> When the ice is open, or the sea navigable, it is either calm, or the wind is adverse, since it is to southerly winds that this state of things is owing: so that the sailing vessel is stopped exactly where everything else is in her favour, while the steam boat can make a valuable progress.

Ross held no doubt that the ship for his Arctic expedition *must* be equipped with steam propulsion. Yet steam power was still a recent innovation in 1829, when Ross commenced his voyage. Even though the U.S. ship *Savannah* had crossed the Atlantic under both sail and steam ten years earlier—thus purporting to have demonstrated steam's utility—she had been under steam for only one hundred and five hours of the twenty-nine-day voyage. Crossing the Atlantic solely under steam power would have to wait until 1838, when the *Sirius* made her historic voyage. In fact, steam propulsion during the first half of the nineteenth century was limited primarily to rivers, harbors, and coastal runs.

Notwithstanding, Ross's *Victory* was a steamer—the first ever in Arctic waters. Her engine drove two eleven-foot paddle wheels, one on each side of the ship. If ice threatened the wheels, the crew could hoist them from the water in about a minute's time. Propellers would have been a far superior arrangement. However, although Ross was ahead of his time and the concept of the screw propeller dates back to Archimedes, propellers were not used on ships until 1837, well after Ross's return from the Arctic.

To compensate for the engine's mass, her manufacturer chose not to install a flue, but to save weight by providing draft through a system of bellows. A series of gears transmitted power from the engine to the bellows and to the paddle wheels. Unfortunately, the design was faulty, and the bellows and gears required constant attention of the crew. That, combined with manning the engine's hand-operated pumps in a steamy ninety-five-degree environment deep in the hold of the ship, quickly exhausted the men. Early in the voyage, at least one man fainted and could not be revived until his mates carried him to fresh air. If this was not bad enough, the engine constantly broke down, and even when working to its fullest, its feeble power hardly made the effort worthwhile.

The first serious trouble with the machinery began just seven days into the voyage, when a key securing the starboard paddle to the main shaft snapped. Without any steel onboard to make a new one, the engineer made a replacement of iron. It, too, broke, rendering the whole contraption useless. Undaunted by the setback, Ross continued the voyage. After a week of repairs and making spare keys, reinventing some of the mechanical works, and rerigging the sails, Captain Ross found that by keeping the weather on the starboard side and operating just the lee paddle, *Victory* beat to windward as well as any vessel along the Scottish coast. With hopes high, Ross and his crew continued toward Loch Ryan for their rendezvous with the *John*, unaware of the tragedy that lay just ahead.

At ten in the morning of Monday, 8 June 1829, *Victory* tacked close to the Mull of Galloway, making fine progress. Down below, principal stoker William Hardy attended to the fickle steam engine. The iron monster hissed and fumed and whistled. Her two sixteen-inch pistons made a deafening blast as they completed each thirty-inch stroke. Connecting rods drove the whirring wheels, meshing gears, and reciprocating rods. In the coal-dust-darkened hold, Hardy reached across the machinery to oil a piston rod. Suddenly, the ship lurched and threw Hardy forward. He tried to catch himself, but his arm slipped between the rotating spokes of the massive guide wheel. In an instant, Hardy's entangled arm was torn asunder.

With extraordinary effort, Hardy managed to extricate himself from the machinery and struggled up the two ladders to Captain Ross on the main deck. Without exclamation or complaint, the dazed man showed Ross his left arm, shattered and nearly severed above the elbow. Eyeing the young man's splintered bone, torn muscle, and skin held together by a section of flesh, Ross knew the arm had to be amputated. Unfortunately, the ship's surgeon, George MacDiarmid, was not aboard. He had sailed ahead on the *John* and was already at Loch Ryan, a day's sail away. With no choice but to perform the amputation himself, Ross bemoaned, "I should have been much more at my ease in cutting away half a dozen masts in a gale than in thus 'doctoring' one arm."

Luckily, MacDiarmid's medicine chest was onboard. But when Ross called for the amputation saw, it was not to be found. Steeling himself, the captain applied a tourniquet, and securing "the only two arteries which I could find . . . I cut off the injured muscles and skin in such a way as I hoped sufficient to remove the dead and hazardous parts, and to leave materials for producing a decent stump." He left the protruding bone in its splintered state for the surgeon.

With a full press of sail and steam built to capacity, *Victory* hastened for the nearest port, just nine miles away. If they could beat the turn of the tide, engineer Hardy stood a good chance for proper medical care that same day. Suddenly, a loud crash told all onboard that the steam engine had failed again. The bellows flywheel had stripped its teeth. To compound the matter, water poured from virtually every seam in the boilers, "as if it had been predetermined that not a single atom of all this machinery should be aught but for vexation, obstruction, and evil," lamented Ross. The injured engineer's frantic mates followed the engine manufacturer's quaint instructions for stopping leaks: They loaded the boilers with potatoes and dung (oxen were onboard as a supply of beef)—but to no effect. The ship slowed. With the tide against them and barely any wind, the crew tacked to make port. But the seas and winds played against them. Hardy's care would have to wait till morning tide.

At eight o'clock the next morning, they moored at Port Logan. A coast guard colonel provided a spring-equipped cart to ease Hardy's conveyance to Ross's home at Stranraer. There, a Dr. Ritchie completed the operation with the assistance of Surgeon MacDiarmid, who had been summoned from Loch Ryan. Captain Ross had done his surgery well. William Hardy recovered sufficiently to return to practice his engineering at the establishment where he had worked before signing with the *Victory*.

With Hardy in good hands, the *Victory* proceeded to Loch Ryan, Scotland, to rendezvous with the *John*, only to find the *John*'s commander involved in a confrontation with the crew. The men refused to weigh anchor unless guaranteed the same pay regardless of whether the *John* came home with her hold full or empty of whale oil. Inasmuch as crew wages were customarily proportional to the catch, this was an outrageous demand, and Ross would hear none of it. Yet the men had an additional concern. They had heard about the *Fury*'s destruction and feared the *John* would suffer a similar fate, especially since the *John* did not have extra strengthening against the ice as the *Fury* had had. The last thing they wanted was to spend a winter trapped in the Arctic. Ross assured the men that they would be home in six months, and he further guaranteed that he would find them an abundance of whales. Catching the whales and filling the ship to earn their fair share, however, was the crew's business, and Ross was not about to guarantee what they might catch. Still, the crew was unconvinced. There was no persuading the "disorderly and dirty crew, who skulked and sneaked about the ship," said Ross.

Ross grumbled to *Victory's* men that such a crew of cowards as the *John's* was unworthy to join his expedition. "Shall we sail by ourselves?" Ross asked of his crew, who responded in unison with three hearty cheers. Even so, the stubborn Ross told the *John's* commander to muster the men of the mutinous ship. He demanded to know who was with him and who was not. Ross started with the first mate, Muirhead. "Are you with me?" shouted Ross. Muirhead retorted that he would not sail without a guarantee of one hundred and fifty tons of oil. "And you, Robb, Second Mate?" asked Ross. Same answer. Next, Ross turned to the boatswain and the harpooners and asked if they would assist in weighing anchor. The sailors swaggered before their mates and shot back a cocky refusal. In the next minute, the *John's* whole crew—with the exception of the cook, the cooper, and two hands—stood with the first mate and his cronies.

With a solid majority on their side, the mutineers tried to convince *Victory's* sailors to join them in a drunken binge. But when the *Victory's* crew remained true to Ross, the rebels moved to commandeer the whaleboats and head for shore. A scuffle broke out. Two boats were stove in, and a man fell overboard. Outnumbered more than two to one, Ross's nineteen men were powerless to stop the deserters. The best *Victory's* men could effect was to hiss the mutineers as they rowed away.

No mere mutiny, however, was going to foil the feisty Ross's plans. He didn't need the *John* and her troublesome crew. He would sail to Fury Beach alone and restock on the *Fury's* abandoned supplies. His loyal crew, joined by three of the *John's* hands, loaded the *Victory* with as much of the *John's* provisions as they could stow and sailed off. (The *John*, with almost the same crew to a man, experienced another mutiny the following year. The master was killed, and Muirhead and several loyalists were cast off, never to be heard from again. Shortly thereafter, the *John* went down off the western coast of Greenland. Most drowned.)

So it happened that, although not crucial to Ross's original scheme, attaining HMS *Fury's* provisions grew to utmost importance.


*Prince Regent Inlet, August 12, 1829.* Ross and his crew had successfully brought *Victory* 2,610 miles from England to the Arctic's Prince Regent Inlet, where the search for the Northwest Passage began in earnest. Now hampered by ice and a swift current that made it difficult for *Victory* to beat to windward, her situation grew alarmingly similar to the lost *Fury's*. Even if the leaky engine had worked, the paddle wheels would never have propelled the ship faster than two or three miles per hour. A thick fog settled in, obliging Ross and *Victory's* crew to wait it out in the lee of the ice pack. First Engineer Alexander Brunton used the quiet time to repair the engine—again.

After eleven hours of aimless drifting, the visibility improved and the *Victory* was on the move once more. Wending her way up the narrow channel between the shore and the ice pack in the center of Prince Regent Inlet, *Victory* worked her way back north toward Fury Beach. Progress was excruciatingly slow. Every couple hundred yards, the engine's steam pressure leaked away. The paddles ceased their slap, slap, slap. *Victory* meandered uselessly. While Brunton worked to rebuild steam, Ross took in the situation. What were his options? He could do nothing while waiting for the steam to rebuild. Or he could resort to the time-tested but back-breaking method of working a ship through ice—warping. Warping a ship involved drawing the ship ahead via a rope wrapped around the capstan, a giant, pulleylike device mounted on the forward deck.

Manning the capstan aboard a nineteenth-century sailing ship was an arduous task. All hands take part in the action at the mate's shout, "Man the capstan!" Hustling 'round, they heave with all their might on the capstan's five-foot bars. To coordinate the action, a chantyman begins to chant with the rest answering the italicized lines,

> O Storm-y he is dead an' gone;
> *To my way you storm a-long.*
> O Storm-y was a good old man;
> *Ay, ay, ay, Mis-ter Storm-a-long.*

To the gnarled old Ross, the choice of waiting to rebuild steam or warp the ship was an easy one. Back-breaking labor was the way of life at sea. Besides, with the exception of the officers, the seamen were all in their early twenties—plenty of robust, young hands for the task. With not a second thought, Ross commanded the crew to warp *Victory* forward.

At the instant of his order, two men jumped from the bow onto the ice. Others ondeck tossed down a hundred-pound ice anchor attached to a ten-inch hawser. The two men carried the anchor ahead about a hundred yards, where they chiseled a hole in the ice. As soon as the anchor was secured in the hole, they signaled their shipmates to start heaving at the capstan. "Man the capstan!" shouted First Mate Blanky.

Slowly the capstan turned, taking up the hawser. Verse after verse, the men kept up a steady pace as they heaved their way 'round and 'round, pushing with all their might against the stout oak bars, polished smooth by two score of rough hands.

> We'll dig his grave with a silver spade;
> *To my way you storm a-long.*
> And lower him down with a golden chain;
> *Ay, ay, ay, Mis-ter Storm-a-long.*

With every turn of the capstan, *Victory* warped ahead about six feet. The ten-inch hawser fortunately withstood the strain, and *Victory* moved forward as her wedge-shape bow divided the ice. Then, as soon as Brunton had the steam up, the crew rested and watched *Victory* paddle her way forward until the pressure leaked away again, usually after just fifteen minutes. Then it was back to the capstan.

After eight hours of alternating between steaming and warping, *Victory* retraced the distance the current had carried her, which brought the ship within five miles of Fury Beach. Every man who could be spared climbed the masts to look for signs of *Fury's* wreck. Commander James Ross, Captain Ross's nephew and a lieutenant aboard the *Fury* when she was lost four years earlier, thought he spotted a familiar headland. Remnants of tents at the abandoned site came into view as they rounded a point. Commander Ross took to a whaleboat to seek a safe harbor, but there were none to be found. Returning to the ship, the younger Ross

HARRISON COUNTY PUBLIC LIBRARY

reported to his uncle that he had located a "harbor" between a large iceberg and two smaller ones. It would suffice. The icebergs were securely grounded in sixteen feet of water and, better still, it was within a quarter-mile of Fury Beach.

With *Victory* safely in her harbor of ice, Captain Ross ordered cook Henry Eyre to prepare a hearty meal for his exhausted crew. While the men ate and rested, the two Rosses, accompanied by Purser William Thom and Surgeon MacDiarmid, went ashore.

Fury Beach is a narrow, stony shoreline backed by towering cliffs two to three hundred feet in height. Limestone formations in the cliffs create images of fantastic castles, fortified walls, and parapets. Icy water streams from deep ravines and dark crevices. Eroded channels in the cliffs and a jumble of pebbles and rocks at their bases testify to torrents during periods of heavy thaw. The steady fall of water accompanied by more rocks randomly crashing to the beach below and the eerie screams of hundreds of glaucous gulls circling above make the site a noisy and forbidding place. Even in August, the cold, salt-sea wind pushes the visitor away.

Four years of Arctic winters and visitations by polar bears had destroyed all but one of the tents. Crooked poles with tattered canvas dangling from their tops marked where the others had stood. Commander Ross looked for his notebook and collection of bird specimens he had left behind, but those, too, had been destroyed by the bears or the severe climate. He found HMS *Fury*'s main provisions, on the other hand, virtually intact: two mountains of canned meats and vegetables, casks of wine, spirits, sugar, bread, flour, cocoa, lime juice, and pickles, all in excellent condition. Donkin's patented canning process had not only done a remarkable job at preserving the life-saving meats and vegetables, but had also prevented foraging polar bears from detecting the contents. The crew dubbed the mound of provisions "The North Pole Victualling Yard."

Although there was no trace of the *Fury*'s hull, her spare sails, mizzen mast, anchors, hawsers, boatswain's and carpenter's stores, candles, cables, chains, carronades, and gunpowder—all of which had been piled ashore with the forlorn hope of heaving *Fury* down for repair—left a delighted Ross feeling as though he were at the dockside warehouses of Rotherhithe, with everything free for the taking.

The purser prepared a list of wants. Ship's steward William Light and Surgeon MacDiarmid rummaged about, selecting the best. For the next day and a half, the men ferried boatload after boatload to *Victory*. The immense bounty moved Ross to quip, "All that we could possibly stow away seemed scarcely to diminish the piles of canisters."

Before leaving the site, Ross abided by Edward Parry's request and ordered *Fury*'s remaining gunpowder blown up to prevent possible harm to Inuit who may happen upon it. Last, Ross placed in a collapsing dog kennel two bottles with notes about the voyage's progress.

The next day, Ross took sightings with his sextant, checked his chronometers, and, noting a difference of just sixteen miles between his observation and Parry's chart, embarked in earnest on his expedition—the quest for the Northwest Passage. "God bless Fury Beach" echoed off the steep cliffs as *Victory* drew away.

*August 15, 1829, Fury Beach.* Captain Ross pointed the *Victory* south for Cape Garry, the farthest landmark in Prince Regent Inlet sighted by Parry in 1825. Cape Garry marks the southern point of the deep Cresswell Bay, which Parry had considered a candidate for an opening to the

Northwest Passage. The loss of the *Fury*, however, had preempted Parry's exploring it. As Ross sailed by the bay, he correctly reasoned that, because there were no strong currents flowing out, it was truly a bay and not the hoped-for passage. They continued south down Prince Regent Inlet into unexplored territory. The terrain changed from the glowering cliffs of Fury Beach to low-lying rugged, barren hills. Ross delighted in the explorer's prerogative of naming newfound lands. About every three miles he named a cape, bay, harbor, island, or other landmark after his sponsor, relatives, or friends. Consequently, along the western coast of Prince Regent Inlet, we find on Ross's map Cape Clara, Fearnall Bay, Cape Esther, Lang River, Mount Oliver, Grimble Islands, Wilsons Bay, Murray Bay, and Cape Farnand.

At two in the morning of August 16, about thirty miles south of Cape Garry, Captain Ross ordered the anchor dropped. Ross and his fellow officers went ashore and took formal possession of the newfound land. They displayed the colors, drank a bumper of gin to the health of both King George IV and Felix Booth—Ross's patron and founder of the expedition—and gave three hearty cheers, which the men on board echoed. Ross named the land Boothia Felix, today's Boothia Peninsula.

As they wandered about their newly claimed land, Ross spotted a few plants and flowers, ancient graves of the Inuit, bones of a fox, and the teeth of a musk ox in the otherwise bleak and barren Boothia Peninsula. The one sign of animal life was a solitary bird resembling a lark. Ross named *Victory*'s anchorage Brentford Bay. An attempt was made to explore to the foot of the bay, but the season was too early and ice blocked the way.

(Brentford Bay actually does lead to the only western opening from Prince Regent Inlet. The passage, discovered in 1852, is named Bellot

Strait after Joseph-René Bellot, a young Frenchman who drowned in 1852 while searching for the lost Sir John Franklin. The twenty-mile-long Bellot Strait, however, is hardly the sought-for navigable Northwest Passage. It is a half-mile-wide dangerous passage where tides from the eastern and western Arctic meet and violently toss about the unpredictable ice.)

Declaring that the Northwest Passage was not to be found there, Ross ordered the anchor weighed and the steam engine fired up. *Victory* moved slowly down Prince Regent Inlet, her paddles more effective at arousing seals than advancing the ship. Hard-packed ice thumped against her hull. As usual, she made just a couple miles per hour—too slow, in fact, to avoid two masses of threatening ice. Fearing for the rudder, it was unshipped and laid across the stern, leaving the ship to drift north and then south at the whim of the moving ice—her steam engine ineffective as ever.

Hour by hour, ice built up along *Victory*'s sides. She was soon beset. The ice was not pressing dangerously, however, so Ross allowed his crew some much-needed leisure time. The bored and frustrated men lolled about, spread their clothing on the decks to dry, and chatted dreamily of summer days back home in England. The low sun shown warmly through crystal blue skies. Narwhals and seals frolicked in occasional gaps that opened between the ship and the ice. The air was thirty-nine degrees. Back and forth *Victory* meandered. South, a mile and a half. Then north. Then south. Then north and then south again.

The next day, a lane of open water was spotted two miles away. Ross ordered his men back to work. By both warping and sailing, the crew brought *Victory* closer to the open water. Suddenly, the ice eased its grip. Engineer Brunton built up steam only to have the cantankerous engine function worse than ever. Top speed: one mile per hour.

"On no occasion was this want of power more provoking; since if it could but have forced us two miles an hour, we should have been able to gain the most distant point of view," complained Ross.

With a late afternoon breeze, they sailed into a fine harbor, which Ross named Port Logan after his childhood village in Scotland.

Ross and his nephew James went ashore and followed a small stream through a valley. Signs of deer, musk oxen, some lichen, and a little moss offered the only hints of life. Continuing their walk, stumbling over broken rocks and ice, they came across the remains of about twenty Inuit huts, fox traps, and graves. Utterly bored with the scenery, Ross remarked that the most interesting features of the landscape were the veins of quartz running through the granite hillsides and the few shells embedded in the limestone masses. The two Rosses climbed a three-hundred-foot hill. The land extended in a southwesterly direction as far as they could see. Open water ran for at least thirty miles in the same direction. If only the wind would arise, they could continue their voyage, as all faith in the execrable—to use Ross's word—steam engine had been abandoned.

By the time the two returned to the ship, the weather had turned thick with heavy fog. Again the crew furled the sails and sat idle. They hunted seals and amused themselves by hanging sealskins overboard and watching shrimp eat every bit of flesh and blubber—making the skins perfectly clean and ready for tanning. The date was August 29, 1829. And with it came the voyage's first snowfall—a welcome sight in that it covered the "barren and repulsive tract," as Ross described the scene of "dark and rugged rocks, without the least trace of vegetation, or the presence of even a bird to enliven them."

The next day, still stalled, the men went ashore to a two-acre pond and replenished the ship's fresh water supply and did their laundry. A bear was spotted, but, alas, too far away to bother with. Nothing else. The next few days passed wearisomely as the ship drifted back and forth, making no real progress along the coast. Taking potshots at a gull and a seal provided the only diversion for the men.

The earlier hazardous sailing and now the doldrums confirmed in Ross's mind—and correctly so—that if the Northwest Passage existed, its commercial usefulness was nil. The ever-practical Ross put it right when he said, "Merchants risk much on commerce . . . but they are not given to hazard everything. They have a test . . . and the barometer is stationed at Lloyd's Coffee-house. On what terms could . . . insurance [for a ship navigating the supposed Northwest Passage] be effected; on what premium?" Yet Ross was fascinated with the pure pursuit of knowledge. He felt that human happiness consisted of such imaginary joys, as he called them. And what did it matter, he felt, if it were obtained by studying the "anatomy of a fly's toe" or filling in the blanks on a map?

*September 3, 1829.* Finally, a gale. But as was almost always Ross's experience while trying to navigate the Arctic ice, the wind was contrary to the direction he wished to sail—and in less than three hours, the storm had driven *Victory* nineteen miles to the north. Disgusted, Ross did not even bother to ask Brunton to get up the steam. The gale and rain continued hard for the next few days. To prevent further loss of progress, Ross moored *Victory* to a grounded iceberg that protruded four feet above the seven-fathom-deep water. A handful of men headed off in a boat to find a safe harbor. What they found was a harbor Captain Ross described as "not exceeded by any in the world . . . a splendid harbour, in which the whole British navy might safely ride." He christened the newfound harbor Elizabeth, after Felix Booth's sister.

Elizabeth Harbor, however, was a trap. Just when the weather cleared and they were set to leave, ice moved in from the north. It streamed through the harbor's north-facing entrance and packed the harbor full. The men feared for the ship's survival as the ice pressed her, raised her up, and heeled her over. Ice grinding and breaking against underwater rocks made a frightful din as it carried *Victory* along. She left a trail of red as the jagged ice scraped the red ochre paint from her hull. Her shallow draft was all that saved her from destruction.

For four days the men hauled and warped, trying to free her from the grasp of the harbor ice. With the help of the changing tide, the crew warped her out only to have her thrown into a powerful whirlpool created by the fast-moving spring tide of the autumnal equinox. 'Round and 'round she spun, while ice blocks like boulders hammered her hull and shook her rigging. By securing an ice anchor to a mass of ice floating right down the center of the channel, *Victory* was dragged free of the whirlpool. When she reached clear water and the current slowed, they cast off from their benevolent ice mass. Nevertheless, the turning tide threatened to carry them back toward the whirlpool. Sighting a small harbor within two cable lengths—one thousand two hundred feet—the men warped. The men hauled. After about four hours of heaving and chanting, *Victory* was secure again. Steward William Light exclaimed that the ordeal had left *Victory*'s bows and sides "as rough as if they had been indented with a hatchet."

The next few days saw good sailing and many landmarks named as they continued south down Prince Regent Inlet. Grace Islets. Louisa Island. Lax Island. Mary Jones Bay. Cape St. Catherine. Eden Bay. Joanna Harbor. Christian's Monument. Ross described this last feature as "a remarkable mountain, shaped like a tomb." He coined the name for his beloved, departed wife, Christy.

Although Ross never expected any of these lands to be of much value, he nonetheless went ashore and took formal possession. They erected a stone cairn and affixed a copper plate inscribed with the ship's name and date of discovery, 14 September 1829. Recalling the ceremony, Ross later wrote, "that which is nugatory or absurd must be done where custom dictates."

Overnight, a storm with high winds and snow squalls came down from the north. Unable to reach a harbor, *Victory* was again moored to an iceberg. Waves churned by the storm split a nearby iceberg that towered sixty feet above the water. The collapsing berg threw ice and water into the air, and eddies created by the cataclysm threatened to swamp *Victory*. A fragment of the berg gave her a violent shock, and another rose beneath the *Victory's* sixteen-ton launch and lifted it completely free of the water. In spite of the violence, the sturdily reinforced ship and her launch sustained little damage. As the storm raged, Ross sought safety on the lee side of a cape.

The next day the wind slackened, and Ross climbed ashore to examine the prospects. A fine harbor, totally clear of ice, stood to the south. If only they could get around the cape and into the channel, they would have free sailing to the harbor. The next day the storm renewed its vigor. The temperature dropped to twenty-one degrees. Icy seas washed over the decks and froze on the rigging. The ice shifted about so rapidly that a channel open one minute closed ten minutes later. Then another lead through the ice would taunt them by opening in another direction. Their position grew more perilous. The seas increased. As the moored ship rolled dangerously close to capsizing, a "whole fleet of heavy ice islands," as Ross described it, came down the channel, grounded, and formed a protective barrier against the heavy swells. "Such is the ice . . . it is far from being an unmixed evil," wrote Ross.

The storm moderated, the seas calmed, and a hard frost set in. Ice froze tightly around *Victory*, freezing her in place in the midst of its pack. Yet although she was protected, the ice pack prevented getting on with the voyage. Their only recourse was to saw and chop a canal to clear water. To saw the ice, the men used ropes and pulleys to work a fourteen-foot ice saw that hung down into the cut from a tall tripod set on the ice. As with heaving at the capstan, the men worked their ice saws to a chanty:

> O th' ladies o' town, Hi-o!
> *Cheer-'ly man;*
> All soft as do-wn, Hi-o-o!
> *Cheer-'ly man;*
> In their best go-wn, Hi-o!
> *Cheer-'ly man;*
> O! Haul-ey, Hi-o-o!
> *Cheer-'ly man.*

While the men worked, an evening breeze came up, and that, combined with the tide, drove off the sawed-out ice. Just when everyone thought they might be free, however, another mass of ice sailed down the channel and grounded itself, blocking the hard-earned escape route. Again, the men set to sawing and chopping—this time in a different direction. Just as before, the wind drove new sea ice into their canal and blocked the route. They began a third time. Fatigued and embittered by the frustrating effort and ever one to rile up the crew, William Light complained to his mates that he felt that all that sawing of ice was merely a ploy on Ross's part to keep them busy. To Ross the need was obvious: They could not simply leave the ship stuck forever! Some of the men joined Light in his grumbling, but by nightfall the wind was in their favor and it seemed that extrication could be completed the next morning.

Their hopes were dashed when they woke up the next morning to find that it had snowed all night and covered everything with a featureless blanket of white. Worse yet, two more large bergs had moved into the canal. At Ross's orders, the men steadfastly renewed their efforts despite Light's agitation. That evening, after three days' continuous effort, the exhausted men warped *Victory* into the main channel.

Down Prince Regent Inlet she sailed, making good progress for about seventeen miles, until heavy-packed ice loomed ahead. Captain Ross ordered *Victory* moored to yet another iceberg. Within hearing of the crew, Commander Ross argued with his uncle that he was "thoroughly convinced of the ineligibility of the situation in which the *Victory*" lay, and he pushed off in a whaleboat to seek a passage through the ice. The crew exchanged glances with one another. What had brought on this sudden disaccord between the captain and his nephew? Although a measure of reticence between the two officers had admittedly been evident, they had apparently worked in unity up to this point. This was soon to change.

The crew had just finished their breakfast when their mooring iceberg loosed its grip from the bottom. The berg, which reached above the masthead, spun around and rammed *Victory*'s bow onto the rocks. The violent action left her in a precarious, exposed position. The crew uncoiled the hawsers and hauled her off, only to have the current and wind take her down a shallow channel. Wide-eyed, the men gazed at rocks less than six feet below the surface as fate carried the seven-foot six-inch-draft ship safely through the perilous rock field. At last, *Victory* reached a quiet pool to await the report from the whaleboat.

The passage Commander Ross found was choked with icebergs that made it barely as wide as the ship, and it was very shallow. An ice anchor was set and the hawser wrapped around the capstan. "Man th' capstan!"

> In Am-ster-dam there liv'd a maid—
> *Mark well what I do say.*
> In Am-ster-dam there liv'd a maid,
> And she was mis-tress of her trade.
> I'll go no more a-ro-o-ving with you fair maids.
> *A-rov-ing, a-roving. Since roving's been my ru-u-in.*
> *I'll go no more a-ro-o-ving with you fair maids.*

*Victory* moved forward. Her keel screeched against the rocks. The capstan turned harder.

> I put my arm around her waist—
> *Mark well now what I do say!*
> I put my arm around . . .

With a shuddering crunch, she stuck. A horrified Captain Ross calculated that the tide was in. Fortunately, he was wrong. The incalculable tide was near ebb. While they awaited the change, several men sawed projecting points from icebergs that nearly reached across the channel. Others used the rowboats to tow the sawed-off ice out of the way. After several hours of preparation, warping again began in earnest. *Victory* bobbed free of the rocks. She was through the channel.

On October 6, the temperature dropped to twelve degrees. The day turned gloomy as a heavy overcast covered the previous day's bright blue sky. A dark "water-sky" to the north indicated a little open water; otherwise, ice was everywhere. With each passing day, the sun's noon-hour height above the horizon was lower. Chances for further progress looked slim. It was time to move *Victory* into a safe position for winter. The crew cut a canal in the ice to a nearby harbor that provided protection from eastern, western, and northern winds and maneuvered *Victory* in place. *Victory* and her crew of twenty-three had advanced two hundred and eighty miles down Prince Regent Inlet—two hundred miles farther than Parry. At last, two hundred and forty miles above the Arctic Circle and three thousand miles from England, they would spend their first Arctic winter.

Ross named the anchorage Felix Harbor—once again recognizing his patron, Felix Booth. The harbor held promise to set them free in the summer in that the water was thirty-three feet deep and a good current flowed. The boats were landed. The men unbent the sails and unreeved the running rigging. They cleared the decks of ropes and spars.

Ross wrote in his journal,

> *Our conviction was indeed absolute; for there was now not an atom of clear water to be seen anywhere; and excepting the occasional dark point of a protruding rock, nothing but one dazzling and monotonous, dull and wearisome extent of snow was visible, all 'round the horizon in the direction of the land.*

*It was indeed a dull prospect. Amid all its brilliancy, this land, the land of ice and snow, has ever been and ever will be a dull, dreary, heart-sinking, monotonous, waste, under the influence of which the very mind is paralyzed, ceasing to care or think, as it ceases to feel what might, did it occur but once, or last but one day, stimulate us by its novelty; for it is but the view of uniformity and silence and death.*

# CHAPTER TWO

# Captain Ross Errs in Quest
# for Northwest Passage

### (March 1818–May 1829)

U NLIKE other voyages and expeditions in search of the Northwest Passage in the early 1800s, Captain John Ross's 1829 voyage was privately financed. Using private funding for his return to the Arctic was the only means for Ross because ever since 1819 he had been effectively blackballed by John Barrow, Second Secretary of the Admiralty, and thus unable to secure command of a navy ship.

The son of a farmer, John Barrow (later Sir John) had moved up to the post of Second Secretary of the Admiralty through both his abilities and patronage. He acquired the position in 1804 at the age of forty. With the exception of a hiatus in 1806–07, Barrow held the powerful office for forty-one years. Although exploration of the Arctic was one of his greatest passions, Barrow's real experience with the Arctic was limited to one voyage on a whaling vessel when he was a young boy. In spite of this and his humble roots, Barrow looked down his nose at whalers and would never consider giving command of a ship of discovery to a whaler. Along this line, Barrow usurped the credit from the whaler William Scoresby for first suggesting polar expeditions in the early nineteenth century. Scoresby had presented a detailed proposal to the Wernerian Society and had even considered becoming an explorer himself after discovering unusually clear conditions of Arctic ice while whaling in 1814. For unexplained reasons, Barrow spurned Scoresby and his expertise.

John Ross was a friend of Scoresby and had spoken out to give the whaler the credit he felt Scoresby deserved as "the father of Arctic discovery." This infuriated the venomous and stubborn Barrow and contributed to his clash with the proud and stubborn Ross.

Barrow was not a man to be trifled with. He was powerful, energetic, literate, and a master at sarcasm. Although Lady Franklin said, "he is said to be humorous & obstinate & exhibited both propensities," his manners turned uncivil and his methods were often devious in what became a thirty-year campaign against John Ross.

Barrow's blackballing John Ross was the direct result of an expedition that Ross had commanded in 1818. By that year, much of Great Britain's Royal Navy lay idle following the end of the Napoleonic Wars. To help keep navy officers occupied, the Admiralty directed its energy into a concerted search for the Northwest Passage. Even at that time, it was clear to many that a route to the Far East across the top of North America or over the North Pole had no commercial practicality. Yet advancement of science, productive employment of officers and men in time of peace, and the belief that "knowledge is power" easily provided justification for the quest. Barrow even still held some hope for a viable passage. He belonged to the camp that believed in the theory of an "open polar sea." That is, the North Pole region is covered by an ocean that is free of ice during summer months as a result of six months of steady sunshine. A ring of ice surrounds this polar sea, and once a ship breaks through the ring of ice, it would be clear sailing across the pole. That was the theory, anyway. Thus, for reasons of either expanding knowledge or to find a route to the Far East, in 1818 Second Secretary John Barrow launched Great Britain into nearly thirty years of steady Arctic exploration.

The renewed quest for a shortcut to the Far East began with a two-pronged effort—one to seek a northwest passage through Davis Strait, and the other to sail directly over the North Pole. The North Pole contingent was commanded by Captain David Buchan, who had recently distinguished himself as leader of an expedition into the interior of Newfoundland. Buchan's orders included instructions to carry out a number of scientific experiments on the ellipticity of the earth, magnetic phenomenon, refraction of the atmosphere over large expanses of ice, and the temperature and specific gravity of seawater.

The Admiralty awarded command of the expedition's Northwest Passage arm to the forty-one-year-old Captain John Ross, who at the time was enjoying command of HMS *Driver*, patrolling off the coast of his beloved Scotland. In the event that Buchan traversed the pole and Ross made the Northwest Passage, Ross had orders to take command of the combined expedition when they met in the Pacific.

Ross's ship was the 385-ton, square-rigged sloop HMS *Isabella*. Her companion ship was the 252-ton HMS *Alexander*, commanded by Lieutenant William Edward Parry. Buchan's ships were HMSs *Trent* and

*Dorothea.* All four ships were put in dry dock and reinforced for the hazardous journey through the ice-infested waters. Mr. Lang, assistant surveyor of the merchant's yard, oversaw the work.

To the *Isabella*'s hull, Lang's shipwrights added a layer of oak strakes seven inches thick. After caulking and paying with pitch and tar, another three inches of oak—with a layer of animal-hair felt in between—completed the hull's strengthening. A twelve-inch layer of timber fortified the bow. Three-quarter-inch iron plates, fastened around the bow stem and down to the forefoot where the bow stem meets the keel, added to her ability to fight through the ice. Elm boards with a layer of felt beneath protected each side of the keel. Internally, large brackets, introduced fore and aft under the beam ends—combined with a tier of beams five feet below the lower deck—supported the sides against pressure, should she be squeezed between advancing ice floes. Solid wood filled the bow to several feet aft the lower deck beams. An extra capstan along the starboard side of the fore hatchway gave added means to warp the ship through the ice. More than 4,000 yards of spare canvas—equivalent to one full set of sails—and a spare rudder completed *Isabella*'s readiness.

Eighteen ice saws, twelve ice axes, and twenty-four ice anchors, plus five whaleboats were on hand to attack the ice. To repair the whaleboats, there were 56,000 nails, 2,700 board feet of fir, and 56 pounds of oakum. HMS *Alexander* was outfitted similarly, as were both the *Trent* and *Dorothea.*

As commander of the fleet, Captain Ross received six months' advance pay at the rate of £46 per month. The thirty-one able seamen each received £3 per month but were advanced just three months' pay instead of six as the officers had received. Sacheuse, an Inuk brought along as an interpreter, was paid the same as the able seamen. Also onboard each ship was a Greenland master pilot, experienced with sailing through ice-choked waters. His monthly pay was £5.

In consideration that the voyage was not only exploratory but of a scientific nature, instruments abounded. Aboard *Isabella* were eleven thermometers, twelve compasses, four dipping needles (to measure the downward force of the earth's magnetic field—of interest as they neared the pole), transits, a hygrometer, a hydrometer, sextants, various barometers, a cyanometer (an instrument for measuring the intensity of the blue sky), drawing instruments, a pendulum clock (to measure the ellipticity of the earth), Sir Humphrey Davy's electrical apparatus (to look for effects of the aurora), deep-sea clams (invented by Ross for collecting specimens and samples of the ocean floor), and seven chronometers.

Naturally, determination of latitude and longitude of newfound lands was of utmost importance. Insofar as the Board of Longitude had approved the use of chronometers as a means for determining longitudinal position, the Admiralty supplied three chronometers for *Isabella* alone. These were made by the firms of Arnold and Earnshaw, both preeminent instrument makers who had played significant roles in establishing chronometers as *the* tool to measure longitude. As instrument manufacturers always welcomed opportunities to demonstrate their chronometers' accuracy, the firm of Parkinson & Frodsham loaned a seventh for the *Isabella*. The other three timepieces belonged to officers—which was common at the time as the Admiralty often had a shortage of the valuable instruments. To protect the box chronometers from jolts the ships might receive as they fought their way through the ice, the devices were suspended by springs from the cabin ceiling. A heavy cotton cord hanging from the bottom of the chronometer trailed on the floor to dampen the oscillations.

Another innovation even more recent than chronometers was onboard: Trengrouse's life-saving apparatus—a rocket-fired rope for rescue of persons adrift on the ice or stranded on a foundering ship. It was not used on either arm of the expedition.

The Admiralty outfitted each seaman against the cold with a flushing jacket and trousers of rough, thick woolen cloth; a monkey jacket; a red shirt; swanskin (flannel) drawers; sea boots; fur cap; mitts; comfortables or woolen scarves; and wolf-skin blankets. About a dozen extra outfits were on hand, but these were to be given out only as needed and at the sailor's expense.

The ships were provisioned for twenty-six months. Stores on each ship were similar to the *Isabella*'s, which included 18,200 pounds of bread and 26,000 pounds of beef and pork. Other provisions ranged from 600 pounds of raisins to 20 gallons of pickled walnuts to 6 pounds of thyme. *Isabella*'s men also had 700 gallons of wine and 1,925 gallons of spirits to enjoy.

In anticipation of encountering Inuit on the western coast of Greenland, hundreds of mirrors, thousands of needles, several hundred yards of colorful flannel, plus innumerable swords, knives, kettles, scissors, razors, guns, ammunition, and forty umbrellas were packed as gifts. Besides the umbrellas and assorted items, the largesse included 129 gallons each of gin and brandy.

Thus equipped, HMSs *Isabella*, *Alexander*, *Dorothea*, and *Trent* dropped down the Thames to Galleons Reach on April 18, 1818. The *Isabella* and *Alexander* reached Lerwick, Shetland Islands, on April 30, where the advance pay was distributed to the men. The *Dorothea* and *Trent* arrived the following day, the *Trent* leaking badly, which is not uncommon after a ship has undergone extensive rebuilding and reinforcement. Usually such leaks fix themselves as the new wood expands while at sea. The *Trent*, however, showed no signs of improvement and so remained another week at Lerwick for repair. HMSs *Isabella* and *Alexander*, meanwhile, took leave of their sister ships and began their quest for the Northwest Passage.

When *Dorothea* and *Trent* finally set sail, their voyage of discovery was short-lived. In mid-July, they met a solid wall of ice a mere forty miles north of Spitsbergen. Wrought by the changing tide, the wall presented an ominous appearance with its hummocks piled as high as thirty or forty feet. The two ships struggled along the edge of the ice pack but never found an opening. Two weeks later, a storm and heavy ice damaged the *Dorothea* so severely that they were forced to seek a harbor on Spitsbergen to attempt repairs. Unable to satisfactorily repair the *Dorothea*, and with her in too dangerous a condition to sail home alone, both ships returned to England in October, having accomplished virtually nothing.

Meanwhile, Ross's two ships sailed uneventfully for Greenland. As they approached the latitude of the fabled Sunken Land of Buss, Ross shortened sail and hove to in order to take soundings. They kept the lead line constantly going, but no bottom was found to depths of 180 fathoms, adding further evidence that no such "land" exists. Ross concluded that the Sunken Land of Buss was a fantasy and that ships that had reported bottoming in heavy seas had merely been shuddered by the violence of the sea.

Belief in the Sunken Land of Buss was a remnant of Buss Island, a supposed island off the southern tip of Greenland. This island was first reported in 1578 by the captain of the ship *Emmanuel*, one of a fleet of ships partaking in Martin Frobisher's third voyage to Baffin Island. *Emmanuel* was a type of ship known as a busse—a Dutch vessel used in the herring fishery—hence, the island's name. Although the island's existence was never established with certainty, it was included on maps into the eighteenth century. As time went on and no one could locate the mysterious island, the story developed that a cataclysm must have sunk the island beneath the waves. Most likely, the *Emmanuel* was off-course and her captain mistook the southern tip of Greenland for an uncharted island.

Sailing along the western coast of Greenland just north of Vaigat Strait, the *Isabella* and *Alexander* encountered hazardous Arctic conditions: fog, fields of ice, and icebergs. The whaler *Everthorpe* hailed the *Isabella* for medical assistance for an injury from an Arctic hazard of a different kind. A polar bear had dragged the *Everthorpe*'s master from a whaleboat. Although his thigh had been "sadly torn," as Ross described it, the wound did not appear to be life-threatening.

That night a calm ensued, necessitating towing and warping as the only means to maintain ships' way. For the next month, progress continued agonizingly slow, as more fog, icebergs, calms, and fields of solid ice detained or harassed the ships. While battling the ice, they spoke to the whaler *Zephyr* and learned that another whaler, the *Three Brothers* of Hull, had been crushed by the ice and sunk. Fortunately, all hands escaped to the ice and were rescued. Ten days later, the *Isabella* and *Alexander* left the whalers far behind as they passed 75° 12' north latitude and sailed into waters that had not seen a ship in two hundred years.

On August 6, while each ship was trapped in the middle of separate ice floes, a gale arose and the floes began to move and rotate. The six-foot-thick ice closed tightly on *Isabella*. Her beams bent and threatened to give way. The ice pressure increased. But instead of crushing her, the ice worked its way under the *Isabella*, raised her part-way out of the water, then thrust her toward the *Alexander*, which was in a similar plight.

The men jumped to the ice with ropes and ice anchors to try to hold the ships from colliding. Closer and closer the two ships drew. The gale increased. The ice moved more rapidly. With a sickening crash, the *Isabella* and *Alexander* collided stern-to-stern, breaking the anchors and chain-plates and crushing a whaleboat that had been on the ice between them. Just as the masts seemed about to go, the two ice fields receded and carried the *Isabella* alongside the *Alexander*. As they swept past one another, their bower anchors entangled. Wrenched from the catheads as the ships separated, the two anchors were soon suspended midway between the ships. Unable to withstand the tension, let alone the force of one and a half tons of iron in midair, the *Alexander's* twelve-inch cable parted in an explosion that shot a whip of hemp, weighing five pounds to the foot, back at the ship. The Greenland ice masters, who had spent their careers in the Arctic, exclaimed they had never had such an experience, and had the ships not been heavily strengthened, surely both would have been lost. The two ships settled into a pool of open water.

Then, 650 miles above the Arctic Circle, they spotted several men on the ice, about six miles from shore, waving and calling out. Thinking they were whalers who had been shipwrecked in the recent gale, Ross ordered the colors hoisted, and the ships tacked toward the men. Upon approaching closer, however, it was obvious that the men dressed in fur were not sailors, but Inuit. John Sacheuse, the expedition's Inuit interpreter, called out to them in his native tongue. The men shouted back in a language unintelligible to Sacheuse, jumped aboard their dog-drawn sledges, and took off for the distant shore. They halted about two miles away and looked back. Ross sent a boat loaded with gifts of knives and clothing, which were placed on a stool on the ice about halfway between the two parties. The natives kept their distance. Another boat was sent, this time with a dog with strings of blue beads around its neck. Again, the natives made no effort to approach the gifts or the dog. Hoping the natives would retrieve the gifts if they left, Ross took the opportunity to sail about four miles to the north to examine a possible passage through the ice. After ten hours of searching, no opening was found and the ships returned to where the gifts had been left. The dog, having been tied to a stake, was asleep; the presents untouched. A sledge darted about in the distance.

Not willing to give up, Ross had another bag of gifts placed on a grounded iceberg between the ship and the shore. Alongside the bag was a flagpole with a picture of a hand pointing toward the ship. As the wind was calm, Ross had no qualms about waiting for the natives to return, even though his orders had been to proceed on his quest with all dispatch.

About ten o'clock in the morning the following day, eight sledges made a circuitous route toward the flagstaff. White flags were hoisted on each ship. Sacheuse volunteered to go alone to try to engage the natives. With a white flag in hand, he trudged over the ice. A chasm in the ice separated the natives from Sacheuse. He walked to the chasm's edge, took off his hat, and waved in a friendly manner for the natives to approach. Standing off about 300 yards, the Inuit shouted. Sacheuse recognized the dialect. He shouted "*Kahkeite*," meaning, "Come on!" The natives replied, "*Naakrie, naakrieai-plaite*," which Sacheuse took to mean, "No, no—go away," and other words that Sacheuse understood to say that they hoped the ships had not come to destroy them. Sacheuse threw strings of beads and a shirt across the chasm. The natives shouted in their own language, "Go away! Don't kill us!" Sacheuse then threw a knife across the chasm. Picking up the knife, the men cheered and pulled their noses, an apparent sign of friendship. Sacheuse returned the gesture. The stalemate had been broken.

In answer to their questions, Sacheuse explained that the ships were made of wood and the sails of cloth and that they had come from the south. The natives, never having seen cloth or pieces of wood thicker than a finger, stared in amazement. They explained that they had come down from the north to hunt narwhals.

Sacheuse returned to the ship for a plank so the natives might cross the ice chasm to visit the ships. Ross and Commander Parry of the *Alexander* walked back with Sacheuse to greet their new friends. The Britons distributed items of clothing, a few strings of beads, and another knife. The Inuit, however, remained reluctant to cross the chasm. Ross sent for more presents: mirrors, knives, caps, and shirts. A native asked what the red cap was for. Sacheuse crossed the chasm and placed it on the man's head, to the amusement of the rest, who each, in turn, placed it on his own head. In exchange, the Inuit offered narwhal horns and walrus teeth. Ross mused in his journal about the "ludicrous scene" in the middle of the ice, miles from land: eight Inuit, Parry, Sacheuse, Ross, and two sailors, all hollering, laughing, and gesticulating amid a cacophony of yowling dogs as the natives whipped them in line.

Finally, Ross, with Sacheuse interpreting, convinced the natives to visit the ships. The Inuit laughed all the way as they flew across the ice with Ross and Parry on their sledges, hanging on for dear life. When the visitors arrived, the crew crowded the ships' bows and climbed the masts, much to the natives' apparent astonishment. A rope ladder was dropped from *Isabella*'s bow, and after considerable encouragement, the eldest climbed aboard, quickly followed by his companions. For the remainder of the day, the guests toured the ship. They sat for portraits, asked what kind of ice made up the glass of the binnacle and skylights, shrunk away in terror from a pig, and showed contempt for a little terrier (apparently of no use to pull a sledge). They received gifts of hammers and nails, tried to purloin an anvil, and wondered if a ticking watch was alive. Wood, by far, received the most attention; the men stamped on the deck, tried to lift the spare topmast, and minutely studied the furniture in Ross's cabin.

When it came time to leave, Ross loaded them with presents of clothing, biscuits, more wood, and even the plank that had been used to cross the chasm. The eight guests promised to return after they had eaten and slept. They separated in a ceremony of nose-pulling. After they had crossed the chasm, the Inuit threw away the biscuits, split the plank among themselves, mounted their sledges and rode off at great speed, laughing and hallooing as they sped across the ice.

The next day a southerly breeze opened a lead in the ice allowing the *Isabella* and *Alexander* to advance about seven miles to the westward, away from shore. Chatting with Sacheuse, Ross learned that the Inuit wondered if the ships, with their great sails, could fly. Had they come from the moon or the sun? Sacheuse also told Ross that the Inuit got the iron for their knives from a giant rock in a mountain about two days away. Believing it to be a meteorite, Ross planned an overland expedition to locate the rock. But as the sailing weather improved over the next few days, Ross was obligated to move onward in pursuit of his mission's original quest and so never had time to look for the rock.

(In 1897, Robert E. Peary, the purported "discoverer" of the North Pole, retrieved the meteorites—there were three, the largest weighing about 38 tons—which he sold to help finance his polar expeditions. In Peary's own words, the meteorites had made it possible "for an entire aboriginal tribe, the most northerly upon the earth . . . whose habitat is metal-barren, to rise from the stone to the iron age." Nonetheless, without shame, Peary took the source of their iron.)

In celebration of the Prince Regent's birthday on August 11, Ross had the ships decked out in flags and colors. However, he forewent the traditional firing of the cannon so that neither the natives would be startled nor would the delicate chronometers be upset. A musket volley sufficed. That same day, ten other Inuit visited the ship. They joined the men on the ice in a version of soccer in which they kicked around an inflated sealskin. But where were the women? asked the Inuit. Is this tribe of sailors made up of only men? Unable to fathom that no women had come on the voyage, the Inuit trooped over the ice to the *Alexander*, at anchor about 200 yards away. Surely, that was where the women were. "But finding their mistake, they soon returned to us, evidently disappointed," wrote Ross.

Before leaving for the day, Ross urged them to bring samples of iron, for which they would be greatly rewarded. The next day, however, the sailing weather improved. Ross was torn between continuing the parley with their friends or getting on with the mission. Nevertheless, orders are orders and, with no excuse to tarry longer, Ross and crew departed before the "Arctic Highlanders"—as the Scotsman Ross had dubbed them—returned. They were never to meet again.

The ships moved northward along the Greenland coast. On August 16, they rounded Cape York, named by Ross for the Duke of York, in commemoration of His Royal Highness's birthday. The snow on the cliffs of the cape presented a novel appearance: It was a deep red color. The crimson cliffs continued for a distance of about eight miles. Examination of samples through a microscope revealed tiny, deep red particles like a very minute, round seed. When melted, the snow water had the appearance of a muddy port wine. Ross concluded that the material must be of vegetable origin. (Ross was on the right track. The red snow is now known to be caused by a species of blue-green algae, *Chlamydomonas nivalis*, which grows in symbiosis with a cyanobacteria that gives it the red color.)

The expedition continued slowly beyond the crimson cliffs as the men tracked, warped, or towed the ships through one ice field after another, often working as many as three days without sleep. Rowing whaleboats towed the ships. Tracking, on the other hand, was resorted to if the ice was either too close to work a whaleboat or too soft for warping. Tracking was simple enough. Crewmen carried a hawser from the bow out onto the ice and heaved. With luck, once the ship began to move they could trudge forward and haul the ship behind them, although they risked breaking through the soft ice. Those in the center of the line were saved from the water by the tension in the hawser. The lead man, however, was in for a frigid ducking. Ross was highly pleased with both the men's labor and also with himself for the method of its undertaking,

> In the course of our tedious, and often labourious, progress through the ice, it became necessary to keep the whole of the crew at the most fatiguing work, sometimes for several days and nights without interruption. When this was the case, an extra meal was served to them at midnight, generally of preserved

*meat; and I found that this kind of nourishment, when the mind and body are both occupied, and aided, no doubt, by the continual presence of the sun, acted as a substitute for sleep, and they often passed three days in this manner without any visible inconvenience . . . without a murmur.*

When the two ships reached the bottom of Baffin Bay, the explorers spotted Smith Sound to the north and Jones Sound opening to the west, just as William Baffin had described them two hundred years before. Ross named the capes flanking the entrance to Smith Sound for his ships: Cape Alexander and Cape Isabella.

Smith Sound was completely blocked by ice. A ridge of high mountains appeared to extend nearly across the bottom of Jones Sound, which, like Smith Sound, was also blocked by ice. Ross stated that if nothing else came from this voyage, he was at least pleased that his rediscovery of these landmarks of Baffin had reaffirmed Baffin's reputation as a renowned navigator. Indeed, as a result of the voyage, cartographers restored to their maps Baffin's discoveries of 1616.

Sailing south along the western shore of Baffin Bay, they reached Lancaster Sound, another forgotten discovery of Baffin. The *Isabella*, being a much better sailer than the *Alexander*, sailed ahead down Lancaster Sound for a distance of about eighty miles. At that point, Ross determined that this sound, too, was choked with ice. Furthermore, he believed the waterway was an inlet and not a sound in that a range of mountains stood across the bottom. These he named Croker's Mountains, after John Wilson Croker, First Secretary of the Admiralty. Because the weather was becoming unsettled, Ross turned about and headed back out the sound to the *Alexander*, which trailed behind about eight miles to the east. Convinced that these inlets off Baffin Bay were each dead ends and not openings to the Northwest Passage, a disappointed Ross ordered his two ships to sail for home.

Unfortunately for Ross, he had missed his opportunity to be the discoverer of the Northwest Passage. Lancaster Sound *is* an opening to the elusive passage. Fog and atmospheric refraction in the tricky Arctic daylight had fooled Ross by creating a mirage of distant mountains—his Croker's Mountains—that appeared to terminate Lancaster Sound. Furthermore, Lieutenant Parry and several other officers on the expedition disagreed with Ross's conclusion that mountains blocked the passage. They apparently, however, never mentioned this to Ross at the time.

Upon reaching home, word began to circulate among officers of the two ships that Lancaster Sound was probably not a dead end and that they should have continued down the inlet rather than quit and head for home. Second Secretary of the Admiralty John Barrow got wind of the murmurings, most likely through Edward Parry and Edward Sabine (a captain of the Royal Artillery, onboard HMS *Isabella* to make magnetical and astronomical observations). He became convinced that Ross had shirked his duty by sailing home without sufficiently exploring the sound. The more he heard and thought about it, the angrier Barrow grew. In January 1819, he vented his rage with sarcasm and facetious acrimony through a fifty-page article in the *Quarterly Review.* Moreover, the article, written anonymously but obviously by Barrow, not only attacked the man, but also nitpicked its way through Ross's published journal of the voyage.

To John Barrow, both the Polar and the Baffin Bay expeditions were total failures. Yet he accepted the failure of Buchan's polar expedition as "owing to one of those accidents to which all sea voyages are liable." To the "failure" of Ross's Baffin Bay expedition, on the other hand, Barrow spluttered, "we hardly know in what terms to speak, or how to account for it . . . for our own parts we cannot conscientiously pronounce it any otherwise than unsatisfactory."

Barrow scoffed that Ross's "wholly unaccountable" abandonment of the quest had virtually no parallel in the history of voyages of discovery. "He knows no more, in fact, than he might have known by staying at home." Not only that, but according to Barrow, Ross's narrative showed "habitual inaccuracy and a looseness of description." And why a whole chapter on the discovery of a heretofore unknown tribe of Inuit, wondered Barrow when "[d]etailing the particulars of the two or three short interviews onboard the ships" would have sufficed? Barrow then filled eight pages of his article lambasting almost every aspect of Ross's account of the natives. For example, to Ross's remark that the Inuit were astonished when they viewed their faces in a mirror, Barrow challenged, "This we cannot conceive; since ice, in which they could not fail to have observed reflected images, is so familiar to them." Here, Barrow seems to be ignorant of an article that appeared in the December 1818 issue of *Blackwood's Edinburgh Magazine.* This article, anonymous but no doubt by an officer of the *Alexander,* not only verifies Ross's report of the natives' reaction to seeing their faces in a mirror, but adds insight to the cause for their astonishment. "To view themselves in a looking-glass, but more especially in a concave mirror, made them frantic with joy and wonder, and drew forth such bursts of laughter and exclamations of surprise, as were never heard before." Thus, it was the magnified image in a shaving mirror that brought such delight, not just a reflection. But Barrow was too busy seeking fault.

Ultimately, the Second Secretary of the Admiralty all but called

Captain John Ross a coward. When Ross turned back at Lancaster Sound, he had remarked that the weather had turned unsettled and "it became advisable to stand out of this dangerous inlet." To that, Barrow said, "Captain Ross talks of danger in Lancaster's Sound, and of the bad sailing of the *Alexander*. A voyage of discovery implies danger; but a mere voyage, like his, 'round the shores of Baffin Bay, in three summer months, may be considered a voyage of pleasure." Barrow's sarcasm was a cruel insult, not only to Ross, but also to the crews of the ten whale ships lost in Baffin Bay that same year.

Barrow's widely read article moved sentiment against Ross. In the eyes of the public, his voyage began to look like sheer folly. A satirical cartoon published by George Cruikshank depicted Ross strutting at the head of a long procession that carried to the British Museum a bucket of red snow, a dead polar bear, and other voyage artifacts.

All the press was not negative, however. In April of the same year, the *Times* printed an admirably objective response to Barrow's venomous article,

> *It is impossible, however, to disguise, that some think, either that more might have been done, or, at least, that the impossibility of doing more has not been rendered sufficiently certain, by the expedition sent into Baffin's Bay. It is hard that a man's justification should depend on future events; yet it is not easy to see with precision, or to determine with assurance, whether Capt. Ross has obtained all the evidence which he might, respecting the nonexistence of an outlet into the Pacific, till other navigators have examined the same sea which he has traversed.*

Moreover, unlike Barrow, the *Times* found Ross's discovery of the unknown tribe of Inuit of paramount interest,

*It is not, however, for the purpose of discussing this subject, that we introduce notice of Captain Ross's book to the public, but with a view to diffuse more regularly the unexpected incident of the discovery of a race of men in Baffin's Bay, never before visited by civilized Europeans and totally unacquainted with the rest of the world.*

Ross's greatest support came through the *Edinburgh Review:*

*[T]here are evident symptoms of very ungrateful satisfaction with Captain Ross and his associates, because they have exposed themselves to great toils and perils, with the same negative success.——But in truth it is absurd to hold that there can be any want of success in an actual survey of regions previously unexplored. Captain Ross appears to have done his duty with great diligence, courage and ability; and to have told his story clearly and honestly.*

Despite Ross's Scottish heritage, the *Edinburgh Review* was not chauvinistic toward Ross. The magazine found his published narrative to be "very heavy reading, and that it appears to us to be encumbered with details which might very well have been spared." Furthermore, "[W]e were rather surprised at the positive manner in which the nonexistence of the passage is here stated." Nonetheless, "In concluding this sketch of Captain Ross's voyage, it is fully apparent that he has established and extended the discoveries of Baffin." And in a particularly insightful passage, the writer puzzles over the heat that Ross had suffered from the hot head of Barrow,

*The real philosopher is distinguished by his anxiety for truth; and we have never been able to understand on what other grounds the discovery of a North-*

*West Passage, to the north of Cumberland Strait at least, has been esteemed a desireable object. The condition of Baffin's Bay, to a late period in the summer, is such, and the uncertainty of effecting a passage through that Strait, if it existed, so great, as plainly to make it impossible that any advantageous commerce should ever be carried on by such a route with the Pacific Ocean.*

Notwithstanding these supportive articles and that most of Ross's fellow officers never spoke out against him (although they leaned toward the powerful Barrow in that getting command of a ship depended on him), Captain John Ross's navy career was permanently stalled. The furious and all-powerful Second Secretary thumbed his nose at Ross and appointed twenty-eight-year-old Parry to command a return expedition to Lancaster Sound in the spring of 1819.

To Parry's great fortune, the ice conditions in Baffin Bay and Lancaster Sound that year were exceptionally favorable for sailing. The voyage was ultimately one of the most successful British expeditions to the Arctic. Parry's two ships, HMSs *Hecla* and *Griper* sailed nearly 600 miles down Lancaster Sound, overwintered in the Arctic, and returned home safely with the loss of just one sailor (to scurvy) out of the combined crew of ninety-four men. It was on this voyage that Parry discovered Prince Regent Inlet.

Although Parry did not complete the Northwest Passage, his search demonstrated the high likelihood that Lancaster Sound is the gateway to the fabled Passage. A pleased Barrow awarded Parry with the command of three more Arctic voyages. Although each was less successful than the previous, Sir Edward Parry ranks as one of the most accomplished nineteenth-century commanders of expeditions to the Arctic. Nevertheless, it was on Parry's 1824–25 journey, his third command in the Arctic, that ice heavily damaged HMS *Fury*, forcing her abandonment on the subsequently named Fury Beach.

While Parry was winning the hearts of Barrow and the public, John Ross was not sitting idly by. He sought to redeem his reputation as an explorer, and throughout the 1820s, he made several proposals to the Admiralty for Arctic expeditions, including using ships equipped with steam power. His proposals, however, brought no fruit . . . Barrow held the controlling reins to Arctic exploration.

Undaunted by the rejections and determined to return to the Arctic, Ross asked an old friend, Felix Booth, to sponsor his expedition. Felix Booth was the wealthy manufacturer of Booth's Gin. At first, Booth refused because Parliament was offering an award of £20,000 for discovery of the Northwest Passage—the philanthropic Booth wanted no part of any awards. In early 1828, however, Parliament abolished the Board of Longitude, which had the effect of nullifying the award. With that, Ross again approached Booth, who was then willing to lend assistance.

Booth put up £10,000 (an additional £8,000 was later added), to which Ross added £3,000 of his own. With his backing in place, Ross bought the *Victory*, an 85-ton packet steamer formerly in service between Liverpool and the Isle of Man. *Victory* was refitted, strengthened, and raised five and a half feet to increase her tonnage to 150. The new steam engine, manufactured by the firm of Braithwaite and Ericsson, was also installed at that time. While *Victory's* refitting was underway, Ross traveled to Greenock and bought the *John*, a whaler, built of teak. The remainder of the funding was used for provisions for 1,000 days and the men's advances.

To determine longitude, Ross had on board five chronometers, including two of his own and one lent by Parkinson & Frodsham. He also had the usual complement of instruments for a ship of discovery, including a telescope, twelve thermometers, and four barometers. Even His Majesty King George IV's government loaned Ross a collection of books that had been used on previous voyages. Besides published accounts of notable voyages, such as Captain James Cook's, the library comprised books on astronomy, mineralogy, geology, botany, histories of Greenland and Labrador, and so forth.

Thus equipped, Captain John Ross and his crew of twenty departed England on 23 May 1829 for the rendezvous with the *John* at Loch Ryan, Scotland. Mr. Felix Booth accompanied Ross to Margate, whence he hailed a fishing boat for the ride home. Paddled along by steam, the trip to Margate (about fifty miles) took more than twelve hours . . . a dark portent for the engine's utility.

# CHAPTER THREE

# Inuit Friendship Brightens *Victory's* Winter

(October 1829–March 1830)

*F*ELIX *Harbor, October 8, 1829.* At daybreak, the thermometer registered 20 degrees. A fresh gale from the east-southeast pushed the
windchill down to about 22 below zero, making it "inconvenient as far
as our works were concerned," wrote Ross. Nor did the dark, gloomy
sky help. Nevertheless, without an excuse to dawdle, the men set about
their tasks to ready the *Victory* for winter.

Inside the ship, carpenters Chimham Thomas and Robert Shreeve
hammered and sawed, making alterations to reposition the cabin door
and move forward by four feet the bulkhead between the engine room
and the men's accommodations. This not only gave more room, but also
made it warmer. Up to that point, it had been impossible to keep the
temperature higher than 28 degrees. With that alteration, 45 degrees
was easily achieved and was deemed quite satisfactory by Captain Ross,

although, according to the steward William Light, the crew muttered among themselves about the cold. Light, who had sailed on Parry's *Hecla*, made a point of boasting to the crew that throughout that Arctic cruise the shipboard temperature never dropped below 60 degrees. Never again, claimed Light, would he sail on a nongovernment ship like the *Victory*. With his increased grumbling and antagonizing the crew, Steward William Light was turning into Ross's bugbear.

Light, however, was not the only cause for disharmony. As *Victory* settled in for the long Arctic night, the chill between Captain Ross and his nephew James grew increasingly apparent. Despite his signing on with full awareness of both the goal of the venture and also the nature of the ship, James was now convinced that taking a steam vessel to the polar seas was a mistake and made his opinion clear not only to Ross but also to the crew. Of course the captain, too, was convinced the steam engine was a folly, but only in its manufacture, not in principle, and Commander Ross's criticism served only to aggravate his uncle's frustration. Yet there was another reason behind the chill. Commander Ross had vastly more experience in the Arctic than his uncle, having sailed not only on the voyage to Baffin Bay in 1818, but also on all four of Parry's Arctic voyages. No doubt this was an important consideration for John Ross when he asked his nephew to join him. But as the adventure progressed, James Ross increasingly behaved as though his experience gave him license to command. "I best understood the nature of the navigation of those seas," James Ross later testified to Parliament, "and, therefore, that I should render some important assistance to [Captain Ross] in his undertaking." While it was true that Ross valued James's experience, Captain Ross *never* would have considered allowing his nephew command over the navigation of *Victory*, which James Ross seemed to think he deserved. John Ross was the *Victory's* captain—period.

To make room to move the bulkhead, engineers Alexander Brunton and Allan Macinnes dismantled the cantankerous steam engine and hauled it out onto the ice. Some of the parts, such as the two iron boilers, had to be cut into sections because they were too large to fit through the hatchway. Outside temperatures as low as 9 degrees made this ordinarily difficult job hazardous when iron parts, brittled by the cold, shattered like glass. Seamen dragged the more manageable pieces to shore, nearly a mile away, but left the massive boilers and larger parts on the ice alongside the ship. Even so, the labor was extreme. Although making more room in the ship was worthwhile, the wisdom of dragging the old parts a mile to shore was questionable and probably pointless. Ross's motive remains unclear. It may have been his way of maintaining authority, for which he was so well noted; but more likely, it was merely a quirk: Ross had a penchant for collecting, and he never wanted to discard anything. William Light thought the whole operation of saving the boilers was absurd and griped that for all he cared, the boilers could drop to the bottom of the sea. He joked that they should paint the inscription "Dealer in Marine Stores" on the stern of the ship. As we shall see, Ross even made provision for future salvage of the doomed *Victory* when she rested at the bottom of a bay in one of the most remote regions on earth.

While Brunton and Macinnes worked at dismantling, Captain Ross ordered others to cut a canal through the ice to haul the ship to a more secure location. Although the ice was but eight inches thick, the first day of cutting and warping brought the ship just six feet closer to shore. Up and down, hour after hour, the men worked the long ice saws and shoved the sawed-out slabs under the ice to get them out of the way. Frigid water splashed onto their woolen jackets and leather boots and turned each foot into a clumsy, icy mass that kept their feet numbed with the cold. Each day the ice thickened, the temperature dropped, and progress slowed. After a mere twenty feet, even Ross thought the effort fruitless and ordered a halt. The ice had determined *Victory's* winter quarters.

The men spent the next week dragging more engine parts and carrying supplies to shore. Snowstorms and gale-force winds cut visibility and hid crevices in the ice. More than once a heavily laden sailor plunged up to his knees in gelid seawater. In a panic to extricate himself, he soaked his leather-gloved hands in the water that bubbled up onto the ice. His gloves, like his boots, stiffened into an ice-coated mass. The stricken sailor hurried back to the relative warmth of the ship, where his mates chiseled the gloves from his hands.

In spite of the shivering cold, the pounding wind, and the hazardous labor, everyone's health remained fine, with two exceptions: James Marslin, the armorer, showed ominous signs of tuberculosis, and Richard Wall, a harpooner, had fallen down the hatchway into the engine room. Ross considered the twenty-six-year-old harpooner an excellent seaman. Though "not powerful; [he] was one of the best men we had." Fortunately, the injuries Wall sustained in his fall were not life-threatening and he was back on the job in a week.

Marslin, on the other hand, was seriously ill and showed no signs of improvement. His situation deeply affected Ross, because Marslin was supposed to have sailed with the *John* and so would have been back home by then if the *John's* crew had not mutinied. As it was, Ross had been unaware of Marslin's condition until they were far at sea, when Marslin let on that only a few months earlier he had been hospitalized. All the way across Baffin Bay, everyone kept alert for a whaler to take the dying man home, but none was ever spotted. Aggravated by the severe cold and dampness, Marslin's health grew poorer each day and confined him to his hammock on the dark, cold lower deck.

Meanwhile, Marslin's mates continued to winterize the ship. They spread a two-foot-thick layer of snow on the upper deck for insulation and to seal out the wind. After they trod it down, they spread a coating of sand and gravel on top to provide traction. Obtaining gravel was in itself a Herculean task. Holes dug through the ice and soil progressed at the rate of a foot a day. After several days of frustrating labor, they at last reached the concretelike stratum of gravel. Yet it, too, yielded only to the blows of a pickax.

To protect *Victory*'s rigging from the Arctic winter's hurricane-force winds, the crew removed every shroud, stay, deadeye, and tackle until nothing remained standing on deck except the lower masts. Then, from the spare sails of the *Fury*, they made a canvas tent that completely enshrouded the ship's upper deck. If the weather was too severe for outside work (such as chiseling out gravel or banking snow around the ship for added insulation), Ross insisted that the men take a daily walk 'round and 'round the deck for an hour or more as a guard against scurvy. Exercise, along with clean, dry bedding and a good diet were the early nineteenth-century preventatives against scurvy. For extra measure, Ross added a prohibition on swearing.

With the housing completed and winter settling in, the crew fell into a daily routine: up at six o'clock in the morning; hammocks taken down; deck scrubbed with hot sand; breakfast of cocoa or tea; watch for wild animals or natives; record the weather, tides, and occurrence of aurora. Dinner was served at noon; tea at five o'clock. Those who wished, attended classes each evening from 6 until 9 P.M. At 10 P.M., the men slung their hammocks and retired.

Classes while wintering in the Arctic were the inspiration of Edward Parry. As commander of the first expedition to intentionally winter in the Arctic (1819–20), Parry realized that his crew needed shipboard occupations to combat the unending boredom with their confinement. Among Parry's ploys were a newspaper, plays put on by the crew and officers, and a school. Ross saw the wisdom in Parry's ideas, and although *Victory* had no newspaper and the men did not put on plays, Captain Ross and his officers conducted evening classes for the men. The curriculum included navigation, astronomy, mathematics, and even reading and writing for the three men who were illiterate. More than once, while the illiterates stammered their way through their ABCs, Captain Ross's listening skill was taxed to its limit. His eyelids drooped heavily, and before long, the portly Ross fell sound asleep; his deep, sonorous snores elicited not a few snickers from the studious jack-tars.

On Sundays, no work was permitted, and the evening instruction shifted to reading scriptures and singing psalms. As with the week-night school, attendance on Sundays was voluntary. Even so, the classes were well attended, remarked Ross, and "the men seemed truly to feel that they all belonged to one family: evincing mutual kindness, with a regularity and tranquility of behaviour which are not very general on board a ship." William Light carried a different opinion. He thought that the classes were an embarrassment and waste of time. "If they could not read nor write when they entered onboard the *Victory*," he wrote, "they were exactly in the same condition when they left it."

As for Ross's Sunday worship service, Light said that the captain's "observance of the duties of the Sabbath was more mechanical than the result of that inward feeling of sanctity and reverence." Even so, Captain Ross's deep voice was distinctly heard to conclude his prayers with, "and that we may return in safety, to enjoy the blessings of the land and the fruits of our labour." Light used even this simple prayer to ridicule his captain. Years later, when they arrived safely at home, Light wailed, "But did he, in return for such a gracious display of divine Providence, give to his men the fruits of their labour . . . did he give those men what was their lawful due?" Indeed, Ross did, and even more so, as we shall see.

At the end of November, ship's purser William Thom gave Captain Ross an accounting of the provisions, which, according to Ross and Thom's reckoning, were satisfactory for the duration of the planned fifteen-month expedition. Up to this point, the twenty-three men had consumed preserved meats at a rate of fifty-four pounds per week. Other mainstays of their diet were nine pounds of raisins every second Monday; nearly three pounds of sugar daily; four and a half pints of spirits on Saturdays; daily cocoa, tea, rice, and lemon juice; and a weekly allowance of twenty pounds of both salt pork and beef. In addition, the crew consumed sixty pounds of bread each week. Fresh bread was baked on Sundays and Thursdays. The men highly welcomed the baking days, not only for the delicious aroma and the anticipated fresh-baked goods, but because the ovens raised the cabin temperature 10 degrees.

The sun made its final appearance for the forthcoming six weeks on December 1. In fact, the sun had dropped below the horizon for the winter six days earlier, but strong refraction of the atmosphere that unusually clear, cold day—the thermometer vacillated between 31 and 35 degrees below zero—gave the men a much-welcomed extra glimpse of the sun's upper limb. "[W]ith the same circumstances at its next rising, we should not be condemned to more than six weeks of its total absence," wrote a hopeful Ross.

In spite of the extreme temperature, working outside those first two weeks of December was tolerable in that the wind was barely a zephyr. The crew took advantage of the quiet weather to construct an observatory on shore for astronomical, meteorological, and magnetic observations. Built of blocks of snow "mortared" in place with more snow and water, the observatory had the solidity of a granite building. Besides the usual telescope, thermometers, and barometers, the scientific instruments included magnetic needles and electrometers to study effects of the northern lights.* Under the direction of William Thom, and weather permitting, instrument readings were taken faithfully every hour of every day.

Through early December, the temperature fluctuated as much as 28 degrees but continued to be bitter cold. On December 5, the high was

---

*At the time of Ross's expedition, the northern lights, or aurora borealis, was a profound mystery. Nineteenth-century voyagers to the Arctic, where the beautiful light show is a regular occurrence, made a point to carry along various scientific instruments for studying the phenomenon. The aurora had been correctly surmised to be a magnetic phenomenon, but its cause and height above the surface of the earth were unknown. The origin of the aurora was not established with certainty until the second half of the twentieth century. Satellites orbiting earth helped to determine that the magnetic field of the earth deflects high-energy plasma from the sun toward the North and South Poles. Upon encountering the earth's upper atmosphere, hundreds of miles above the poles, these high-energy particles produce the glow as a result of collisions with oxygen and nitrogen atoms.

just 8 degrees below zero. On December 17, a clear but nearly dark-as-night day, it was so cold that the mercury thermometers froze. (Mercury freezes at 39 degrees below zero; the alcohol thermometers continued to be workable.) The men amused themselves by making bullets of frozen mercury and firing them through a one-inch-thick plank. Another bullet shot through the board was molded from frozen almond oil.

During the third week of December, the days grew blustery and the men confined themselves to the ship. The canvas roofing flapped and the lower masts shook when winds, approaching forty miles per hour, howled in the twenty-four-hour darkness. Shifting floes collided, rumbled, and rattled the ship. As the temperature plummeted, icebergs cracked asunder, fell into the sea, and sent percussions that shook the men in their hammocks. No one dared to venture ashore to the observatory. The bored men picked oakum, made spun yarn, and attended their evening classes.

The piercing wind and bitter cold affected even the wildlife. A starving ermine climbed aboard the ship in search of warmth and food. It hid beneath some tanks but was captured when it scampered across the deck. Although the men fed and cared for it like a pet, the little animal died after four days.

*Felix Harbor, Christmas Day, 1829.* The temperature rose to 16 degrees below zero, and a light breeze gave a windchill no worse than about 20 below. Ross stepped outside to survey his ship, proudly decked out for the occasion in all her flags and highlighted by the cold light of Venus that pierced the clear, black sky. "The elements themselves seemed to have determined that it should be a noted day to us, for it commenced with a most beautiful and splendid aurora, occupying the whole vault above." And although Ross and his nephew failed to procure fresh game on a hunting trek, Christmas dinner, notwithstanding, was a wondrous fare: roast beef, minced pies, vegetable soups, plum pudding, and iced cherry brandy with fruit, all washed down with a generous allotment of that favorite of sailors—rum. Following their repast, the men made merry with singing and dancing, although the dancing, as William Light sighed, "felt the want of those objects which impart the greatest charm to it; for there was no sparkling female eye to give animation to the scene, nor a rosy lip on which a passionate kiss could be pressed."

New Year's Day was celebrated with extra rounds of grog and a generous portion of preserved meats. And again the men spent the evening in song and dance. As was not unusual for a navy officer, Captain Ross declined to join the men in their merrymaking. Light took the opportunity to remind his mates that, when he sailed with Edward Parry, Parry joined the crew to put on plays and even published a newspaper and led "them from gloom and discontent to comparative cheerfulness and happiness." In truth, even the gregarious Parry distanced himself from the crew. As he wrote in his journal, he "directed a small increase in the men's usual proportion of fresh meat at Christmas dinner," but otherwise spent the day dining with his fellow officers.

Yet there is no question that Captain Ross was more aloof than Parry and oftentimes behaved as a hermit. That New Year's Eve he sat alone in his cabin, sipped his gin, and reflected with pleasure on their situation. He rejoiced that not one man had been injured by the frost, congratulated himself on the arrangements for insulating and ventilating the ship, was pleased that the men had been kept well occupied with his classes, saw their good position to advance explorations come the eventual thaw, and expressed gratitude to his never-to-be-forgotten "spirited and liberal London merchant," Felix Booth.

Ross's one anguish, as the year closed, was the sorry state of James Marslin, whose consumption was rapidly taking him to his end.

During his voyage to Prince Regent Inlet in 1824–25, Edward Parry had conducted experiments to measure the speed of sound at various temperatures. To effect the experiments, his men fired a six-pounder cannon from the top of a hill. Two miles away, observers on HMS *Hecla* measured the elapsed time between sighting the flash from the cannon and hearing its boom. From this length of time, they calculated the sound's velocity, much as one estimates the distance to a lightning strike by counting seconds from the bolt to the thunderclap. Along with everything else, when Parry abandoned HMS *Fury*, he left the cannon on Fury Beach. Ross retrieved the cannon to continue the experiments.

On January 6, Ross's men took advantage of the day's clear weather and relatively moderate temperature (8 degrees below zero) to haul the long, brass cannon to the top of a hill overlooking Felix Harbor. Strong winds a couple days beforehand had cleared much of the hillside of snow, which made the task of dragging the half-ton cannon over the rocks and up the incline somewhat easier. For the next three days, they conducted their sound-velocity experiments—the cannon's boom raced through the deep-purple-and-red-tinted sky and echoed off the surrounding hills and icebergs. The concussions reached not only the hills and the icebergs, but also disturbed the peace of an Inuit village located about three miles away. *Victory's* little band of adventurers was about to see a considerable change to their humdrum daily routine.

. . .

*January 9, 1830, 11 A.M.* Allan Macinnes was at work in the observatory when he thought he heard strange voices. He looked outside, and, to his surprise, saw four men standing near an iceberg about a mile from the ship. Macinnes shouted to his shipmates to summon the captain.

Captain Ross, Commander James Ross, George MacDiarmid, and Macinnes gathered together and, backed by several seamen, approached the strangers. As the officers drew near, the four natives retreated behind the iceberg but quickly reappeared with twenty-seven companions, including an old and infirm man seated on a sledge. The old man's companions shoved him out ahead of the assembly. Apparently selected as a sacrifice to see whether these strangers to their land were friend or foe, the old man sat with his arms folded and "with a countenance perfectly resigned to his fate," as Captain Ross described him in his journal.

"*Tima tima,*" shouted Ross, knowing the word for salutation between meeting tribes. The Inuit answered with the same. Ross and his men advanced to within sixty yards and threw down their guns as a symbol of peace. Dozens of spears and knives sailed into the air in every direction, amid cheering and hand waving, as the natives reciprocated.

Commander James Ross, who had some familiarity with the Inuit language, spoke to and embraced the old man. "Even then he seemed to doubt that he was not destined to be the first to receive the poniard; and it was not until unequivocal proofs of friendship were interchanged with the whole party that he appeared satisfied his last moments had not arrived," wrote Captain Ross.

Ross sent a sailor back to the ship for gifts, stepped up to the natives, and embraced each in turn. "This seemed to produce great delight, expressed, on all hands, by laughing, and clamour, and strange gestures: while we immediately found ourselves established in their unhesitating confidence."

By that time, Ross's messenger had returned with hoops of iron for each man, which "excited universal delight." In return, the Inuit offered their spears and knives, which Captain Ross refused to accept, much to the natives' astonishment but obvious satisfaction.

Ross then invited their new friends to visit the ship, and Ross, himself, drew the old man's sledge. According to Ross, the seventy-year-old man, whose name was Alictu, "was much pleased" with the honor.

Upon arrival at the ship, "they expressed no surprise... nor did they show any of those marks of astonishment, at either the ship itself or the quantity of wood and iron before them, which we had found among the northern savages of Baffin's Bay in 1818," remarked Ross. He concluded that the natives were no strangers to these materials and had had previous communication with Europeans, or, at least, had had contact with other tribes who had. In fact, one of the Inuit possessed a knife blade that still showed the English maker's mark. And although the knives the natives had thrown to the ground were made from bone or the antlers of reindeer ("a very inoffensive weapon," noted Ross), once the natives were aboard *Victory*, Ross discovered that each man had a knife of steel concealed beneath his clothing.

As to their overall appearance, Ross observed that it "was very superior to our own; being at least as well clothed, and far better fed; with plump cheeks, of as rosy a colour as they could be under so dark a skin."

The visitors stared wide-eyed as Ross, like an excited schoolboy at open house, guided them on a tour of his ship. He led them three at a time down to his cabin, where he showed them whatever caught their attention or would impress them the most. Then they trooped back up to the main deck, where he fetched another group of three. His guests wanted to know the name and use of everything and had no difficulty comprehending Ross's explanations in spite of his ignorance of their language. They especially enjoyed viewing themselves in mirrors and seeing the light produced by candles and lamps. And they expressed delight upon recognizing their own race when shown portraits in Edward Parry's *Journal of a Second Voyage for the Discovery of a North-West Passage*, a published account of Parry's 1821–23 voyage to the Arctic. They did not like, however, the preserved meats offered them. Although one man said the meat tasted good, he later admitted to the younger Ross that he had lied, and after requesting permission from their hosts, the rest of the visitors threw away their portions. Yet when offered whale oil, they swallowed it with gusto, prompting Captain Ross to comment, "Thus admirably are the tastes of all these tribes adapted to their compulsory food . . . nor, assuredly, had these men, amidst their blubber and their oil . . . any reason to envy the refined tables of the south."

Just like John Ross's "Arctic Highlanders" of his 1818 voyage to Baffin Bay, the Inuit of Boothia Peninsula could not believe that the men of *Victory* had not brought along their wives. How or why, they wondered, could these men be without their wives? Every Inuit man has a wife and every woman has a husband, they told Ross, although the only way to effect this within such a limited populace was through an occasional bigamy. This was fine with everyone, however, as each sincerely wished the other a life of fulfillment and happiness. As friendships developed between the two cultures, the accommodating women filled many a void created by the sailors' missing wives and lovers. The steward, who took delight in portraying Ross as stuffy and "trebly steeped in the starch of official dignity," tells us that the women were "not allowed to experiment their seductive wiles on the callous heart of Capt. Ross." Notwithstanding, Ross was not a judgmental prude, and he had no qualms with extending to his men permission to visit the Inuit women. While his crew were trysting with the women of Boothia Peninsula, Ross was quite content to sit alone in his cabin with his ubiquitous tumbler of Booth's Gin.

The visitors stayed aboard *Victory* the whole afternoon and even danced a hornpipe with several sailors while another played his fiddle. Down on the ice, meanwhile, a native and an officer ran a foot race. Out of "equal politeness on both sides," no victor was declared.

Finally, it came time for their new friends to depart. Ross accompanied them homeward for about two miles, where they made a mark in the ice with the understanding that they should meet at that spot the next day to take Ross to the village to meet the women and children.

That evening Ross recorded in his journal,

*This was a most satisfactory day; for we had given up all expectation of meeting inhabitants in this place; while we knew that it was to the natives that we must look for such geographical information as would assist us in extricating ourselves from our difficulties and in pursuing our course. It was for philosophers to interest themselves in speculating on a horde so small, and so secluded, occupying themselves so apparently hopeless a country, so barren, so wild, and so repulsive; and yet enjoying the most perfect vigour, the most well-fed health, and all else that here constitutes, not merely wealth, but the opulence of luxury; since they are as amply furnished with provisions as with every other thing that could be necessary to their wants.*

The following day, the temperature was 37 degrees below zero. The sky was clear and the air calm. It was Sunday. As usual, Ross conducted the worship service; but, eager to visit the Inuit village, he held the service unusually early, hurried through it, and departed immediately thereafter.

With armloads of glass beads and needles for the women, Ross and his officers set out for the meeting place. Upon arrival at the agreed-upon spot, they found the Inuit men milling about, waiting as promised, in spite of the severe cold. Weapons were again thrown in the air, embraces exchanged, and upon completion of the formalities, everyone headed for the village. After a hike of about a half-hour, they arrived at the village of about a dozen igloos, each having the appearance of an inverted basin, joked Ross.

Crouching down on his hands and knees, the imposing captain crawled through the long, crooked tunnel that formed the entryway to an igloo. Once inside, he could stand erect—as long as he stood in the center of the ten-foot-diameter dome. Ross caught his breath and choked on the disagreeable redolence as he peered through the greasy haze that filled the strange, round chamber. His eyes slowly grew accustomed to the dim interior, lighted by smoky oil lamps and the feeble January daylight that filtered through an oval skylight of ice. John Ross gazed with wonder at the exotic scene that surrounded him.

Opposite to the entranceway, several natives, "with little discrimination of wives, husbands, and children," lounged on a communal bed. A bank of snow about two feet high covered with a sealskin "bottom sheet" and a deerskin blanket formed the bed. A woman sat at the end of the bed and tended to an oil lamp, which not only provided light, but also served as a cooking stove. The lamp was a dished-out stone filled with blubber. A moss wick along the edge of the bowl held the flame. Spare moss hung nearby in handy reach. Simmering in a stone dish, suspended above the flame from a tripod of bone, was a mixture of oil, deer, and seal meat.

The inhabitants told Ross that seal, musk ox, reindeer, fox, hare, and fish constituted their main diet. Although fish were eaten raw or dried, they preferred the other meats cooked in oil if they had enough fuel, which was always a precious commodity. Ptarmigan, when they could be caught, were delicacies reserved for the children and women. Another lamp, nearly two feet in length and holding a gallon or more of blubber and oil, heated the igloo.

Ross observed,

*[T]he apartment [temperature] was perfectly comfortable . . . and of such provisions, there seemed no want. Everything else—dresses, implements, as well as provisions—lay about in unspeakable confusion, showing that order, at least, was not in the class of their virtues.*

Eager to gain information regarding his springtime prospects for locating the Northwest Passage, Ross embarked on a string of geographical inquiries of his hosts. To his surprise, they were familiar with Igloolik, Winter Island, Repulse Bay, and Ackoolee, all of which were places to the south and east that Edward Parry had visited previously and had charted in considerable detail. Ross was disappointed, however, that he could not get confirmation for any westward-leading channels from the southern end of Prince Regent Inlet. To the best of his understanding of the natives' replies, no such channel existed. Although frustrated with the news and difficult communication, Ross still held hope that others in the tribe might provide clearer information. But it was time to head back to the ship.

Before he left, Ross invited a native named Tulluahiu to come to the ship to see Surgeon MacDiarmid. Tulluahiu had lost his left leg in an encounter with a polar bear, and Ross thought that perhaps a wooden leg might be fitted. Tulluahiu promised to come the next day.

On the way back to the ship, a blast of wind froze one of Ross's cheeks. Unaware that his cheek had been bitten by the frost, Ross was surprised when one of his Inuit guides made a snowball, rubbed the frozen flesh, and, he later wrote in his journal,

> . . . thus certainly saving me from a disagreeable sore. After this, he always continued near me, frequently reminding me to put my hand to the same part, for fear of a recurrence of the attack. This was good-natured, and aided, with all else, to give us a favourable impression of these people.

When the crew awoke at 6 A.M. the next day, the outside thermometer registered 35 degrees below zero. The temperature never rose higher than 30 below the entire day, and not one sailor dared venture outside. Nevertheless, at one o'clock in the afternoon, the crippled Tulluahiu arrived for his appointment with the surgeon, drawn on a sledge by his friend Tiagashu.

Tulluahiu was about forty years old and, as many other men in the tribe, sported a goatee and mustache and kept his hair clipped short. Although a worried expression marked his countenance, he was a cheerful man, who was amused by the Europeans' idiosyncrasies, such as Ross's insistence on measuring everyone's stature. At five feet eight inches tall, he was of median height for the men of the village.

Although much plumper than his companions, his excess weight may have resulted from lack of exercise because he was unable to partake in the village hunts. Indeed, he told Ross that it was a rare day when he could join the others. To get around, neighbors pulled him on a sledge or, if he wished to walk, one or two supported him at his side.

Tulluahiu's friend Tiagashu was the eldest son of Alictu, the old man Captain Ross had drawn on a sledge to the ship on the first day of their encounter. Tiagashu represented the exact extreme in build from Tulluahiu in that he was more slender than the others were, although he looked roly-poly when outfitted in all his furs. His disposition was mild and, according to Ross, he was an exceptionally warm and intelligent man who was industrious and cared deeply for his large family, which consisted of his elderly mother and father, his wife, their three children, and another child from his wife's previous marriage. Yet he was physically weak, and providing for his family taxed him so severely that at times they were on the brink of starvation. Others in the community— always willing to divide their provisions even if they did not have enough for the next day—helped. Even so, there were times when Tiagashu and his family suffered so dearly that they had no recourse but to turn to Ross, who unhesitatingly helped them through their famine.

Surgeon MacDiarmid examined Tulluahiu's leg, which had been severed just below the knee, and he found the wound well healed and a good candidate for a wooden leg. Tulluahiu explained that the healing was a result of the care he had received from his companions. He told MacDiarmid that when the bear mauled his leg, his friends formed a tourniquet of thongs around his thigh and stripped the loose flesh from just below his knee with their razor-sharp knives. Like Ross's amputation of Hardy's arm, however, the splintered bones presented a problem.

To create a clean break, the native "surgeons" bored a hole in the ice and told Tulluahiu to insert the tip of his mangled leg in the hole. Then, in a quick, sideways motion, they snapped off the protruding bones. They completed the operation by cauterizing the wound with burning moss.

While Tulluahiu related his horrific experience, carpenter Chimham Thomas sat down next to him and made measurements for the wooden leg. Until that moment, Tulluahiu apparently had not fully grasped what the carpenter and surgeon hoped to do for him. Then, realizing their plan, the excited Inuk suddenly turned even more openly communicative.

*Ah ha!* thought Ross. Here might be an opportunity to gain information on the prospects for the Northwest Passage. Ross spread out before Tulluahiu his and Parry's charts of the region. Without hesitation, Tulluahiu pointed out the location of both his village and the ship. Ross handed him a pencil. Tulluahiu drew a line showing the route the families had taken from their previous encampment to their present location and counted nine fingers to indicate that they had slept that many times during their journey. A beaming Ross looked on.

Next, Tiagashu took the pencil and drew the unknown (to Ross, anyway) coastline to the southwest, indicating capes, bays, rivers, nearby islands, and a fine lake to fish for salmon.

Tulluahiu then took the pencil back from Tiagashu and marked a nine-day overland trek to the west that would bring Ross to the salt sea. But was there a water route to this western sea? Ross wanted to know. Neither man could say. They said, however, that someone else in their community was more knowledgeable on the topic and that they would be happy to bring him the next day.

The geography lesson over, Ross offered the two men plum pudding and brandy, both of which they turned down. Instead, Tiagashu and Tulluahiu amused each other by holding up a large magnifying glass between them so that each saw the other's grotesquely magnified face. Deeply touched, Ross looked on and mused,

> [O]ur brandy was as odious [to them] as our pudding; as they have yet, therefore, to acquire the taste which has, in ruining the morals, hastened the extermination of their American neighbours to the southward. If, however, these tribes must finally disappear, as seems their fate, it is at least better that they should die gradually by the force of rum, than that they should be exterminated in masses by the fire and sword of Spanish conquest; since there is at least some pleasure, such as it is, in the meantime, while there is also a voluntary, if slow suicide, in exchange for murder and misery. All which it is our duty to provide for, is that this event be not hastened by oppression and wrong, that it may not be attended by the suffering of individuals.

When at last Ross snapped out of his reverie, it was time for the two Inuit to head back to their village. Captain Ross presented each man with an empty meat canister and explained to Tulluahiu that his new leg would be ready in three days. Gleeful over their gifts, the two men departed in high spirits. Ross reflected further,

> It is delightful to be able to overwhelm the needy with gold; not less so, I imagine, than when it is done at no cost; and here we had made these poor men as rich and as happy, with what was little better than an old saucepan, as if our canisters had been made of silver and were to be purchased with gold. Let no man imagine that he knows what a present is worth, till he has found what

*happiness can be produced by a blue bead, a yellow button, a needle, or a piece of an old iron hoop.*

As promised, Tiagashu showed up the next morning with his friend, Ikmallik, the purported geography expert. Ikmallik's wife, Apellagliu, also came along. She was Tulluahiu's sister, who not only looked like Tulluahiu, but also shared his tendency for corpulence. Ross observed that Ikmallik and Apellagliu made a charming couple who had a "mutual desire to oblige each other." Along with Tiagashu, Ikmallik would become one of Ross's favorites. Ikmallik obviously liked Ross, too, and brought for trade anything he thought Ross might want. He even helped Ross rebuild his magnetic observatory, "which he did cheerfully and extremely well," wrote the captain. Ikmallik's stature, at five feet ten inches, combined with his unusual strength and high intelligence, garnered him the respect of the whole tribe.

An array of tattoos ornamented the thirty-six-year-old Apellagliu's face, which was the practice for most of the women. The tattoos consisted of straight, black lines on her brow, her chin, her cheeks, and each side of her mouth. (Somewhat later, a young woman named Kemig unabashedly posed for Ross to show how the women's tattoos extended across their breast, along their shoulders, and down their arms. To make a tattoo, the woman used a piece of deer sinew that had been moistened with oil and saliva and coated with lampblack. She threaded the sinew on a bone needle and drew the blackened string through a series of deep stitches—about twenty to the inch—in her skin along the pattern she wished to create. When finished, she rubbed the area with oil to stanch the bleeding. The process was quite painful, according to Captain George Lyon, Parry's second in command on his 1821–23 Arctic voyage. Lyon had submitted himself for a tattoo two inches long, and when finished, he remarked, "I could now form an idea of the price paid by the [Inuit] females for their embellishments.")

Invited to Ross's cabin, Ikmallik, Apellagliu, and Tiagashu sat around a table on which Ross had spread out his charts. While Ross and his nephew James watched, Ikmallik drew coastline after coastline: to the south, the west, and east. Every feature, be it river, lake, hill, or bay, had a name, which Ikmallik delighted in telling Ross. All the while, Apellagliu sat at the table with her arms folded and proudly observed the impression her husband's mapmaking had on the visitors to her country.

To the onlookers' amazement, Ikmallik's coastlines even included Wager Bay, more than 340 miles south of *Victory's* present location. This bay, which extends off the northern end of Hudson Bay, was well known to European explorers and had at one time been considered a likely candidate for the Northwest Passage.

Ikmallik drew "very correctly" (remarked Ross) landmark after landmark with which the two Rosses were already familiar. He went on to point out that, when the waters to the south thawed in summer, they would be open until autumn for sailing. This was good news. But what about a waterway to the west? None existed, Ikmallik replied. According to Ikmallik, the only waterway that led westward from Prince Regent Inlet was in the north.

(Ikmallik was correct. Prince Regent Inlet leads to a dead end, as Ross later confirmed. The westward route to the north that Ikmallik mentioned was probably Bellot Strait, at Brentford Bay, which Ross had sailed past on his way down Prince Regent Inlet five months earlier.)

From that day on, Ikmallik was known as the "Hydrographer." He was not, however, the only person in the community who could provide such detailed charts.

The following day, Ross paid a visit to Tulluahiu's igloo. When he arrived, however, Tulluahiu was absent, having taken advantage of the calm air—which rendered the 35-below-zero temperature less danger-ous—and had braved to accompany his friends on a seal-hunting expe-dition. Tulluahiu's wife, Tirikshiu, had stayed at home, though, and she invited Ross to come in for a chat.

Seated inside the igloo with Tirikshiu were Tulluahiu's elderly mother, Ajoua, and the couple's three children. Their eldest child, Shul-lanina, was a pretty girl, whose rosy, tattooed cheeks added a decidedly feline air to her beauty. She wore her hair tied in two long bundles that draped over her slender shoulders. Captain Ross did not fail to observe that the nubile girl had the "best figure" in the community. Her con-genial thirty-eight-year-old mother Tirikshiu (whose name meant "ermine") was one of the tallest women at five feet five-and-a-quarter inches, according to Ross's ever-handy measuring tape. Although Ross measured the heights of adults and boys, he never mentioned whether he measured the height of a teenage girl. Perhaps the gentlemanly cap-tain felt it inappropriate—although the pleasure he experienced judging the charms of the youthful maidens was unmistakable.

Like Ikmallik, Tirikshiu was well versed in the local geography. As a matter of fact, she was a sister to the Hydrographer. (Ikmallik and Tul-luahiu had each married the other's sister.) Much to Ross's wonderment, the charts she drew were even more detailed than her brother's. Not only did she draw miles of coastline as he had, but she also added many islands and marked locations where Ross should sleep and others where he might obtain food on his travels. Her enhancements to the invaluable information already provided by Ikmallik astounded Ross—what a bonanza for his forthcoming explorations!

As Ross thanked Tirikshiu and stooped to crawl from the igloo, she halted him—she had a gift, she said, for his wife—apparently unaware that Ross was a widower. Ross trundled back to the snow bench and settled down among the furs with the children and mother-in-law while Tirikshiu pulled a bulky bundle from a darkened corner of the igloo. Ajoua and she watched with pride as the courtly captain opened the bundle. Inside was a complete woman's outfit. Sewn chiefly from deerskin, it consisted of a double layer jacket, trousers, boots, and overshoes. Ross held the jacket up to Tirikshiu. It reached from her chin to the middle of her thigh and had a pointed flap that dangled down to about mid-calf in both the front and rear. The jacket was made with two deerskin layers constructed such that the hair of the inner layer was next to the wearer's body and the hair of the outer layer faced outward. Long sleeves reached to cover the fingers. The matching trousers, which reached to just below the knees and were designed to cover the tops of the boots, had drawstrings to hold them up. The boots, like the jacket, also consisted of a double layer of deerskin, except the hair of both layers faced inward. To complete the ensemble, there was a pair of ankle-high, watertight sealskin overshoes.

This talented woman, remarked Ross, was not only an accomplished hydrographer, but she was also a splendid seamstress. He noted the unusual care she had taken with the symmetry and matching the colors on each side of the jacket and trousers. She had added a fringe of white hair (from the thighs of deer) along the bottom of the jacket, around the opening of the hood, and at the ends of the sleeves. Her workmanship was "a first-rate specimen of mantua-making, and it was my business to estimate it as a London lady would have done the loftiest production of the highest dress-maker in the calendar of fashion." Although he had nothing with him but a silk handkerchief to give her in return, Ross was gratified that his small gift "attracted her chief attention."

Just then, Tulluahiu and the hunting party returned in high spirits with a large seal. Several of *Victory's* hands had witnessed the capture, and they described their hunting adventure to the captain on the walk back to the ship.

To begin the hunt, the sailors explained, the Inuit walked quietly across the ice while keeping a constant lookout for a seal's breathing hole. The hole is about two inches in diameter and may be in the center of a small volcanolike mound. If the hole were active, the animal could be heard, from time to time, as it worked at the ice with its claws to enlarge the hole so it could climb onto the ice. As the animal enlarged the hole, it scraped the ice thinner in a broader and broader circle, but the initial two-inch breathing hole remained about the same size. When the ice was thin enough for the hunter to hear the seal's breathing, he speared the hapless creature right through the thin ice. Waiting for an opportunity to strike, however, could take hours, if not all day.

To prepare for the wait, the hunter built a semicircular wall about four feet in height to protect himself from the wind. Within the arc of the wall he sat motionless on a stool formed from a solid block of snow. To prevent rustling his clothing while he sat, he tied his legs together at the knees. Within easy reach by his side were his spear and knives, which rested on fork-shaped sticks that poked up from the snow. This arrangement allowed him to pick up the weapons without making the slightest sound. Finally, when it was time to strike the seal, he quietly lifted his spear from its fork rests and plunged it through the ice using both hands and all his strength. He then enlarged the hole with his knife, stabbed the seal again, wrapped a line attached to the spear around his foot, and dragged the animal from the water.

January 15, the day scheduled for fitting Tulluahiu's wooden leg, opened with a gentle breeze blowing about ten miles per hour and the thermometer at 41 below. Even this breeze, which registered just force 3 on the Beaufort Scale*, created a windchill around 70 below zero. No one expected Tulluahiu to come. But show he did.

Captain Ross led the one-legged man to his cabin, where Carpenter Thomas waited with the wooden leg, elegantly carved with the date and the ship's name. To everyone's delight, the leg was a perfect fit, and in no time, Tulluahiu "began to strut about the cabin, in apparent ecstasy,"

---

*Devices for measuring the speed of the wind have been around since the seventeenth century, but were not in common use and Ross did not have such a device aboard the *Victory*. He reported wind speed in terms of Admiral Sir Francis Beaufort's 12-point scale (developed in 1805), which assigned a name and number for the wind based on the wind's effect. For example, a wind of force 2 on the Beaufort Scale was called a "light breeze," and its effect on the sea was "small wavelets still short but more pronounced; crests have a glassy appearance but do not break." On land, a force 2 wind would result in "wind felt on face; leaves rustle; ordinary vane moved by wind." As another example, a force 9 wind on the Beaufort Scale was called a "strong gale" and on sea produced "high waves; dense streaks of foam along the direction of the wind; sea begins to roll; spray affects visibility" and on land "slight structural damage occurs; chimney pots and slates removed." In the early part of the twentieth century, the Beaufort Scale was equated to wind speed in terms of miles per hour. It is these equivalents that are quoted throughout this work.

As we have seen, Ross was well aware of the extra cooling effect caused by the wind, along with the danger of working outside in freezing temperatures when a strong wind was blowing. Quantifying the combined effect of the wind and cold on exposed flesh, however, was not done until the 1940s, when the well-known windchill factor was worked out.

wrote Ross. He was so excited with his newfound mobility that he did not want Thomas to remove the leg when it came time to head for home. Walking in snow, however, proved difficult, and Tulluahiu had to be satisfied to sit on the sledge with his leg packed alongside. As the happy Inuk pulled away, Chimham Thomas called to him that he would carve a wooden foot to make it easier to walk in the snow.

In a gesture of gratitude for Tulluahiu's wooden leg, Otoogiu, the village physician, or *Angekok,* who had brought Tulluahiu to the ship, offered to heal James Marslin, whose tuberculosis had worn the man to a near skeleton. Ross turned down the *Angekok*'s offer, in consideration that "our poor man's case was too serious to permit our countenancing such trifling."

Marslin died five days later. That day, the upper limb of the sun was briefly visible for the first time after an absence of more than seven weeks. We can only hope that the frail man's shipmates carried him to *Victory*'s main deck for one last glimpse of the sun before he died that evening. Although the forty-five-year-old armorer's one wish, that he be buried on his home soil, was impossible to gratify, the severe cold delayed for four days even his burial in the Arctic. His shipmates finally laid his remains to rest in a shallow grave, just over two feet deep, the deepest they could carve into the granitelike frozen soil. "He seemed to be an inoffensive man and departed this life quite prepared for the great change. He deserved praise indeed for his spirit; though, for many reasons, we could have wished he had acted otherwise," eulogized Ross, who regretted that Marslin had not told him of his illness. If only he had, Ross would never have signed him on the risky voyage.

On the last day of January, accompanied by relatives and friends, Tulluahiu's mother, Ajoua, came to the ship and asked to see the man who had made her son's wooden leg. When Chimham Thomas came forth, the frail, bent-over old woman, who could barely walk without a staff, looked into Thomas's blue eyes, threw her arms around him, and engaged him in a powerful *kunik* (affectionately rubbed her nose against his) "with as much fervour and ardour as she might have evinced in her more juvenile days," observed William Light.

Afterward, the sailors entertained their guests with wonders such as magnets, firing a pistol, and—what produced the greatest surprise—an exhibition of snapdragon. Snapdragon was a Christmastime game in which the participants snatched raisins out of a bowl of flaming brandy and ate them while afire. The game especially impressed Otoogiu, the *Angekok*, who awarded the sailors for their daring feat of magic with one of his conjuring songs.

Outdoors, meanwhile, Ajoua's relatives and friends joined other members of the crew in games of leapfrog and soccer, even though the temperature hovered around 30 degrees below zero and the sun had already set after its brief appearance. Smoke spewed from *Victory's* flue and formed a dense cloud that hung just a few feet above the ship. Amber light from her oil lamps streamed through the scuttles and illuminated the scene down on the ice. The sailors, enveloped in white clouds of steaming breath, laughed at the Inuit's leaps, made awkward by their bulky clothing. And the Inuit laughed at the sailors' poor footing on the ice, which often resulted in a hardy tar sliding into a pool of frigid salt water.

Several days later, Tulluahiu visited *Victory* to drop off an arrow as a gift of thanks. He showed tremendous pride in his new leg—now augmented with Thomas's wooden foot and a slip-resistant leather boot sewn by Tirikshiu—and walked with considerable skill, often advancing far ahead of his companions. Furthermore, not only was Tulluahiu able to go on a seal hunt, but for the first time since his loss he was an active participant. He loved showing off the leg; there was no question that he and his friends were overwhelmed with the gift and enjoyed the company of these strangers to their land. Tulluahiu's brother-in-law, Tia-gashu, howled in laughter when Ross showed him the portrait he had drawn of the wooden-legged Tulluahiu. Ross's primitive portraits of the Inuit always elicited their mirth, but the one of a man with a wooden leg was especially laughable to the cheerful, good-tempered natives of Boothia Peninsula.

To Ross, the month of January "had passed away like a dream . . . our visitors prevented time from dragging on in a tiresome uniformity" and had furnished the crew with outfits "much more useful . . . than those which we had brought from England." If John Barrow could only see him now: with volumes of geographical knowledge from the natives—natives like the Arctic Highlanders whose encounter Barrow had savagely ridiculed; having sailed hundreds of miles farther down Prince Regent Inlet than Parry; miles of newly charted coastline in hand; snug in a safe harbor; and ready to find that elusive Northwest Passage come the summer thaw. With the one exception of the loss of James Marslin, the first month of 1830 had been exceptionally reward-ing for *Victory*'s band of explorers.

Early February weather continued where January's had left off: tem-perature regularly more frigid than 40 degrees below zero and at one stretch reaching 47 below for four straight days. On these mid-winter days, the wind was merely a light breeze at less than seven miles per hour, which made it less dangerous for the men to take daily walks. Even so, the sailors made it a point to remind each other to remove their gold earrings, which could result in an instantly frozen earlobe.

The extreme cold made the sledges drag hard, as though on gravel instead of slippery ice. The ice crunched and squeaked underfoot. Overhead, the sky was a transparent, cloudless, navy blue.

The cold, however, did not deter the Inuit from visiting the ship. Finally, after one too many knocks on his cabin door and the constant giggles and laughter from above decks that interrupted his solitude, Ross restricted the number of visitors to five or six persons at a time. "The perpetual crowds were really inconvenient," he complained. Still, every day the natives flocked to the ship and gathered in crowds outside to wait their turn to board. On one occasion, a mother nursed her perfectly naked baby while she waited—though the thermometer stood at 40 below zero.

Ross's restriction was prompted not only by the "crowding," but by the realization that items were disappearing from time to time: a candle snuffer here, a hammer there, a table knife, Ross's large magnifier, and even a lens from his eyeglasses.

Ross suspected the *Angekok* Otoogiu had taken the magnifier. Otoogiu had been in the captain's cabin for treatment of a swollen face, and Ross had shown him the magnifier at that time. When Ross paid a visit to Otoogiu's igloo, he found that, sure enough, Otoogiu had the magnifier. Not only that, but also one of his children had the missing lens from Ross's glasses. Accused of the theft, Otoogiu made no secret about it and greeted the accusation as a matter of merriment. Ross threatened Otoogiu that if he did not return the magnifier, the other side of his face would swell from the "magical glass." Poor Otoogiu—

the village conjuror and a great believer in magic (although none of his fellow citizens thought much about his antics)—was so terrorized by Ross's threat, that he returned not only the magnifier, but also a harpoon that Ross had given him as a gift. To fully stress his point, Ross took back the harpoon and returned to Otoogiu the bow and arrow that the *Angekok* had originally given to Ross in exchange for the harpoon.

About that same time, an Inuk named Milluctu, who "was rather inclined to possess himself of what he saw," to quote Captain Ross, complained that he could not walk on his leg and asked to have a wooden leg made—no doubt for the valuable wood. MacDiarmid informed Milluctu that he would have to cut off his leg first, to which Milluctu replied that he did not have time and that he would return when it was more convenient. When MacDiarmid saw Milluctu aboard ship the next day, he said his leg was better.

Still, objects continued to disappear: a dog chain, pieces of wood, thimbles, hooks, a telescope, a pulley. Frustrated, Ross put out the word that, if anyone were caught stealing, they would no longer be permitted aboard the ship. Even this, however, did not bring a complete end to the purloining, although the thievery did decrease significantly. Ross wrote in his journal, "after we had taken some trouble to explain to them that to steal was 'bad,' very few instances of a similar nature occurred. In one case, [Tulluahiu], aware of his wife's propensities, always brought back what she had taken away." Captain Ross further remarked, "we had no right to expect absolute honesty among this tribe above all others; and, at any rate, we were bound to expose them to no temptations."

The daily visits continued. In exchange for knives, needles, files, and other treasured items, the Inuit brought seal meat, bear meat, fox meat, and even wolverine, all of which Ross greatly welcomed. He especially welcomed the fresh seal meat, which he knew was essential to ward off scurvy. The men fed the other kinds of meat to the dogs, to a pet Arctic fox, and to *Victory's* four cats. But far more than just for the fresh meat, the officers and crew—to a man—welcomed the Inuit for their companionship, in spite of any inconvenience from thefts or other annoyances, such as disruption of the Sunday worship. As a rule, Ross made the visitors wait until he had concluded his service before he let anyone come aboard.

One afternoon, Ikmallik and a group of women came by to entertain the crew with a performance of traditional songs and dance. While Ikmallik danced, the women arranged themselves in a semi-circle around him and sang with "all the power of their throats and lungs." As the ceremony proceeded, many a woman sidled up to a lonely sailor and whispered *"kunik"* in his ear—provided, that is, that the young man did not use snuff, a decided turnoff to the nose-rubbing ladies of Boothia Peninsula. Later that evening, more than one sailor was observed heading toward the igloo village, arm-in-arm with his new sweetheart. Captain Ross, on the other hand, retired to his cabin, poured a little glass of gin, filled his long-stemmed clay pipe, sat back in his armchair, and propped his feet on the stove fender. Passing by the cabin door, a crewman might have heard the muffled, baritone voice of his venerable captain, softly humming his favorite sea song, "The sea, the sea, the open sea! The blue, the fresh, the ever free . . . ," which the steward loved to parody as, "The gin, the gin!"

As to the natives' singing, Commander James Ross "made up his mind, that if Okkaru [the soloist] ever visited the ship again, never to invite her to sing." Most certainly Captain Ross, too, thought the music hideous; yet he withheld judgment: "I fear that we were not musicians enough to analyze and estimate the peculiarities and merits of this national music."

On March 2, Tiagashu climbed aboard *Victory* in tears. He sobbed that his father, Alictu, the old man pushed forward on the sledge the day of their first encounter, had died. Besides his wife and children, Tiagashu took particular care of his father and mother, and his father's death greatly bereaved him. Tiagashu's mother, Kanguagiu, was about sixty years old and quite infirm herself. She never left her igloo except when the tribe moved to a new location, but, even so, she managed eventually to acquire a new companion. Like Alictu, this man was also elderly and feeble. Hence, Kanguagiu's remarriage did not alleviate Tiagashu's familial responsibilities. The change was quite the contrary for the good-hearted but sickly Inuk, whose family came dangerously close to starvation in the ensuing months.

Shortly after Alictu's death, the whole community abandoned their village and moved about seven miles to the northeast in a first step toward establishing their summer quarters. With their departure, MacDiarmid visited Alictu's igloo, having correctly surmised that Alictu's corpse would have been left behind. MacDiarmid examined the body and found a long incision in the abdomen, evidently made after his death. He reasoned that the wound had probably been made to prove that Alictu was dead. MacDiarmid noted that the old man "was corpulent and seemed to have no disease but old age." He buried Alictu's body to prevent its being devoured by foxes—but not before he removed the skull for Ross's collection. Actually, Ross hoped to present it to the Phrenological Society, which represented a "science" of great interest to the captain. The old man's skull was left behind, however, when the crew were forced to abandon *Victory* in the spring of 1832.

Throughout March, Commander James Ross, accompanied by Ikmallik, set out on one-day journeys to reconnoiter the surrounding countryside to gain a better understanding of the region's terrain so that they would be ready for overland expeditions when the weather moderated. Another goal of these short outings was to establish a trigonometrical baseline from which to conduct detailed surveys of the Felix Harbor region. To effect the mapping operation, Commander Ross and his men built cairns at precisely measured locations on hilltops and other prominent spots.

Although these journeys took the men as far as thirty miles from Felix Harbor, they returned to the ship by evening without fail. The weather was still far too dangerous to risk an overnight stay in the open. Thus, everyone feared for the safety of George MacDiarmid and William Thom when they disappeared on a short hike to study the geology of an unusual rock about ten miles away. Somehow, MacDiarmid and Thom got lost when a light snowfall masked familiar landmarks. For nearly three hours, the two men wandered aimlessly, until the crack of guns and the glow of blue flares, fired by their anxious shipmates, directed them homeward. Exhausted and frightened when they at last clambered safely aboard *Victory*, MacDiarmid and Thom no doubt relished the warmth of the cabin and the comfort of a hearty meal prepared especially for them by the cook, Henry Eyre.

While the younger men went exploring, the fifty-two-year-old Captain Ross oversaw what few duties there were aboard ship and mostly confined himself to his cabin. Ross truly relished his quiet time alone. His chief activity on these dark, late-winter days was poring over his vast collection of trousers, jackets, mittens, narwhal horns, walrus teeth, bows, arrows, miniature kayaks, and other gifts from the natives. His collection eventually filled three 336-gallon barrels.

On a particularly idle day in mid-March, Captain Ross got the idea that it would be helpful if an Inuk learned English as well as John Sacheuse had, who was Ross's interpreter on his voyage to Baffin Bay in 1818. To this purpose, Ross brought a young native named Poowuty-ook under his wing. Poowutyook had free run of the ship and even joined the sailors in their evening classes.

According to William Light, one day Poowutyook stole a hare and a ptarmigan that had been prepared for the captain's table. He hid them in his trousers while he sought a hiding place to devour his booty. In a corner of the steward's cabin was a large tub about three-quarters full of flour, which, perhaps to Poowutyook, resembled snow. Whatever the case, he climbed into the tub to enjoy his meal. When Light notified Captain Ross that his meal had disappeared, Ross and Light suspected Poowutyook and searched throughout the ship for him. Upon entering his cabin, Light tells us, he and Ross beheld

> . . . a strange, unaccountable figure rising gradually from the midst of [the flour tub], like a ghost from a tomb, his shaggy vestments so covered with the contents of the vessel, and his visage apparently so crusted with the farinaceous substance . . . that had the minds of the astonished spectators been imbued with superstition, they would have thought that one of the Domdaniel caves had been opened by the wand of a magician.

Sadly, Captain Ross did not see the humor and ordered a dozen lashes for Poowutyook. As harsh as this may sound, flogging was still practiced in the Royal Navy at that time. It was not banned until 1879.

Even Light's revered Edward Parry ordered thirty-six lashes each for two men for drunkenness on his Arctic voyage of 1819–20. Although Ross ordered the flogging of Poowutyook, he was not a proponent of the cruel punishment and preferred less-drastic means. In his treatise, *On Temperance in the Royal Navy*, published in 1852, Ross advocated ridicule over flogging as the best punishment for drunkenness. Indeed, Ross took mercy on Poowutyook. In consideration of the severe cold and in view of the Inuk's naiveté, he allowed Poowutyook to keep his back covered and ordered that the lashes should not be heavily applied. As a consequence, each lash merely raised a cloud of flour that "threatened to suffocate the bystanders." Light wrote that Poowutyook probably thought the *Kabloonas* (Europeans) were aiding him, in that "the stick was applied solely to his back, as being the only part which he could not cleanse himself."

Perhaps needless to say, Poowutyook's days as a protégé were all but over. The last straw for Poowutyook was when a gun went off in his hand while hunting with Commander Ross. The flash of the gun, recoil, and smoke startled the boy so, that, although fifteen miles from home, he darted away, dashed over the snow-covered hills, and was soon out of sight. He never again returned to the ship.

On the last day of March, Ikmallik invited the men of *Victory* to see how he and his wife, Apellagliu, construct an igloo. Although overcast and snowing, the temperature rose to 20 degrees *above* zero, which made it a relatively good day to mill around and watch a demonstration.

Ikmallik first prodded the snow with a pole to ascertain if the snow was sufficiently deep. Having determined that it was, he next used a shovel of bone to level the snow within a circle about ten feet in diameter, making certain that a layer of hard-packed snow at least three feet thick remained. He then cut out wedge-shape blocks of snow about two feet long and a foot thick from the center of this circle, trimmed them to shape with a knife, and positioned them around the outer edge of the circle.

As he added blocks of snow around the perimeter, the wall spiraled upward and inward, and before long, it formed a perfect dome. Apel-lagliu stuffed the joints with snow from the outside while her husband positioned the blocks from the inside. Ikmallik completed the structure by inserting a square, tapered keystone at the apex. Older boys in the neighborhood pitched in and built attached kennels for the dogs while the smaller children played nearby and built toy igloos of their own. Ikmallik finished the new home with the addition of an ice window.

Because clear, fresh-water ice from a pond was not available for the window, Ikmallik cast the skylight himself. He first laid a piece of seal-skin on the snow with its edges turned up to create a bowl about two inches deep. He then filled this shallow bowl with water from snow melted over his oil lamp. The water quickly froze and yielded a perfectly transparent windowpane. Windows made in this fashion were highly esteemed for the fuel required to melt the snow and so were carried with them when the family moved from igloo to igloo. The whole process of constructing the igloo (excepting the time to melt the snow for the sky-light) took barely forty-five minutes. Impressed with the demonstration, Ross wrote, "A tent is scarcely pitched sooner than a house is built here."

The translucent walls of the newly constructed igloo illuminated the interior in beautiful shades of verdigris green and blue, according to the varying thickness of the blocks of snow. Nevertheless, the beauty disappeared in a day or two as smoky lamps coated the walls with a black, oily dirt. Soon piles of putrid blubber, the stench of dogs, and the odor of unbathed humans made the interior less than inviting to a European, to which John Ross remarked,

*They cannot well avoid contamination from the oil which they use as food and fuel; as, in a confined hut, where everything must be dried at the flame of the lamp, the effects of smoke are equally inevitable. The expenditure of fuel required to thaw what they drink is very great . . . very often they cannot pro-cure enough, or suffer severely from thirst should their oil be expended: so that we need not be surprised if they do not wash themselves . . . Yet they wash their faces at least, by using a piece of wetted bearskin towel.*

Moreover, when invited on board *Victory*, both the men and women enjoyed having their hair cut and combed by First Mate Thomas Blanky. An Inuk by the name of Konyaroklik was unique among his fellow tribesmen in that his head was bald, of which Captain Ross chuckled, "he had one son, called Ulla, of whom he was very proud; he was still more so of his bald head. . . . He was . . . rather good-looking . . . and was delighted when he saw his portrait, which I had made of him."

When it came time to abandon the igloo after several weeks or more, the interior presented "an appearance of wretchedness, which baffles all description," recorded Light. The lampblack, the blood, the filth, the melting and dripping walls disfigured by holes cut to facilitate removal of goods . . . all presented but a cheerless, unnerving sight. Light told of the worst of all when he wrote, "The sight of a deserted habitation is at all times calculated to excite in the mind a sensation of dreariness and desolation . . . but this feeling is even heightened rather than diminished when a small portion of these inhabitants remain behind to endure the extreme of wretchedness." Light's words referred to the Inuit practice of leaving behind the hopelessly ill, old, or infirm. Forced to move to new hunting or fishing grounds, it was not unusual for a tribe to abandon those who could not carry on. This was according to Light's experience with a related tribe while on Edward Parry's expedition in 1821–23. In truth, the cruel, unforgiving Arctic environment left little choice. Yet Captain Ross noted that *Victory's* crew never saw evidence of this practice. He thought their behavior quite the contrary, in light of the kindly treatment of old Alictu and the one-legged Tulluahiu.

# CHAPTER FOUR

# Inuit Friends Assist with Explorations

(April 1830–September 1830)

*F*ELIX *Harbor, April 4, 1830.* The thermometer registered 22 degrees Fahrenheit in the shade. Snow melted rapidly in the sun. Water streamed in rivulets over black rocks exposed by the disappearing snow. Sailors spread out their laundry to dry. Winter had departed, or so it seemed.

With the warmer days, twenty-nine-year-old Commander James Ross prepared to embark on his first overland expedition. His objective was to explore a river known by the natives as Neitchillee. According to the charts Ikmallik and Tirikshiu had drawn for the two Rosses, Neitchillee was about 150 miles southwest of Felix Harbor. It was a large westward-flowing river, they said, that emptied into the polar sea. Young Ross doubted that it was a river and hoped Neitchillee might actually be a strait—the Northwest Passage. No, the Hydrographer and

his sister insisted, there was no strait from the southern end of Prince
Regent Inlet. But Commander Ross would take no chance; he had to see
it with his own eyes. Captain Ross, on the other hand, had become convinced that no strait existed south of the 70th parallel. The two bick-
ered back and forth until the captain stormed into his cabin to sulk; the
stubborn James turned his attention to prepare for the journey.

Two young men, Awack and Ooblooria, had volunteered to guide
Commander Ross on his jaunt. They had already planned to go to
Neitchillee to retrieve kayaks they had stored there, so serving as guides
for Commander Ross was a good deal because Ross promised to give
them each a steel file for their assistance. Awack came well recommended in that, not only was he one of the most expert hunters of the
community, but also he was the twenty-two-year-old nephew of
Ikmallik. If being related to the Hydrographer was a recommendation,
Ooblooria's credentials were even higher—he was Ikmallik's seventeen-
year-old son. Captain Ross considered Ooblooria "a fine, active, and
intelligent lad," and he was always a favorite with the crew. Besides being
the Hydrographer's son, he was married to Shullanina, the pretty daughter of Tulluahiu and Tirikshiu, which no doubt added further to the
young Inuk's high standing with the sailors.

Eager to get started on the journey to earn their files, Awack and
Ooblooria arrived at Victory the afternoon before the planned departure
with their sledges, dogs, and provisions. After they spent the day con-
firming the travel plans with Commander Ross and the captain, who
had come out of his sulk and agreed to James's plan, the two Inuit
attended Captain Ross's evening worship service, where they followed
"the example of the members of other congregations," wrote William

Light, and promptly fell asleep. Afterward, they popped wide-awake to stuff themselves on a supper of nearly five pounds each of seal meat. They concluded their dinner with the almost ceremonial licking of their platters, and by nine o'clock were fast asleep in their berths aboard ship.

Licking things was a common Inuit custom, especially of plates and items received as gifts. The ceremony could lead to trouble, though, if the item were foreign to their experience. During a wintertime visit to *Victory*, a young boy, unaware of the danger of ice-cold metal, licked the iron band of a cask. The boy's tongue instantly froze to the metal. In a panic to detach himself, he left behind a layer of skin. "A disagreeable accident," wrote Captain Ross.

The next morning, the explorers were packed and ready to leave when a stiff breeze arose, the temperature dropped nearly to zero, and an ominous sky threatened bad weather. Captain Ross beseeched his nephew to delay his departure, and even Awack and Ooblooria tried to persuade him to wait for a better forecast. Yet, plead as they might, the eager young commander prevailed, and at six in the morning the four men—James Ross, Thomas Blanky, Awack, and Ooblooria—set out for Neitchillee in a swirl of light snow.

They had not been gone three hours when the wind increased to 25 miles per hour and a heavy snowfall pelted their faces. By evening, it blew a fresh gale—about 45 miles per hour. Back at *Victory*, Captain Ross ordered rockets fired and blue lights lit atop the mainmast to guide the travelers back to the ship. The gale-force wind raked across the deck and blew out the beacons nearly every fifteen minutes. While one crewman worked to reignite the blue lights, a second fired off more rockets. The rockets screamed skyward, but the wind blew them sideways before they scarcely reached the height of the mainmast. As the blue glow washed over the scene, all hands stared into the blizzard on the lookout for shadowy figures that might be their errant shipmates.

Meanwhile, out on the trail, the storm pounded the four adventurers with high wind, driving snow, and extreme cold. Winds above 40 miles per hour can make walking under any circumstances difficult, let alone climbing over icy hummocks and snow-covered hills. When they had first set out, the men easily made six miles per hour, but the storm brought their progress to a mere crawl. Awack, normally a good-humored young man who broke into laughter whenever he or someone else tumbled from their sledge, begged Commander Ross to make camp. James Ross ignored Awack's pleas and insisted that they press onward. He never saw the blue lights or rockets, but even if he had, it would have made no difference; the young commander was resolved upon completing his mission.

Suddenly, a blast of wind-driven snow blinded Awack, who was at the lead of the party. In the whiteout he lost his way and drove his sledge over an embankment. Down the steep incline he tumbled and landed with a bone-jarring crash at the bottom. Although he was uninjured in the fall, Awack's sledge was wrecked. To continue with the broken sledge was impossible, and to head back to the ship—against the wind—would have been suicidal.

Blanky suggested that Awack use the shaft of his spear to repair his sledge. But Awack, not seeing any reason to risk his life to hurry onward, ignored the suggestion, and he and his cousin began to construct an igloo in which to sit out the storm.

Livid over Awack's "insubordination," Commander Ross grabbed both Ooblooria and Awack's spears, broke them in half, and demanded that Awack use the pieces to repair his sledge. The two Inuit youths were both stunned and furious. In an attempt to pacify his guides, James Ross promised to give them new, steel-pointed spears when they returned to the ship. In any regard, finding themselves suddenly weaponless left Awack and Ooblooria with little choice but to abide by the commander's dictum, and so they set to work on the sledge, mollified by thoughts of new spears.

Once the repairs were completed, the four men pushed onward— only to have the storm worsen. After two hours of blind meandering through fields of rough, hummocky ice, and with visibility not quite twenty yards, Commander Ross finally agreed to call a halt. In less than a half-hour everyone was sheltered in Awack and Ooblooria's expertly built igloo, "affording a shelter at least, as perfect as we could have obtained within the best house of stone . . . in the wretched plight that we now were," wrote a by then grateful James Ross.

For nine hours, the men had fought the wind and snow without food or water. Then, settled in their igloo, an agonizing thirst overwhelmed them. Ross melted snow over the blue flame of an alcohol lamp, and in a few minutes he had enough water for everyone, much to the amazement of Awack and Ooblooria, who would have waited at least three hours to melt the same quantity of snow with their stone vessels and oil lamps.

Before long, the igloo's warmth left Ross and Blanky soaking wet as snow that had sifted into their woolen coats melted. The two sailors pulled off their soggy outfits but were hardly any better off as a steady drip, drip, drip from the igloo's roof added to their misery. The two Inuit, on the other hand, were perfectly comfortable in their outfits of animal skin and fur. Ross and Blanky finally found a modicum of comfort inside their sleeping bags, although dampened to the very soul.

The four dead-tired men had just fallen asleep when a ruckus jolted them wide awake. Outside, the sledge dogs had broken loose and were fighting among themselves over Awack's sledge. His sledge, like many Inuit wintertime sledges, had been constructed entirely of frozen fish and deer. To build it, Awack had formed the two seven-foot-long runners from narrow cylinders of salmon wrapped in skins and tied with thongs. He then plated the surface of the runners with a two-inch-thick layer of mossy earth and water, which he polished to a slick finish with a bearskin rag moistened with water and saliva. The crossbars were constructed from frozen loins of deer. The method provided a wonderfully efficient way to carry emergency provisions . . . and made a tempting feast for the dogs. Fortunately, the men awoke in time to stop the dogs, and Awack was able to salvage his edible sledge.

The next day the weather moderated, and the four travelers returned to their journey. They made good progress throughout the day and reached the western sea in mid-afternoon. While Ooblooria and Awack went to look for their kayaks, Commander Ross stood on the headland of a cape and gazed out to sea, now convinced, and with a dent in his ego, that the land on which he stood was connected to the North American continent. He named the cape "Isabella" after his sister, whose birthday was that day. Commander Ross and Blanky erected a cairn, went through the usual ceremony of taking possession of the land, then headed back to the igloo to rejoin their native guides.

Awack and Ooblooria were already at the igloo when Ross and Blanky arrived, and to a surprised and rather condescending Commander Ross, Awack had "displayed considerable ingenuity" in starting a fire by "procuring a light by means of the oxymuriatic matches which he had seen us use for that purpose; and he had thus provided us with an ample supply of water; a refreshment of which we were much in need." Matches, like the alcohol burner, were not magical to the natives, but assuredly, they were marvels that the Inuit were eager to understand. Ordinarily, Awack would have started the fire by repeatedly striking together two pieces of *inneuk*, or iron pyrite, until sparks fell on some dry moss. Then, he would cup the moss in his hands and gently blow on the glowing embers until the moss caught fire.

With his thirst quenched, thanks to Awack's attentive skills, the commander continued, "we are living among water, walking on water, and eternally annoyed by water . . . and always forgetting that the snow and ice . . . is . . . not to be converted into drink without great labour and expense of heat."

The evening's fare was ptarmigan soup for Ross and Blanky and boiled seal's flesh for Awack and Ooblooria. Fatigued by their 40-mile trek, the men slept until 10 a.m. the following morning, the dogs having been tied up well removed from the tempting sledges.

On the way back to the ship, Ooblooria suffered terribly. His eyelids were red and swollen and tears streamed from his snow-blinded eyes. To look at light was painful, and his eyes felt as though they had been scratched with sandpaper. The intense radiation from the sun, dazzling off the fresh snow, had burned his corneas. The natives knew very well the danger of the sun's glare, and they usually protected themselves with *ittuyaga*—goggles of bone with narrow slits through which to see. Yet even with this protection, the ultraviolet rays can do their damage. And perhaps the seventeen-year-old Ooblooria may not have been as cautious as he should have been. For the next two days, Ooblooria's only recourse was to shield his eyes from all light.

If his agony from the snow blindness was not bad enough, Ooblooria's frozen trousers scraped the flesh from his knees with each step. He hobbled along, trying his best to keep up with the others, but the sores turned raw and he fell behind. Ross and Blanky put the blind and crippled teenager on their sledge while Awack dragged both his and his cousin's sledges, which carried their kayaks.

After a long and tiring fifth day on the trail, the four men arrived safely aboard *Victory* at six o'clock that evening. Both Commander Ross and his uncle were highly pleased with the success of the first overland expedition on Boothia Peninsula. The men had traveled about seventy miles to the south-southwest from Felix Harbor, explored the Neitchillee, and determined to Ross and Blanky's disappointed satisfaction that the Neitchillee was, indeed, a river.

As promised, Awack and Ooblooria each received files and new spears plus a bonus of wood to repair their kayaks. Despite the squabble over repairing the sledge, Commander Ross was impressed with Awack and considered him a "superior young man." Why not, thought the young commander, bring Awack back to England and "humanize" the bright, young Inuk? With that in mind, when Commander Ross awarded Awack his file, he asked the young man if he would like to move aboard *Victory* and sail to England. Awack was surprised by the offer and told the commander that he needed time to think it over. When he returned two days later, he shocked Commander Ross and the other officers by stating that, no, he would not live aboard the *Victory*, nor did he wish to visit England. When asked his reasons, Awack let on that he was betrothed and that he had had a most tearful discussion with his beloved, Narluwarga. "A woman's tears had again determined the destiny of a human being," wrote William Light, who said the bewildered officers considered Awack, "A fool! A motley fool!"

Toward the end of April, Commander Ross prepared to make another exploratory mission. As both Rosses were now convinced that there was no east-west strait south of the 70th parallel, the Northwest Passage, if it existed at all, must be to the north, as Ikmallik had said three months earlier. Although *Victory* had sailed down the coast from the north the previous year, it would have been easy to have missed a narrow strait through the snow and ice-covered jagged coastline. (Indeed, unbeknownst to them, they had already failed to discover Bellot Strait.) And the very last thing John Ross wanted was to miss the Northwest Passage and return home only to have someone else—Parry perhaps?—find it later. Captain Ross had had enough of John Barrow's caustic rancor. The only way to assure nothing had been overlooked was to explore to the north on foot, and James Ross was eager to make a detailed survey in that direction.

Early in the morning of April 27, Commander Ross set out on just such an expedition. His plan was to stop at the village to pick up a guide, then explore as far north as possible. Second Mate Thomas Abernethy and Surgeon George MacDiarmid accompanied him. MacDiarmid's role was to go with them to the village, learn the plans for the journey from the Inuk guide, then report to Captain Ross. Captain Ross, then, would establish caches to provision the explorers on their return journey.

The three officers were surprised when they were not greeted by the usual shouts and cheers when they approached the village. Where was everyone?

As they walked among the silent igloos, a couple dogs barked the alarm, which brought several men crawling from their igloos, each armed with a large knife. A man named Poweytak rushed forward and drew back his arm as if to hurl his knife at Ross and MacDiarmid, who were just a few yards away. But the sun blinded the man, and before he could launch his weapon, his son ran up and restrained him.

Commander Ross, Abernethy, and MacDiarmid retreated to their sledge to get Ross's gun. Poweytak's sons wrestled with their father and tried to pin his arms behind him. The majority of the village's men, however, appeared ready to back Poweytak in his assault on the officers.

In the next moment, the mob brandished their knives again and made a move to surround Commander Ross and his two companions. Ross brought his gun to his shoulder and aimed. He was a split second from firing when most of the Inuit ran back to their igloos, evidently frightened by his action. In the next moment, they were outside again and gestured wildly with their knives.

For half an hour, the two parties stood face to face as Commander Ross pleaded for an explanation of what was wrong. Again, the Inuit advanced, evidently about to hurl their weapons. Ross again raised his gun to his shoulder. If he fired, the natives would overwhelm and probably kill him and his two companions. Nonetheless, he aimed and prepared to shoot. Just as his finger touched the trigger, a pretty woman of about twenty-five years of age scrambled from one of the igloos and shouted to Ross not to shoot. She boldly walked past the men and confronted the three officers.

Kakikagiu, as that was her name, explained to Commander Ross that Poweytak's seven-year-old adopted son was killed the previous night when a falling rock struck him on the head. She went on to explain that the community felt that, somehow, Victory's crew was to blame and that the boy's father sought revenge. Commander Ross stressed that he knew nothing of the tragedy and that he had nothing to do with it.

She related all Ross had said to Poweytak's two sons, who had been restraining the enraged father while she negotiated with Ross. After much conversation, the men accepted the commander's claim of innocence, but with obvious reluctance. Undaunted and with his mind set on his exploration, Commander Ross cautiously approached the men and offered a large file to anyone who would guide him and Abernethy. The men huddled among themselves for a few minutes, and the tension eased somewhat further.

Kakikagiu suggested to her husband, Poyettak, that he should accept the offer of the file and go with Commander Ross. Poyettak hesitated. Kakikagiu insisted. Still, Poyettak hemmed and hawed. At last, after repeated entreaties by Kakikagiu, the hen-pecked Poyettak agreed to accompany Commander Ross and Abernethy. Poyettak's teenage friend, Illictu, then stepped forward and said that he, too, would go along.

Perhaps Kakikagiu wanted Poyettak to go with Ross and Abernethy not only for the valuable file, but also to get Poyettak out of the house for a few days. The vivacious Kakikagiu (about whom Captain Ross later wrote, "her figure . . . was completely *en bon point*.") had a second husband, Aknalua, who, according to the captain, was the more handsome of the two. John Ross told how on one occasion the young wife sent Poyettak on a hunting trip so she could spend the day alone with Aknalua. When Poyettak returned, the three of them shared the success of the hunt. Perhaps the wily Kakikagiu saw James Ross and Abernethy's need for a guide as an opportunity to spend time alone with Aknalua.

Whatever the case, the crisis seemed resolved, and Commander James Ross, Thomas Abernethy, Poyettak, and Illictu set out on their journey to the north. George MacDiarmid headed back to the ship to inform Captain Ross of what had taken place and that Commander Ross and Abernethy expected to be absent for five days.

After traveling about twelve miles, Poyettak told Commander Ross that he wanted to examine a seal hole in hopes of making a catch. Ross, however, was skeptical and refused to let Poyettak go alone. He feared that the Inuk was still disturbed over the circumstances regarding the boy's death and that he planned to abandon the party. As they looked for the breathing hole together, Poyettak suddenly turned toward Ross, struck the commander in the chest with his hand, and told Ross that he (Ross) was *ajungitsok* (good). Poyettak then reminded Ross that he had left his gun behind and handed him his spear and said that Ross "should be armed as well as he." Although taken aback by Poyettak's punch to his chest, Commander Ross then understood that the rift between the two groups was healed and they proceeded in good cheer to find the seal hole. When they reached the hole, Poyettak lay down on the ice, put his nose to the hole, and declared that the seal had deserted the breathing hole a number of days ago. The travelers would have no fresh meat that night.

Dinner the next evening promised to be better when the four men came across tracks of a musk ox. Poyettak and Commander Ross loosed their dogs, which dashed away at full speed over the hummocks and hills after the shaggy animal. For two hours, the men followed the trail until they reached where the dogs held the exhausted animal at bay—barking and dodging and nipping at the ox's hooves. Poyettak approached as close as he dared and discharged an arrow, only to have it strike a rib and fall out with no apparent effect. Poyettak shot several more. Again, no effect.

Commander Ross aimed his gun and fired both barrels. The musk ox crumpled to its knees but quickly got up and charged Ross and Poyettak, who leapt behind a rock just in time as the enraged animal slammed into the rock with a thud. Poyettak tried to stab at the writhing beast but missed. The musk ox struggled to its feet and again charged Ross. Poyettak screamed at Ross to take cover, but the confident commander held his ground. When the charging beast was just five yards away, Ross fired twice more. The musk ox fell down dead, one ball having pierced its heart, and its shoulder shattered by the other.

That was the first time Poyettak had seen the effects of firearms. Commander Ross wrote, "it was the state of the broken shoulder that surprised [Poyettak]; nor would it be easy to forget his look of horror and amazement, when he looked up at my face and exclaimed, 'Now-ek poke!' (It is broken!)"

That evening over their musk ox steak, Poyettak brought up the subject of the crisis over the little boy. He thanked Commander Ross for not shooting his father and breaking the man's shoulder as Ross had done to the musk ox.

The commander was curious to know how Poweytak could be Poyettak's father when their ages appeared so close—both in their late twenties or early thirties. The answer was simple. Poweytak was Poyettak's stepfather. Shortly after his birth, Poyettak explained, his natural father had wanted to migrate westward, but his mother wanted to stay in place with her family. So the couple agreed to an amicable separation, and Poyettak's mother, Kanguagiu, remarried. She had four more sons by her new husband, but then found herself single once more when her second husband drowned. Her five sons made her a desirable catch, nonetheless, because Inuit children are essential to their parents' survival in their old age. Kanguagiu soon married Poweytak, her first husband's younger brother. They had no children, however, and so Poweytak and Kanguagiu adopted two children—one was the little boy killed by the falling rock.

All the while Ross and Poyettak were chatting, Poyettak and Illictu, without interruption, wolfed down strips of raw meat cut from the musk ox. Poyettak crammed a strip of meat into his mouth as far as he could, cut it off with his knife so close as almost to cut off his nose, then passed the slice to Illictu. Illictu did the same, then handed the remainder back to Poyettak for another round. Back and forth it went until it was gone. Then one of them carved another piece from the musk ox's ribs, neck, backbone, or side, and the two gourmands continued their meal. "This enormous stuffing caused our guides to pass but a restless night: If they had possessed a term for the nightmare, we should probably have heard of it in the morning," wrote Commander Ross in his narrative. Each night of the journey was spent in a similar fashion.

In the meantime, back at *Victory*, the days passed peacefully although not always quietly. On April 23, St. George's Day, Captain Ross ordered the ship decked out in her flags and a royal salute fired. "There was no one, indeed, to witness this customary loyalty," wrote the captain, "but it was right to maintain the etiquette of the service." Twenty-one times *Victory*'s cannon roared its salute. It is not known what Tiagashu and his family, who were camped right alongside the ship, thought of the racket, but the crew no doubt enjoyed the deafening commotion.

Tiagashu and his family were living next to the *Victory* because a disastrous streak of poor hunting had reduced them to near starvation. As usual, Tiagashu ventured almost every day onto the ice to hunt seals. Nevertheless, the days he returned home empty-handed, weakened and exhausted from the long wait by a breathing hole, greatly outnumbered the increasingly rare days he made a capture. Most every day, either no animals were seen or, if he did have the fortune to spear one, the powerful animal escaped from the frail man's line. Days without success turned into weeks. Ikmallik had tried to help, but even he was unable to provide enough to feed both families.

Faced with almost certain starvation, Tiagashu appealed to Captain Ross for help. His hopes soared when he saw the captain take sightings with the sextant. Could that thing pinpoint the location of seals? he wanted to know. Captain Ross explained to the disappointed Inuk that it would not, but he offered food and invited Tiagashu to move his family closer to the ship. Tiagashu and Adlurak promptly built an igloo and moved their family alongside the *Victory* and Captain Ross ordered Seaman Anthony Buck to pull a seal from the ship's stock, thaw it, and cut it up for the family. Tiagashu watched Buck fumble with the half-frozen animal. The starving children gathered around and cried pitifully. Unable to restrain himself, Tiagashu grabbed the knife from the inexperienced butcher, expertly sliced the seal up, and doled out the precious food to his family. Over and over Tiagashu thanked Captain Ross and expressed regret that he had nothing to offer in return.

Meanwhile, Captain Ross grew anxious for the safety of Commander Ross and Abernethy, who had failed to return when scheduled. Had the men got lost or run afoul of the natives again? Ross sent teams to search an area about five miles broad in the direction from which they should return. The teams failed to locate the missing men but brought back the good news from the natives that they had been spotted and should be home soon. Three days later, Commander Ross and Abernethy returned uneventfully.

The extensive overland journey provided the proof that at last convinced Captain Ross that the Inuit were correct: An east-west strait in the southern regions of Prince Regent Inlet did not exist. Ross correctly concluded that Boothia Felix was a peninsula of the North American continent. From that point on, he and his nephew concentrated their searches for the Northwest Passage to the north and the west.

By that time, the season for exploration was rapidly passing. Although it was only May, a mere two months of suitable weather remained for overland exploration. Overland journeys were impossible beyond the middle of July because warmer weather made the land intolerably soggy for travel, and hordes of vicious mosquitoes appeared that drove near mad any man foolish enough to venture on land. And most important of all, with the advancing thaw it was time to prepare *Victory* for voyage and to extricate her from her dock of ice.

On May 17, Commander Ross, Abernethy, and two crewmen embarked on the last overland expedition for the season—an unguided journey that lasted twenty-eight days and reached as far as 200 miles west of Felix Harbor.

Commander Ross was compelled to travel without guides because most of the natives had left their village at the end of April for new hunting and fishing grounds. Captain Ross wrote, "it is probable that we were more sorry than they, at a parting, after which, as we then thought, we were not likely to meet again."

Now on their own, Commander Ross's plan for the expedition was

Hibluna jumps for joy and exclaims, "Owhee! Owhee!" after receiving a knife from one of the crew of *Victory*. Although she was extremely dirty, sloppy, and had no front teeth, her good humor won the affection of the sailors.

*Photo by Joe Pellingra, from the author's private collection.*

On Stone by J. Brandard, from the original Drawing by Captain Ross.

HIBLUNA.

On Stone by J. Brandard, from the original Drawing by Captain Ross

POYETTAK.          KAKIKAGIU.          AKNALUA

Kakikagiu stands between her two husbands—Poyettak on the left and Aknalua. Captain Ross said, "She was . . . by far the most robust woman we met with; her stature was five feet three inches and a quarter; her face was broad, her eyes, nose, and mouth small, as also her hands and feet, in proportion to her figure which was completely *en bon point*."

*Photo by Joe Pellingra, from the author's private collection.*

Seated inside her warm igloo, Kemig shows off the traditional tattoo patterns of the women of Boothia Peninsula.

*Photo by Joe Pellingra, from the author's private collection.*

KEMIG

On Stone by J.Brandard from the original Drawing by Captain Ross

KONYAROKLICK             NEWEETIOKE

THE BALD HEAD

Konyaroklik, remarkable as the only member of the tribe who was bald, stands beside his friend Neweetioke who was a brother to Ikmallik, the Hydrographer.

*Photo by Joe Pellingra, from the author's private collection.*

Interior of an igloo. While the mother, wrapped in furs, nurses her baby, a second Inuit reaches in from the right side of the scene to stir the bowl of meat that simmers over the flame of an oil lamp. A semicircular woman's knife, much like a vegetable chopper, lies next to a bone and bits of offal on the snow bench. Other pieces of meat and offal thaw on a shelf that rests on bone brackets stuck into the snow of the igloo wall.

*Photo by Joe Pellingra, from the author's private collection.*

An Inuk patiently huddles behind a windbreak while he waits for an opportunity to strike at a seal through the ice. His legs are tied together above the knees to prevent rustling. His spear rests on bone forks stuck into the snow so that he can pick it up quickly and silently. He may sit this way all day.

*Photo by Joe Pellingra, from the author's private collection.*

Out on the ice, an Inuk checks a seal hole for recent activity while a second native prepares to spear a seal through the ice.

*Photo by Joe Pellingra, from the author's private collection.*

Inuit build an igloo. The igloo toward the left rear has been fitted with a skylight of ice. In the background, a kayak rests on piers of snow to keep it out of the reach of the dogs who would relish the skin of the kayak as a fine meal.

*Photo by Joe Pellingra, from the author's private collection.*

Fast moving ice forces a severely damaged *Fury* onto the rocky shore of Fury Beach. HMS *Hecla* waits a few hundred feet away in a small, but safe, pool of open water.

*Photo by Joe Pellingra, from the author's private collection.*

The crew of HMS *Fury* heave her down (roll her over) to attempt repairs to her battered hull and keel. The damage, however, was fatal to the ship.

*Photo by Joe Pellingra, from the author's private collection.*

Traveling among the ice hummocks of the polar sea was a daunting task. Mountains of ice, thirty or more feet in height, often blocked the way.

*Photo by Joe Pellingra, from the author's private collection.*

*Sir John Barrow Bar^t*

*Secretary of the Admiralty from 1804 to 1845.*

*From the Original Picture by Jackson R.A 1824.*
*In the possession of Mr Murray*

Sir John Barrow

*Photo by Joe Pellingra, from the author's private collection.*

to proceed to Cape Isabella, discovered and named for his sister on his trek in early April, cross the waters at the western shore of Boothia Peninsula, and make his way westward along the North American coast. Ultimately, he wanted to reach as close as time and provisions allowed to John Franklin's Point Turnagain, the easternmost point reached by Sir John nine years earlier. If he were so fortunate as to reach the point, his journey would connect the known parts of the Northwest Passage and, thus, in essence, he would have completed the elusive passage.

It was evening when the men set out on their mid-May journey. The next day the sun shone brilliantly through a cloudless sky, and the thermometer registered a crisp 9 degrees. Indeed, the sun was too brilliant. In just a couple hours, Thomas Blanky suffered a painful case of snow blindness and MacDiarmid had to lead the stricken man back to the ship. Unfortunately, MacDiarmid's abandoning the expedition would have severe consequences for the well-being of the others. The plan had been for MacDiarmid to travel with Commander Ross until they found a suitable depot for extra supplies. MacDiarmid was then to head back to the ship and, at the right time, return to the agreed-upon spot to stash provisions for the returning travelers. When MacDiarmid and Blanky turned back prematurely, no one had yet determined the location for the depot, and so Commander Ross could not count on extra provisions on his return journey to the ship. This unfortunate gap in the plan left Commander Ross and his men provisioned for a round-trip journey of just twenty-one days. Notwithstanding the almost certain shortage of provisions on their return, the undaunted Commander James Ross made no adjustment and pushed forward.

By the end of the second day out, the four explorers had crossed the narrow isthmus that separates Prince Regent Inlet from the polar sea. They hailed the frozen sea (today's James Ross Strait) with three hearty cheers and then embarked across the ice toward Cape Isabella.

Sunlight dazzled off the snow and threatened to blind the men with its brilliance, just as it had done to Blanky. To protect themselves from snow blindness, Commander Ross switched their traveling from daytime to night. During the daylight hours, they camped in hollows dug into the snow because they had not developed the expertise to build igloos.

As further testament to Commander Ross's ignorance of the skills of the Inuit, after only ten days of travel he complained that his dogs had become "worse than useless, from the continued labour which they had exerted, and which we could not diminish by giving them occasional rest for a day or two, since we could not afford to hazard the loss of that fine weather." Consequently, James Ross lost to exhaustion all but two of his eight dogs. According to Steward Light, the commander killed the weaker dogs to feed the two that managed to survive his unrelenting drive. Commander Ross later admitted, "It was plain we had over-worked them . . . we ought to have followed the system of the natives, who never drive these animals for more than four days at a time."

Daily temperatures hung just above freezing and made travel worse than if the temperature had been in the teens. The sledges sunk into the softened, slushy, wet snow and required the greatest effort to drag them free. Where the ground was laid bare, the sledges scraped and screeched across the rocks. Worse yet, the frozen waterways, until then the most efficient highways, turned unpredictable and treacherous. Some ice still looked solid but cracked asunder when stepped on. In other places, the ice highway had turned to a torrent that was impossible to ford.

The four men struggled along the north coast of America until their fifteenth day out. At that point, they were about 250 miles from John Franklin's Point Turnagain. Commander Ross had come within halfway to closing the 500-mile gap in the Northwest Passage. There, the men erected a six-foot-high cairn of stones, unfurled their flag, took possession, and deposited a canister containing a note describing their proceedings. Commander James Ross named their farthest "Victory Point" and established its location as 69° 38' north latitude, 98° 36' west longitude.*

---

*Throughout the journey, Commander Ross determined his latitude by means of a sextant. The method is fairly straightforward. In mid-May—the period of Ross's journey—the earth's tilt causes the noon-hour sun to appear about 18 degrees to the north, rather than directly overhead, when viewed from the equator. Every degree that one travels to the north from the equator, the noon-hour sun appears one degree farther toward the south. Thus, at about 18 degrees north latitude, the noon-hour sun appears directly overhead. At Victory Point, Commander Ross would have used his sextant to measure the angle of the noon-hour sun above the horizon and found it to be about 51 degrees south of directly overhead. To this figure, he then added about 18 (he would find the exact value in his copy of the *Nautical Almanac* published by the Royal Greenwich Observatory), which established his position as being about 69 degrees north latitude.

Commander Ross determined the longitude of Victory Point with the aid of his pocket chronometer. Inasmuch as one 360-degree rotation of the earth takes 24 hours, the earth rotates at a rate of 15 degrees per hour. Therefore, if in Greenwich, England (defined as 0 degrees longitude), a particular star is observed to rise at 9 P.M., the same star would not rise until 10 P.M. when viewed at a location 15 degrees to the west. All Ross had to do, then, was observe a certain star rising above the horizon and note what time this occurred according to his chronometer, which was tracking the time in Greenwich, England. If the observed star was known to rise at 9 P.M. when viewed in Greenwich, and Ross saw the same star rise at 3:30 A.M. the next morning at Victory Point, he then knew that Victory Point was about 98 degrees (at 15 degrees to the hour) west of Greenwich.

Unlike lines of latitude, which are parallel, lines of longitude converge at the poles. The

With more than half of their provisions consumed, the commander reluctantly concluded, "There was nothing, therefore, left to us but to submit; and thus, however mortified at the necessity of such a resolution, I was compelled to settle finally for our return to the ship."

On the nineteenth day out they calculated that, with the few ptarmigan, foxes, and hares they had caught and by reducing their daily ration, they had maybe five days' provisions left. Yet they were still eighty miles from the ship, and progress had slowed to ten miles per day. Nevertheless, Commander Ross issued the incredible order to continue exploring—even though four days previously he had said that he would head for the ship; even though two more dogs had died; even though, in his own words, the men "suffered great fatigue." Onward, Ross led his men over the rugged, ice-covered terrain. After several grueling miles, Ross took a longer look at his exhausted companions, the used-up dogs, and the winding coastline. "Unless the coast should assume an easterly direction the next day, I must abandon the intention of completing this whole line of shore."

The coast did not assume an easterly direction. And so, much to the chagrin of the spunky commander, on the twenty-first day of their journey, the four explorers turned about and headed for home. Fortu-

---

farther one travels from the equator, the shorter the distance between degrees of longitude. Thus, although each degree of *equatorial* longitude is about 69 miles, at the high latitude of Victory Point, each degree of longitude is reduced to about 24 miles. Once Ross had determined Victory Point's longitude (about 98 degrees west), he then knew he still had about 250 miles to go because Point Turnagain was about another 10 degrees farther west.

nately, the closer they got to the ship, the lesser the effect of the thaw and traveling was somewhat easier.

Two days later, the exhausted and hungry men reached an encampment of Inuit. Atayaraktak, a brother of Ikmallik, welcomed the men and led Commander Ross to a cairn that John Ross had constructed to alert his nephew to a cache of provisions. When the four half-famished travelers located the depot, they discovered that the natives' dogs had ravaged it. Another Inuk, Milluctu (the man who had tried to con Mac-Diarmid out of a wooden leg), had taken what was left. Milluctu's mother, Topaka, offered the men what little remained, although she had thrown away the rum and lemon juice, calling it "very dirty water." To make up for what the natives had eaten of the cache, Atayaraktak gave the near-starving explorers some cod and also helped them build a hut of stone, since the softened snow was no longer suitable for an igloo. After three days of rest with Atayaraktak and his family—and all the fish they could eat—the four men departed for *Victory*.

Onward the men trudged until just a day's travel from the ship, where a shallow bay blocked their progress. On the outbound they had walked across the frozen bay and had not given it a second thought. Now, it was water. To go around the bay would have added several more days of renewed starvation to the journey. Faced with an unacceptable alternative, the four men gritted their teeth, took a deep breath, and stepped into the icy water.

Immediately soaked through, their woolen pants and leather boots weighed them down and made each step a forced, awkward shuffle. Staggering along the uneven bottom, the men kept their balance by clinging to the sides of a small skin boat in which they had piled their supplies. With the air temperature at just 35 degrees, a fall meant almost certain death from hypothermia. For two miles the four men shivered, and waded, and slipped, and sloshed their way across the bay. Although soaked and miserable, they somehow managed to reach the opposite shore without a deadly mishap.

Two days later, their mates welcomed the ragged, waterlogged travelers aboard a warm and dry *Victory*. Although everyone returned safely after nearly a month's absence, Steward William Light wrote,

> *On the arrival at the ship, the men appeared like human skeletons: their flesh shriveled, their countenances wan and doleful, their gait feeble and tottering, and their general appearance bespeaking the liberated inmates of a prison, or a few miserable objects, who had escaped from the city of the plague.*

*Felix Harbor, June 1830.* A heavy rain poured from the gloomy sky. Fortunately, the crew had completed caulking the upper deck and was spared a drenching from rainwater that tried to seep into their quarters. The temperature climbed to 50 degrees but dropped to freezing at night.

Torrents of meltwater streamed down the hillsides, over the rocks, and splashed noisily into the sea. An occasional bumblebee and other small insects buzzed the air. Large flocks of king ducks flew overhead. George MacDiarmid shot a brant goose and a swan. A sailor found the egg of a Canada goose. Snow fell, mixed with rain. The thaw continued.

The bird migration increased dramatically. Hundreds and thousands of plovers, buntings, ducks, gulls, geese, sandpipers, and kittiwakes streaked overhead and flocked to the rocky shores. Captain Ross encouraged shooting expeditions and directed that each bird be brought to his cabin so he might determine its value for his collection. If the bird was a suitable specimen, Ross ordered it skinned and preserved. Otherwise, the bird was the shooter's to enjoy for dinner. William Light despised Captain Ross's directive. He went out of his way to fool Ross by shooting upwind of the ship so Ross would not hear the gunshots. Then he smuggled the birds onboard and had them cooked in secret. If the bird were one he knew Ross was especially interested in, he mutilated the bird to destroy its value as a specimen and then showed it to Ross, all the while laughing under his breath at his captain's disappointment.

Captain Ross's bird collecting not only irritated Light, but aggravated the ongoing fits of jealousy between the captain and his nephew. "I was the only person," whined James Ross, "who at all understood the nature of those subjects [of natural history], but I was not ordered to undertake them." And so it went. Barely a month went by without a period in which the two Rosses did not speak to one another, "the one taking to the sulks in one corner of the cabin, and the other following his example in an opposite one—one due north, the other due south," wrote the steward. Captain Ross's inherent taciturnity undoubtedly added to the irritation of his gregarious nephew, who, perhaps feeling alone, befriended the crew. To the elder Ross, however, fraternizing with the crew was flat-out forbidden for an officer.

Notwithstanding the bickering or the cool silence in the cabin, preparations for *Victory*'s release increased steadfastly as the days grew warmer.

Snow that had been piled on the ship for insulation melted and flowed into the hold. Carpenter Chimham Thomas fixed the pumps, and the men pumped the bilge clear, which caused the steward to exclaim, "[I]t being the first time that it had been performed in nine months, the stench of the bilge water was ... so great as almost to sicken a man."

In the midst of all the activity, Tulluahiu arrived at the ship, drawn by his friends on a section of sealskin that replaced their sledges of salmon, which they had eaten. He had broken his wooden leg and hoped Chimham Thomas would make another. The kindly carpenter-doctor—as Captain Ross loved to call him—somehow found time among his other duties to make Tulluahiu a replacement.

To hasten melting, men spread gravel on the ice around the ship and along an escape route that led to the main channel of Prince Regent Inlet. The gravel enhanced the effect of the sun's rays, and before long the ice in the canal melted to just two feet thick. While some of the crew spread gravel, others cut the ice from *Victory*'s port side. She rose fourteen inches, which eased a heavy starboard list—a great improvement for a crew who had long since tired of living in a canted home.

Steadily, the sailing preparations to *Victory* continued. Encouraged with the prospects of being at sea again, the sailors cheerfully pulled down the canvas tent, rerigged the mainmast and foremast, resecured the bowsprit, hoisted the fore-topmast, and painted the mastheads.

Meanwhile, Captain John Ross and four of his men made a short reconnoiter to the west. On July 1, he spotted an Inuk across a small bay and fired his gun to gain the man's attention. The man appeared startled, but then went through the customary throwing his weapons in the air as a sign of peace. When Ross finally reached the native, he realized he was Ikmallik's nephew, Awack. Awack, who always got excited over the most trivial of things, burst into laughter and danced a little jig when he realized it was Captain Ross. Even William Light got a chuckle out of Awack's antics and remarked that if the Inuit "could have been induced to form themselves into a theatrical company, Alwak [*sic*] would undoubtedly have been chosen as the most proper person to fill the character of a clown."

Captain Ross handed Awack his gun as a sign of friendship, and together they walked to Ross's tent. As they walked, Awack told Captain Ross that his uncle was camped about ten miles away and that Ross was welcome to join them. Ross wanted very much to see Ikmallik again, so as soon as they reached the captain's tent, he and his companions packed up and went with Awack to Ikmallik's. When they reached the Hydrographer's camp, Ross "was received with open arms by our old friend Ikmallik." The captain gave his friend a sovereign to wear around his neck and told Ikmallik that the likeness of George IV was Ross's "great chief." Ikmallik should preserve the gift and show it to any European he might happen to meet, Ross told him. "It was not likely to be spent, whatever else might happen," joked Ross, who added that Ikmallik would have been utterly astounded if he knew the quantity of fish-hooks, axes, knives, and needles the coin could buy.

At that time, Ikmallik and Tulluahiu and their families were the last to remain in the area; the other Inuit had already headed south to better fishing and hunting. Ikmallik told Ross that the fishing season in the region had ended and that he, too, was about to set off for the lakes to the south, but that he would stay another day if Ross would remain with them. John Ross immediately set up his tent, and Ikmallik reerected his, which he had just pulled down. "They were highly delighted when I displayed the flag above Ikmallik's tent instead of our own," wrote Captain Ross.

However, when the twelve members of Ikmallik and Tulluahiu's families crowded into Ross's tent for a salmon dinner, Ross was at a loss

HARRISON COUNTY
PUBLIC LIBRARY

over how to cook for everyone in the cramped confines. "We were soon relieved from all anxiety about cookery, finding that they preferred their fish raw," chuckled a relieved Ross. (The word *Eskimo* is a derogatory Danish word of Algonquin origin for "he eats it raw.")

Captain Ross described in his journal the manner in which the fish were prepared and eaten. First, Ikmallik and Tulluahiu cut off the fish's head and removed the backbone. Next, they slit the fillet longitudinally into sections. These they rolled into cylinders of about two inches diameter—not unlike sushi—and stuffed them into their mouths as far as they could, after which they cut off the excess, in the same manner Commander Ross had described their eating the musk ox meat.

The next day, the two Inuit families sold Ross a quantity of salmon (deep-frozen in a pit) for the price of three knives. Ross was astonished to learn that no less than a ton of frozen fish was in the pit. For three days, he and his four crewmen dragged the booty on sealskin blankets to the ship. He admitted that he had no idea how large a volume of salmon was stored in the pit and that, if he had known, he would have offered far more than just three knives. (Ross does not say whether he ever offered Ikmallik or Tulluahiu additional payment.) After a fond farewell, Ross's friends headed off to their original destination. "To our communication with the natives I must also add that they endeavoured to entertain us in their best manner," summarized Captain Ross.

The frozen fish arrived just in time, because back onboard *Victory* some of the men showed incipient signs of scurvy. Ross ordered each man to consume three pounds of fish every other day. Unfortunately, the Inuit had not gutted the fish before putting them in cold storage. This left the fish with a less-than-pleasant taste, especially those parts near the liver. It was no mean task for the crew to gut and clean several hundred fish. Nonetheless, the task was done, and the diet worked! In three to four weeks the men's health improved significantly.

On the tenth of July, clouds of mosquitoes appeared over the land and marshes. By the twenty-second day of the month, the swarms had found the ship and the men. Thousands of hungry insects, excited by the warm-blooded bounty, buzzed and crawled everywhere. They crept up sleeves, settled in the men's hair, walked on their food, and followed them to their hammocks. At any given moment, hundreds of insects covered each sailor, seeking out the tiniest opening through his clothing. And when the bugs could find none, they bit right through the material with fierce, needle-like pricks. With no screens or mosquito repellent, relief was impossible. Escape was impossible. The venomous insects and the still, oppressive, humid, 70-degree air brought all work to a halt for five days straight. Heavy rain, lower temperatures, and a stout breeze finally ended the men's torment.

By the end of July, *Victory* was completely refitted. Even her crow's nest had been reinstalled. She looked good in her new paint. And Thomas's repaired pumps easily controlled any leaks. Ross wrote that *Victory*

> . . . *had never been so trim, neat, clean, and comfortable. We had obtained abundant room by the dismissal of the engine; and that was no small gain, to compensate a loss, if that machinery can be esteemed a loss, whence we have derived so little advantage and undergone so much inconvenience and vexation. It was probable that the [Inuit] would profit for a long time to come by the caches of Messrs. Braithwaite and Erickson [manufacturers of the steam engine.].*

Yet look as hard as he might, Captain John Ross could see no clear water in Prince Regent Inlet, nor did the ice appear to be on the move.

His one hope was that a strong southerly gale would break up the ice. Even so, on his 1821–23 voyage to the region, Ross's predecessor, Edward Parry, had already escaped his winter quarters by July 2. Ross was a month behind. If he were stalled another month, he could count on a month's sailing weather, at the most, in consideration that in the previous year ice had blocked them in by early October.

While the men waited for *Victory* to get free, they fished for trout, lolled about, and played with their pet rabbit and foxes. Earlier in the season, a couple sailors had captured a mother fox and her four kits, but the mother died after eating a specimen of a willow partridge, which had been preserved with arsenic. The four kits thrived and became the sailors' favorite pets. Light told how the young foxes ganged up on the *Victory*'s tomcat to steal its meal. A fox would crouch in front of the old cat while he ate. A second fox would bite his tail, and when the cat spun around to attack it, the first fox would dash off with the old cat's meal. According to Light, the old cat never caught on, even though the foxes repeatedly pulled the stunt.

*Felix Harbor, September 1, 1830. Victory* remained fixed in place—the same location in which she had been for eleven months. Ice completely barricaded her originally planned deep-water escape route from Felix Harbor. The alternate route, in which the ice appeared more likely to break up, was a channel in which the water varied in depth from thirty to less than three feet, depending on the tide. Worse yet, the bottom of the channel was strewn with jagged rocks and boulders so that *Victory*'s only chance to traverse the waterway was during the highest of tides.

The depth of the water was so variable and the tide so unpredictable that the slightest error to port or starboard could leave her keel impaled on the rocks. The men took soundings and marked the channel with buoys. *Victory's* escape required not only great caution and speed, but also considerable luck.

Then, the temperature dropped to 29 degrees—the first time below freezing since mid-June. Snow fell steadily and covered the hills. A gale blew out of the northwest. Ice packed together in a single mass. The men were heartsick.

Suddenly, the ice moved. Moreover, its movement coincided with a spring tide—the highest tide possible.

"Man th' capstan!"

With three hearty cheers, the men laid out the hawsers and fixed the ice anchors. Slowly, *Victory* crept over a bar toward an open pool as the capstan creaked its way 'round and 'round. The tide, however, dropped precipitously, and before they got her through the channel, she settled on the rocks in just fourteen inches of water. The men jumped from the ship, shored her up, and began unloading her. They pumped out four tons of water and put another ten tons of articles in the whaleboats to await the incoming tide. The wind shifted, however, and the next tide did not rise nearly high enough. The men built a twenty-four-foot-long bridge of planks from the ship to the rocky shore. For the entire day, the crew carried everything movable to shore. Steward William Light moaned,

> *A foreboding, not of a very pleasant nature, did not fail to come across the minds of some of the crew, whether their present situation might not be looked upon as the counterpart of the fate of the* Fury; *and whether their stores might not be the fortunate means of saving some future navigators from starvation.*

The returning tide flowed around *Victory*. At three-quarters tide, she was still marooned. Anxious eyes watched the water slowly creep up the numerical marks on her rudder. The sea gurgled and sloshed at her hull. A wave rolled in. The watch on the bow shouted, "She floats! She floats!" With a mighty heave on the hawsers, the crew hauled the empty ship free of the rocks.

In the meantime, a heavy snowfall had buried the provisions and supplies on shore. Should the supplies be brought on board, which would increase *Victory*'s draft and possibly ground her again? the men wondered. Or should they wait until she was moved to deeper water, but then might be caught in the current and driven too far from shore?

Ross determined to re-ship the supplies. Even with all hands at work, the men spent three days' labor to bring everything back onboard. Fortunately, *Victory* floated free during the whole time; yet she was still encumbered by ice that choked the channel—ice that pressed dangerously against her hull and threatened to stove her in. She had to be freed.

The men cut. The men sawed. The men chopped at the ice. They heaved at her hawsers. They worked at the capstan. At times, even with three hawsers wrapped around the capstan, *Victory* barely budged an inch. Little clouds of hemp dust wafted through the air as the hawsers drew tightly against one another and popped and creaked their way around the capstan. Inch by inch, foot by foot, *Victory* advanced. In four days, she moved just ten feet closer to the open water. Two days later, she was two ships'-length closer. The next day, nearly 1,500 feet. Hour after hour spent at the capstan turned into days upon days.

On 17 September 1830, Captain John Ross rejoiced,

*Under sail—we scarcely knew how we felt, or whether we quite believed it. He must be a seaman to feel that the vessel which bounds beneath him, which listens to and obeys the smallest movement of his hand, which seems to move but under his will, is a thing of life, a mind conforming to his wishes; not an inert body, the sport of winds and waves. But what seaman could feel this as we did, when this creature, which used to carry us buoyantly over the ocean, had been, during an entire year, immovable as the ice and rocks around it, helpless, disobedient, dead.*

# CHAPTER FIVE

# The Ice Refuses to Release *Victory*

## (September 1830–April 1831)

*P*RINCE *Regent Inlet, September 18, 1830.* Nature did not let Ross simply sail away. No sooner had *Victory* been under sail than the wind shifted to the southward. The ice floes, which were just beginning to break up, swept before the wind and tide and blocked *Victory*'s route. In a matter of minutes, the rapidly moving ice piled up against her sides, halted her progress, and threatened her security. Fortunately, just like occasions the previous year, icebergs moved in, created a little harbor, and protected *Victory* from the onslaught of the ice.

By six o'clock the next evening, the storm had increased and the wind shifted to a gale that blew out of the north-northwest. Winds raced across the ice at fifty miles per hour. Snow covered the hills, the ship, and even the men down on the ice who had been attempting to cut a breathing space around *Victory*. Within an hour, the wind increased to a whole gale: sixty miles per hour. The ice rumbled and moved violently. *Victory's* protective icebergs lost their grip on the sea floor, moved en masse with the floes, and pushed *Victory* before them. By 4 A.M., the wind howled at seventy miles per hour. *Victory* rolled and pitched. Her rigging rattled. The masts shook. Suddenly, a devastating blast yanked the fore-topmast stay from the bowsprit. In an instant, the standing backstay followed. With the fore and aft supports gone, the fore-topmast split from its lower mast and plummeted to the deck. The lower masts creaked and cracked. The hurricane seemed intent on blowing away the entire upper rigging, which loosened and then snapped taut as the typhonic wind punished first from one direction and then another.

Not yet through with the ship, nature gathered together her forces of wind, ice, and tide and drove the schooner onto the rock-strewn shore. Up and down *Victory* bobbed in the turbulent, shallow water. Her keel ground against the bottom with the water's ebb, and her stern slammed into the rocks with its flow. For sixteen hours *Victory* beat against the rocks and bergs as the wind wailed at fifty miles per hour and often exceeded seventy. Then the wind eased. Then it started up again. For five days, the capricious hurricane pounded *Victory*.

When at last the storm relented, *Victory* came to rest with her keel on a layer of ice congealed to the bottom of the channel. She careened nearly onto her side. Somehow, the lower masts had withstood the assault, but her deck was a shamble of tangled shrouds, stays, tackles, blocks, deadeyes, and splintered wood. Clearing the deck and rerigging the fore-topmast, however, would have to wait. *Victory's* position was far too precarious, and all hands set to work at clearing the ice from beneath her. By the close of day, she floated free with the high tide, but settled to the rocky bottom and fell on her broadside at ebb. The surrounding ice left no means to sail into clear water, which was a distant two miles away. Worse yet, she was badly exposed to the assault of sea, ice, and tide. Captain Ross ordered her rudder unshipped to protect the priceless apparatus from further attacks.

*Victory*'s sad situation precipitated a stormy dispute between Captain Ross and his nephew. Captain Ross believed that if they had not waited for the inlet to clear of ice before moving from Felix Harbor, but instead had attempted to creep along the shore, perhaps they may have escaped. But the captain had deferred to his nephew's judgment in that Commander Ross had had previous experience with Prince Regent Inlet when he had sailed with Parry—albeit the younger Ross's experience was hundreds of miles to the north of Felix Harbor. And now, Captain Ross put much of the blame for their predicament on James Ross. "That his anticipations were wrong, the event has shown; whether we might really have succeeded by adopting [my] plan, will never be known," wrote the angry captain in his journal. To Commander Ross, however, the fault lay entirely with Captain Ross. He complained to the crew that "a want of skill and judgment on the part of Capt. Ross, and particularly to a lack of boldness and determination" were to blame for *Victory*'s treacherous situation. The renewed frigidity between the two men lasted for days. While both men sulked about and avoided one another, the embarrassed crew tiptoed carefully around the feuding officers. Finally, with the help of a "magnum of Booth's best cordial," as William Light put it, the rift was repaired and the business of the ship carried on as usual.

With a truce in place and *Victory*'s safety again foremost in his mind, Commander Ross climbed a hill to look for a secure harbor. When he trudged over and examined the only harbor in view, he discovered that it was too shallow. Yet even if the harbor's depth were adequate, *Victory* was immovably trapped by the ice floes. The only recourse was a narrow bay some 300 yards away—300 yards of solid, 16-inch-thick ice. The men hauled out the fourteen-foot ice saws and got to work. The temperature dropped to 5 degrees. A light snow fell. A moderate breeze gave a wind-chill of about 25 degrees below zero.

After a full day of cutting the ice, *Victory* advanced a mere 18 feet. Captain Ross wrote in his journal,

> *It seemed almost a fated period for us; as it was the very anniversary of the day which had fixed us not three miles from the spot which we were now seeking to occupy; while we were perhaps again captives—who could conjecture?—for another year. It had been a busy and a labourious month; but it was busy idleness, as far as any result had followed, and all the labour had produced no return. It was in every sense, a wasted month; and it had been an amply provoking one. . . . We had now to hope again, for nearly another year; to count months, weeks, even days, yet with less confidence than we had done during the last winter.*

In the previous year, gales from the west and south had opened leads in the channel ice, which permitted Ross, in spite of the difficulties encountered, to sail *Victory* as long and as far as he had. Now, the winds constantly blew from the north and drove masses of ice into the increasingly rare leads and pools of clear water. On top of that, the September of 1830 was colder than the September of 1829, which further augured for a worse winter.

*October 1, 1830.* The men renewed sawing the canal at the break of day. Although the ice was only about sixteen-inches thick, the shallow water made the task far more difficult than it was the year before. To advance a canal in 1829, the men had sawed the ice into slabs, which they then shoved under the ice and out of the way with long pike poles. In their present situation, the shallow water prevented shoving the slabs underwater, so their only recourse was to attach an ice anchor and haul the pieces up and out of the canal with help of the capstan.

To make matters worse, the wind and tides of the recent storm had created a mess of buckled, hummocky ice that varied tremendously in thickness. In some places the ice was higher than *Victory*'s gunwales; in others, less than two-feet thick.

After five days, when the canal had advanced about 100 feet, the men encountered ice that was regularly three to four feet thick, or more. Progress was excruciatingly slow and uneven. Some days *Victory* advanced as much as fifty feet. Others, as little as six feet. And some days, if the weather were particularly cruel, no advance whatsoever.

All hands worked the whole of each day. At night, they set to work sawing in two or three shifts, depending on the tide and any advantage the ebb and flow might offer. "[W]orking like horses . . . [s]ome of the men would fall in the canal, head over ears; and before they could get to the ship, their clothes would be frozen, the jacket to the waistcoat, and the former so hard, that it would almost stand upright," wrote William Light.

The first half of the canal never had more than four or five feet of water at low tide. *Victory*'s draft was over seven feet, so the men often had to stop sawing at low tide to take time to prop her up. Otherwise, she would topple onto her beam ends. To complicate matters, the currents, the wind, and the ice combined to make the tide entirely unpredictable. On one occasion, the waters rose more than eight feet; on another, just one inch.

With *Victory* propped up, the crew once more sawed the ice, chopped at the ice, and hauled the slabs out with the capstan. If a tide sufficiently high to float *Victory* returned, one team set to the capstan and warped her forward, while another continued to labor at the saws. For thirty days the men worked, day by day and night by night.

On October 24, the ice sawyers ran into a section that was sixteen feet thick. As before, sinking the cut-out ice was impossible and the slabs were impossibly heavy to raise with the capstan. In the surrounding ice field, not far from their canal, the men located a region of thinner ice. They cut a spur canal to the thinner ice, floated the sixteen-foot-thick chunks down the spur, and lodged them out of the way in a bay they had cut in the relatively thin ice. *Victory* did not advance one foot that trying Sunday.

On October 30, the progress was but six feet. The next day, *Victory* refused to budge another inch. "[T]he whole month had been employed in making a worse-than-tortoise progress, the entire amount of which, after all our toils, was but eight hundred and fifty feet. I believe that some of us could not help calculating the number of centuries it would require to make a single north-west passage, at this rate," quipped John Ross as the Arctic settled on *Victory*'s home for the second winter. He named the site Sheriff's Harbor in respect to his patron, Felix Booth, who, besides owning a gin distillery, was the sheriff of London. Sheriff's Harbor was less than what Captain Ross had wished for *Victory*, but at least the ship was protected from advancing icebergs, and the harbor's ten-foot-deep water would prevent her bottoming at low tide.

Ross ordered the sails unbent, the remaining topmast unrigged, snow walls built around the ship, a gunpowder magazine constructed on shore (as a fire precaution), the lower decks painted white to make it more cheerful, and other similar preparations for wintering as had been done the previous year. These included reinstallation of Ross's apparatus for condensing the water from the cabin's humid air. A serious aggravation and health hazard with overwintering in the Arctic in the nineteenth century was the condensation that formed on everything in the ship: walls, ceiling, bedding . . . everything grew wet with moisture. In the worst case, moisture dripped from the ceiling onto the crewmen's hammocks, where, because the hammocks were against the hull of the ship, the moisture froze, only to be thawed at nighttime by the warmth from the sailors' bodies. William Edward Parry had remarked on his 1819–20 Arctic voyage,

> *[W]e found the steam from the coppers, as well as the breath and other vapour . . . began to condense into drops upon the beams and the sides, to such a degree as to keep them constantly wet . . . it . . . accumulated in the bed-places occasionally to a serious and very alarming degree.*

Parry's solution was to raise the inside temperature to over 100 degrees near the stove and close to 70 degrees throughout the ship. Captain John Ross, however, had nowhere near the abundance of fuel that Parry's larger, 370-ton ships carried. To solve the problem, Ross had had *Victory* fitted with an array of copper flues that carried the vapors from the men's berths, cabins, and galley to three downward-opening iron tanks mounted between the decks. By convection, the warm, moist air traveled to the cold, iron tanks, where the moisture condensed and froze. Every week, a crewman chiseled out about four bushels of frost that had accumulated within the condensing tanks. This arrangement not only kept the interior air relatively dry, but also provided an additional source of salt-free water.

At Captain Ross's request, purser Thom gave an accounting of the *Victory*'s remaining stores. These included 17,364 pounds of flour, 13,250 pounds of salted and preserved meats, and 2,738 pounds of sugar. Also left were 120 gallons of rum and gin, 250 pounds of rice, 6 cases of cocoa, and quantities of split peas, lemons, pickles, mustard, and barley. Thom estimated *Victory*'s provisions would last somewhat less than two years, at which time they would have to sail to Fury Beach to replenish their stores from what remained of *Fury*'s abandoned provisions. To carry them through the next six months—until hunting and fishing might provide fresh meat—Thom worked out the following ration for each man:

Mondays and Fridays: ¾ lb. salt beef and ¾ lb. flour
Tuesdays, Thursdays, and Saturdays: ½ lb. preserved meat and ¼ lb.
    meat in barley soup
Wednesdays and Sundays: 1 lb. pork with pea soup
Alternate Mondays: ¾ lb. preserved meats with vegetable soup

A satisfied Captain Ross wrote,

*Thus, the men would have soup on six days out of every eight—and on the other two, beef and pudding—while a constant succession of diet would be obtained. Thus, we trusted that their health and strength would be kept up, so as to enable them to go through the fatigue of traveling in the spring.*

In fact, as a result of hunting when weather permitted, the officers enjoyed roasted hare every Sunday. Although it was common in the nineteenth century for officers to eat a different and better diet than the crew, Steward William Light wrote, "Deep, however, were the murmurings of the crew, at the great difference, which was observable between the fare of the cabin [officers' quarters], and that which was doled out to them in their respective berths."

A new blizzard roared for sixteen hours on November 11. The temperature dropped to 16 below zero. Gale-force winds up to thirty-five miles per hour created windchills around 75 below zero. Ross ordered that all work outside the ship cease for the duration of the storm. He noted that the temperature on the same date the previous year was 26 degrees *above* zero. As soon as the weather cleared, the men attended to the next preparation for wintering, which was to cut a fire hole. A fire hole was nothing more than a hole cut through the ice to assure a source of water in case of a fire onboard the ship. Twice a day throughout their stay, a crewman chopped away new ice that closed over the hole.

On the fifth of November, the thermometer registered 39 degrees below zero. The temperature had not reached that low the previous winter until January 14. As Ross had feared, the winter of 1830–31 was off to a severe start. Ross walked the three miles to Felix Harbor to examine the ice. To his chagrin, the harbor was far more hampered with heavy ice than it had been the previous year. He went on,

> *I certainly thought our present one preferable, independent of the fact of its being so much farther to the north, which was our intended direction. It, indeed, seems trifling to talk of two or three miles as a great space gained; but*

*when it is recollected that we were a whole month navigating scarcely three hundred yards . . . even two miles were a subject of congratulation.*

While he was there, Ross erected signposts at Felix Harbor to direct the Inuit to *Victory's* new wintering site. On the discarded steam engine boilers he drew figures of large hands that pointed toward Sheriff's Harbor. And on a hill overlooking Sheriff's Harbor, he erected a flagstaff in hope of attracting the Inuit's attention. Ross's actions amused the steward, who wrote,

> *[W]hen, however, the trifling distance is considered, which the second harbour was from the first, it was not likely that a roving people . . . would not discover the vessel; for, although she might not be exactly visible from Felix Harbor, the sound of her guns . . . would have been a sure indication to them that the Kabloonas were still in their vicinity.*

Such was the strength of John Ross's desire to be reacquainted with his old friends.

On the first of December, Ross tried to track down a brace of willow partridges, but the 2 P.M. Arctic nightfall brought his quest to a halt. Looking about, Ross mused,

> *[I]t is the [Inuit] alone who here know the true secret of happiness and the rational art of living . . . [he] eats but to sleep, and sleeps but to eat again as soon as he can. What better can he do? The adaptation is perfect, his happiness absolute. Had we been better educated, we should have done the same; but we were here out of our element, as much in the philosophy of life as in the geography of it.*

The month of December dragged on uneventfully, and, in his lonely ennui, Ross continued to wax philosophical,

*Man is a strange animal when he can live in so many different countries, in climates so opposed, and on food so diverse. He would be a stranger one, if, having ever known another country . . . he had made a voluntary choice of the America of Prince Regent Inlet. But he has contrived to wander hither, whencever he might have come; if he ever knew bananas, he has learned to prefer fish oil, has made bones a substitute for bamboos, and blubber for pineapples; learning also that a seal skin is a more fitting dress than a cotton wrapper, and that snow may be substituted for wood and stone. . . . Man, in the mass, is equally happy in all conditions of life, all regions of the earth, and all states of cultivation. It is a very different thing to maintain that, individually, all are equally happy, or that, to all, there are equivalent compensations of happiness and suffering.*

A few days before Christmas, Captain Ross and his fellow officers took a stroll over the snow-covered hills. The temperature hovered around 25 below zero. Snow fell in occasional squalls. A light breeze blew. Walking along the smooth snow struck him as "almost agreeable," except that there was nothing on shore to amuse them. The land provided a place to exercise—that was all. "In the calendar, this was the shortest day; that was tolerably indifferent to us, who had no day at all," Ross wrote as he sunk deeper into his depression and boredom.

*Sheriff's Harbor, Christmas Day, 1830.* Violent weather forced the men to cancel their Christmas Day parade. A thirty-mile-per-hour wind shook *Victory's* canvas covering and brought the 17-below-zero temperature to a windchill around 74 degrees below zero. Snow squalls blew throughout the day. Deep inside *Victory*, nonetheless, the other festivities of the day went on as planned. The crew's Christmas dinner was ox cheek soup, pudding, raisins, carrots, and grog. For the officers, there was smoked tureen of hare soup, beef, dried and pickled fish, vegetables, plum pudding, and Stilton cheese. The difference between the two menus further added to Light's resentment toward Captain Ross.

After dinner the men sang "The Army and Navy," "The King, God Bless Him," and "God Save the King." William Light wrote, "The choruses equaled in noise and loudness, but not exactly in harmony, those which are bellowed from the mouths of our professionals on the stage when it is their particular desire to tickle the ears of royalty." Perhaps if the men had known that George IV had died six months previously and that his far more popular brother, William IV, reigned, they might have sung even louder.

On New Year's Day "the temperature remained at minus 47 degrees, it was calm, and the cold was not severe to the feelings," wrote Captain Ross in his journal. The men hoisted *Victory's* colors and dressed her out with her signal flags and pennants, but otherwise no special New Year's celebrations took place. Five days later, the temperature dropped to 59 below zero, the coldest *Victory's* crew would ever record. Captain John Ross's only comment was, "Saturday ended a dull week, without any change in the weather or the temperature." The whole month of January saw few notations in Ross's journal: a comment here and there about the rise or fall in temperature, a ptarmigan shot, an aurora, a gloomy sky, a sun not yet visible, a sun finally seen. "It was a welcome sight, even now; though it was long yet before we should derive much advantage from it, in respect to heat at least."

After the religious service on Sunday, January 30, some of the men walked the six miles to the Inuit's encampment of the previous year, but they found nothing except a deserted campsite. By that same day the previous year, Tulluahiu's wooden leg had been made, Ikmallik and Tirikshiu had drawn maps for Ross, gifts had been exchanged, Otoogiu had offered to heal Marslin, and daily visits by all had brought wonderful cheer to the doldrums of Arctic winter.

How different the January of 1831. *Victory's* decks stood mournfully quiet: just the occasional thump of sailors' boots across the cabin floor; the sputter of a dying candle; the rustle of reread, eighteen-month-old love letters; the trickle of water leaking through *Victory's* battered hull; the slosh, slosh of her hand pumps. Quiet conversation, muttered Sunday evening prayers, singing of psalms, the clatter of dinnerware, the hiss of pudding steaming in the copper, a sailor's ditty on the fiddle, the muted scratch of an ink-dipped quill in an officer's journal. The scamper of a cat, the howl of a dog, the shoveling of coal, the wind's moan, the rigging's creak, the pops and cracks of expansion and contraction with the cruel temperature.

"We had been disappointed in not receiving the expected visit from the natives but attributed their absence to the badness of the weather," wrote Ross. So ended January 1831.

February was not much better. Thom, Commander Ross, and others made their hourly trips to the observatory to check and record the readings on their instruments: temperature, barometric pressure, magnetic observations, wind speed. "[B]ut we could make no observations with the instruments on [days when the temperature approached 50 below zero], since it was impossible to touch the metal as if it had been red hot." Measured the thickness of the sea ice: four and a half feet. Sky cloudy. Sky clear. Temperature at 9 degrees above. Temperature at 49 below zero. Played with the pet foxes. Shot frozen balls of mercury into a board. Trapped a fox, a ptarmigan, a hare. Ennui.

February's highlight was the escape of one of the foxes that had harassed the tomcat. With a short length of chain still around its neck, the young fox dashed across the deck and down onto the ice. Its freedom was short-lived, however, as it was found the next day in the fox trap. The poor thing had frozen its tongue to the iron bars of the trap. The sailors returned the errant fox to join its caged companions on the lower deck. Captain John Ross concluded February 1831 with, "Not having yet seen the [Inuit], we now gave up the hope of their joining us till May."

About this time a dispute again developed between the two Rosses. Although no details exist, the disagreement was apparently a renewal of the one begun way back in September when each blamed the other for *Victory*'s entrapment. As always, both men avoided one another, neither speaking nor exchanging even common courtesies. James escaped to the observatory for days on end, coming aboard ship only for his meals and sleep. Captain Ross confined himself to his cabin. Then one day, the frigid atmosphere exploded in a heated argument of shouting and accusations, mostly regarding management of the ship. Cowed by the outburst but curious of the substance and outcome, the crew strained to hear the exchange, muffled by the cabin's solid walls. Gradually, the shouting diminished to barely audible conversation. As day turned to night, the cabin door opened and Captain Ross called for the steward to set the table with two glasses. Peace had been found and toasted, reported the steward, who snickered that uncle and nephew had "thoroughly convinced themselves that the cabin of a ship blocked up in the ice, in a latitude of 70 north, is one of the most improper places in the world for two persons to live in who are at enmity with each other."

The next day the crew and officers returned to amusing themselves by firing musket balls of ice, almond oil, and mercury at a wooden plank. The plank split.

By mid-March, even though the temperature lingered around 30 degrees below zero, the strength of the sun had increased sufficiently to melt snow on some of the rocks. Ross ordered the men to spread gravel on the ice to hasten melting a canal for *Victory's* escape. Although backbreaking, the work was no doubt welcomed by the men as a relief from their daily tedium and a sign that the voyage might again proceed. Ross noted that, although some snow on the rocks was melting,

> *[T]he effect was of no long duration . . . [and] the preceding year . . . the water was running down in streams. It was an adverse prospect as our future plans were concerned; and had, at times, some effect of casting a damp on the men, which their tiresome sameness of occupation had no tendency to remedy.*

Boredom aside, the crew remained healthy. None had been on the sick list, and scurvy had made no signs of appearance. In his published journal, Ross wrote for the last day of March,

> *Our disappointment in not seeing the [Inuit] continued daily increasing, as their expected arrival was the longer delayed. We still looked forward to their visits with hope.*

With April, the weather improved somewhat. The thermometer registered zero on April 2. Two weeks later, the arrival of a snow bunting heralded the passage of winter. Ross had the men prepare for an overland journey. Carpenter Thomas worked on the sledges. Engineer Brunton constructed a traveling kettle for cooking.

"*Manig tomig!*" Over the western hills trudged three Inuit, shouting in their native tongue, "All hail!" Poweytak (the father of the little boy killed by the falling rock), Poweytak's stepson Noyennak, and a third Inuk named Neytaknag had returned.

# CHAPTER SIX

# The North Magnetic Pole

(April 1831–June 1831)

*SHERIFF's Harbor, April 20, 1831.* The day before the three Inuit had returned to *Victory*, Commander Ross and five others had set out on an overland journey to hunt musk oxen and explore yet another candidate for the Northwest Passage thirty-seven miles due north. On their first day out, Commander Ross scanned the countryside with his spyglass and spotted a mound that appeared to be a newly built igloo. As he and his comrades neared the dome, three occupants came out with their knives drawn and quickly approached. Ross laid down his gun. To his relief, the natives threw down their weapons, too, and in the next moment welcomed Commander Ross and his company with open arms. The three men were Poweytak, Noyennak, and Neytaknag.

Poweytak told Commander Ross that toward the end of the previous summer they had been camped a few miles to the north where they waited for *Victory* until the advancing winter compelled them to leave. The three Inuit were surprised to hear from Commander Ross that ice had prevented *Victory's* northward advance, because where they were camped, the sea was practically clear of ice.

Poweytak went on to say that they had accumulated an abundance of salmon and reindeer meat that they had wanted to sell to the men of *Victory*. When *Victory* failed to show, they buried the meat in the snow and now Poweytak wished to sell it to Commander Ross for two knives. Commander Ross agreed to the bargain, but because he had no means to carry the meat, he asked Poweytak to go to the *Victory* and tell his uncle about their barter. Commander Ross wrote a note for Poweytak to give Captain Ross that explained the deal.

When Commander Ross and his comrades had shown up outside the igloo, the three Inuit were in the process of packing up to cross the isthmus of Boothia to the western sea via a chain of lakes. Hearing their plans, Commander Ross asked if he might accompany the Inuit to the western sea because his calculations had indicated that the North Magnetic Pole must lie in that direction. First, however, Ross wanted to complete his planned journey to the north, and he prevailed upon the three men to join him in that direction. The natives, however, held no interest in James Ross's northward trek and told him they would proceed to the *Victory* and wait there for his return if he still wished to join them.

Consequently, everyone agreed to regroup when Commander Ross returned to *Victory*, and the next day at six in the morning the two companies went their separate ways: Poweytak, Noyennak, and Neytaknag to *Victory* to close the meat sale with Captain Ross; James Ross and his five companions to travel northward along the coast.

When Poweytak, Noyennak, and Neytaknag arrived at the ship, Captain Ross warmly welcomed the three natives and invited them to his table. Over dinner, they discussed what had transpired since they had last seen each other the previous fall. Ross was amused to hear that a family had named their newborn *Aglugga*, for his nephew, James. *Aglugga* was the Inuit's nickname for the young commander and referred to his "activity and fortitude." (Shortly after their first meeting, the Inuit had assigned names to each of *Victory*'s crewmen. Captain Ross had been nicknamed *Tullugak*, the Raven.)

In other news, Ross was crushed to hear of the death of Tiagashu. Of all the Inuit he had met, John Ross was especially fond of Tiagashu and his pretty wife, Adlurak, "one of the best-looking . . . remarkable for having large eyes . . . and perfectly aware of the peculiarity she possessed." Tiagashu had been one of the first to come aboard *Victory* to draw charts of the coastline, had been generous with his gifts to Ross, and had even helped Ross build the observatory. In return, Ross had aided the frail man and his family when they had been reduced to absolute starvation. Ross never learned the cause of Tiagashu's death and regretted "that we had not been at hand, since it might have been within the power of our medicines." Adlurak later married an Inuk named Auowahriu, a widower with three children of his own. Although crippled in an accident, Auowahriu was an excellent fisherman and provided well for his then expanded family of wife and seven children. Adlurak was able to remarry quickly because of her four children, which brought Captain Ross to remark,

*The because would not be a very good reason in England, it is certain; the ready-made family of another is not often a source of much comfort. . . . But*

*here ... the children were a commodity of price, a great fortune, a source of profit instead of loss, and happiness instead of vexation and torment. . . . It is on them that the helpless aged depend.*

Captain Ross eulogized his friend Tiagashu, "Whatever he might be as an [Inuk], he at least died an amiable and an exemplary man," and mourned his loss.

The next day, the three natives guided Captain Ross and four others to the store of frozen meat about sixteen miles away. Although the cache totaled only about 180 pounds, a disappointed Ross made no complaint and paid the agreed price of two knives. After all, that previous July Ross had bought about a ton of fish from Ikmallik and Tulluahiu for just three knives.

The party then proceeded to the Inuit's encampment, where Ross and his men spent the night while Poweytak, Noyennak, and Neytaknag went to retrieve a second cache of frozen meat, for which Ross agreed to pay a third knife.

While waiting for the three men to return, Ross and his men chatted with their wives and played an Inuit game called Bear and Dogs with the children. Captain Ross did not describe the game in his journal, but it's amusing to try to picture the rugged Captain of the Royal Navy as a polar bear and the Inuit children as dogs darting about, nipping at his ankles.

Poweytak, Noyennak, and Neytaknag returned later that evening with the meat cache, which, combined with what Ross had bought earlier, totaled 250 pounds—enough fresh food to feed *Victory's* crew for two weeks, thus allowing them to economize on their dwindling supply of antiscorbutic lemon juice.

Ross summarized the month of April 1831,

*The health of the men was still good, and the supply of fresh provisions I had procured was likely to maintain them in an efficient state. We had at length found out the long-wished-for natives, and at last also had been able to commence our traveling by land.*

While Captain Ross visited the natives and brought home the stores of fish and reindeer meat, Commander Ross continued his trek to the north. Before long, fog and newly fallen snow overtook the six sailors and reduced visibility to a few yards. Each morning the fog lingered until about 9 A.M., only to be replaced by blinding sunlight that glinted off the fresh snow. Severe snow blindness affected three of the six men and forced a halt for the day. From then on, they traveled at night.

By the sixth day out, Commander Ross was satisfied that he had completed his survey "after considerable suffering from the lameness of some of the men, consequent on the freezing of their boots, and from the blindness of another" and was at last completely convinced that the Northwest Passage was not to be found in the region, as the Inuit had said all along. Yet, in spite of the poor condition of the men, Commander Ross chose to explore the undulating coastline on the way back to the ship rather than to take the overland beeline route that they had taken outbound.

As they worked their way along the coast, ice forced forty feet up the rocks by the winter sea hampered their progress. Then drifting, knee-deep snow and winds at nearly thirty miles per hour brought the party to a halt on the second homebound day. The strong breeze soon turned into a violent gale, which, combined with temperatures in the single digits, pinned the men down for twenty hours. While they waited out the storm, Third Mate George Taylor removed his soaking wet shoes and socks to try to dry and warm his feet. When the storm finally let up and Commander Ross called them to be on the move again, one of Taylor's socks was still wet. Nonetheless, pressed to get going, he slipped his foot into the soaking wet sock, put on his shoe, and headed out with the others. The wind, still strong, had shifted to blow directly into their faces. The temperature was near 18 degrees below zero. The men suffered dearly, but because their provisions had run low with delays caused by storms and snow blindness, Commander Ross insisted they march onward for ten hours before camping again.

At the end of the day's hike, Taylor complained to his commander that his right foot was numb. He yanked off his boot and sock and, to his horror, his foot was frozen solid along the sole and part-way up the heel. James Ross applied the usual remedy—he rubbed it with snow and immersed it in ice-cold water—and "the injury was checked, though with considerable consequent suffering from inflammation," wrote the commander.

The next day they were on the move again, but because poor Taylor could no longer walk, his companions dragged him on the sledge. He suffered miserably from the "concussions the sledge underwent" when they crossed a five-mile-wide ice field with ridges thirty feet or more in height. After twelve hours of clambering up and down the ice hummocks, the men stopped, completely exhausted from hauling their wounded mate. Twenty miles lay between them and *Victory*. Commander Ross set out alone for help. He arrived at *Victory* nine hours later.

Captain Ross immediately dispatched all available hands to the aid of Taylor and the others. Shortly after midnight that same day, the stricken Taylor and his mates were safely aboard *Victory*. Both First Mate

Thomas Blanky and Harpooner Richard Wall suffered from extreme exhaustion and were "ill with a complaint of the bowels." Wall was confined to the sick bay for two weeks before he recovered with "no ultimate bad effects," wrote Captain Ross.

Taylor, on the other hand, was gravely injured and was put under the care of Surgeon MacDiarmid. Notwithstanding Commander Ross's treatment—or perhaps because of it—George Taylor's frozen foot swelled up like a "bladder of hogs-lard," as William Light described it. MacDiarmid lanced the translucent blisters, but gangrene had already set in and MacDiarmid prescribed amputation as the only recourse for the hideously mortified foot. For some reason, Taylor begged MacDiarmid to wait for the return of Captain Ross, who had left on another mission with his nephew. Although MacDiarmid feared that any significant delay could result in Taylor's death, the foot was by then so swollen that surgery had to be delayed, regardless. MacDiarmid applied poultices of soft bread and oatmeal to reduce the swelling. Taylor waited. Nearly a month passed before the surgeon felt comfortable with performing the amputation. By that time, Captain Ross had returned. On June 2, MacDiarmid removed much of Taylor's foot. "This was accordingly performed by the surgeon, with credit to both parties; that of suffering well, to the patient," wrote Captain Ross in his journal.

While Taylor had suffered in his hammock below decks waiting for his captain to return, the captain was on the overland trek to explore the chain of lakes leading to the western sea. The plan for the excursion was that upon arrival at the western shore, a party under command of Captain Ross would return to the ship, while another under command of Commander Ross would continue in search of the North Magnetic Pole.

To the crew, the coordination of this two-part overland expedition must have come as somewhat of a surprise. Rarely were uncle and nephew in concordance with one another on any plans. Indeed, the early planning stages for even this expedition resulted in a squabble. Commander Ross "did not consider himself as acting under, or being subject to the immediate orders of Capt. Ross," said the steward, and he was not about to allow his uncle any say in his plans to locate the North Magnetic Pole. And whatever discoveries he made, "he seemed much disposed to keep them within his own breast." Strong words were exchanged, and Commander Ross refused to attend the Sunday service but instead went for a walk. The cold air must have helped, because shortly thereafter the two men were speaking and "evidently saw that they must either relinquish travelling together, or a reconciliation must be effected between them."

On the way out, the whole party was guided by an old woman named Alurak, her son Ookurahiu (a nephew of Ikmallik), and Ikmallik's brother, Atayaraktak. Captain Ross described his entourage of May 1831,

> Our march had a very nomadic and new appearance, as the line of it also was somewhat picturesque. The mother of the two men led the way in advance, with a staff in her hand; my sledge following, with the dogs, holding some of the children and some of their goods, and guided by a wife with a child at her back. Another native sledge followed in the same manner; next to which was Commander Ross's, and lastly the other [Inuit] sledge; the rear being brought up by a native drawing two skins of oil, and, at a distance, ourselves with one of the little boys.

The woman with the child at her back was Eringahriu. Her husband, Ootoonina, was also along. The ship's crew found it difficult to pronounce Eringahriu's name and nicknamed her "Nancy," to which she answered with "perfect readiness." Although she was missing her front teeth and was "extremely dirty . . . badly clothed . . . [and of] unseemly appearance," she was a favorite among the crew for her good humor and merry nature. Eringahriu had a sister, Hibluna, who Ross said, "was remarkable for being the plainest-looking woman in the whole tribe." She, too, had no front teeth and, like her sister, was given a nickname by the sailors: "Owhee." Hibluna's nickname was for her habit of exclaiming "*Owhee! Owhee!*" and jumping about in delight whenever presented with a gift. "Her joy knew no bounds," as Captain Ross put it.

On the fourth day out, the little band of travelers came across a remarkable river, which Ross named Saumarez, after Admiral Lord de Saumarez, Ross's mentor and idol under whom he had served in the Royal Navy from 1803 to 1812. In defiance of air temperature that fluctuated between zero and the freezing point that day, the river measured 34 degrees and flowed with considerable strength. The Inuit told Ross that the water never froze and originated in a spring-fed lake about a mile upstream.

Vertical walls of black igneous rock soared eighty feet straight up on each side of the torrent and created a gorge "so narrow that we might almost fancy we could jump across it." The eerie gorge appeared as a sharp gash in the earth's surface, as though caused by some cataclysmic event eons in the past. The warm, spring-fed waters and the igneous rocks all pointed toward ancient volcanic activity.

They set up camp alongside the lake, which, in spite of the warm, spring-fed waters, had a thick layer of snow-covered ice. While camped lakeside, the Inuit carved two elliptical, basin-shaped sledges from the clear ice of the lake. When it was time to move onward, they fastened the two bowls together, loaded them with their goods, a woman climbed on top, and off they "traveled with great rapidity." A couple days later, the Inuit demonstrated further ice-carving skill. Ross described this new sledge,

> . . . which we found no less beautiful than extraordinary. It was of the shape of an ordinary one, but made entirely of ice, runners and all, and, while very neatly made, having a most delicate appearance. Being transparent, it seemed indeed to be a sledge of crystal, while it was strong enough to bear the weight of all the stores the owner heaped on it.

On May 27, Commander Ross and his contingent of five men separated from Captain Ross to begin the search for the North Magnetic Pole. Captain Ross turned back for the *Victory* and, although the remainder of Captain Ross's journey was relatively uneventful, rare days of fine weather followed by days of snowstorms and gale-force winds left him and his men utterly exhausted and broken down when they finally arrived back aboard ship, after a trek of just fifteen days. The weary men restored their vigor in a steam bath.

Captain Ross remarked that he was greatly dismayed when he compared the condition of the ice around *Victory* to the way it had been the previous year. Furthermore, the weather for the month of May "had been a great contrast to that of the same month in the last year. The sun had scarcely made any impression on the snow, and no water had yet been seen." He could not help but wonder, *Would* Victory *be trapped for a third winter?*

Meanwhile, Commander James Ross, Thomas Blanky, Thomas Abernethy, and three other hands sought the location of the North Magnetic Pole.

That the North Magnetic Pole does not coincide with the (geographical) North Pole has been known since at least as early as Columbus's time. Voyagers had observed that, although the needles of their magnetic compasses pointed generally north, the needles almost never pointed exactly toward the pole. Not only that, but the discrepancy varied from location to location and even from time to time. In 1350, in the mid-Mediterranean, for example, the compass pointed to true north, but 300 years later it pointed east of north.

In 1698, Edmund Halley embarked on the first of two long voyages for the sole purpose of mapping these variations of the compass, as they had then become known. His effort not only produced accurate charts that indicated to mariners how much to compensate for the variation in the compass, but also led to predictions for the whereabouts of the North Magnetic Pole.

Over the years leading right up to Ross's *Victory* expedition, navigators refined their calculations for the location of the North Magnetic Pole. These included the results of extensive magnetical observations made by both Sir John Franklin and Sir Edward Parry during their respective excursions to the Arctic. At the time of Ross's departure, the location of the pole had been pinpointed to be at 70° north latitude, and 98° 30' west longitude. Based on that prediction, Commander Ross knew that he had been within ten miles of the sacred spot on one of his overland forays from Felix Harbor in 1830. At that time, however, he did not have instruments with him to verify the location of the pole.

An ordinary compass is virtually useless at locations as near to the North Magnetic Pole as Felix Harbor. At this high latitude in the Canadian Arctic, the direction of the magnetic force on a compass needle is nearly vertical so that the needle tries to point downward. This downward force causes the needle to bind on its bearings, and it cannot spin. The instrument of choice to ascertain the pole's location, then, is a device called a dipping needle, which is essentially a compass with a needle that swings in the vertical, rather than horizontal, plane. All things being equal, at the equator, the dipping needle would lie horizontal like a normal compass. (Due to local variations in the magnetic field of the earth and the misalignment of the magnetic poles with the geographical poles, the needle might not lie exactly horizontal at the equator.) Then, as one moves north toward the magnetic pole, the needle begins to exhibit a downward tilt. When finally standing at the pole, the dipping needle will point directly toward the ground at the observer's feet.

Efforts to pinpoint the North Magnetic Pole are complicated by the diurnal wanderings of the pole. That is, the pole moves in an elliptical pattern every day, which at times takes it as much as forty miles from its "home" place. Commander Ross was well aware of this and knew that the only way he could accurately determine the central location of the pole was to make many observations throughout the day. Up until just a few hours before leaving the ship on May 17 to begin the search for the pole, Commander James Ross made dozens upon dozens of observations.

. . .

On May 27, Commander Ross spent another whole day making magnetical observations with his dipping needles. As the day progressed, the
temperature dropped to 13 degrees. Snow squalls with winds approaching twenty miles per hour pummeled the men and shook Ross's delicate
instruments. The 20-below-zero windchill made it impossible to handle
the brass instruments. His best estimate was that the North Magnetic
Pole was about fifty miles to the northwest. Unable to make further
observations, Ross and his small band of men packed up their equip-
ment and pushed onward. His supplies were running low, and if he was
going to find the pole, they had to move quickly.

At eight the next morning, snow blindness that had affected four of
his men compelled Ross to halt. He lamented that he had gained but ten
miles. A break in the weather, however, consoled him, and he took up
his observations while he waited for his snow-blinded men to recover.
The dipping needle registered 89° 41' (90° 00', or perfectly vertical,
would indicate he had reached the pole) with a slight lean toward the
north. He egged on his sluggish horizontal compass by tapping the side
of its case until it settled down and indicated that the pole must be
northwest of where he stood. Commander Ross wrote of his elation in
his journal, "I need not say how thankful I was for this fortunate, if
temporary, clearing of the weather, since it thus placed us in the right
track, and served to encourage even the weary and the ailing, by showing
them that the end of their toils was not far off."

In spite of his anxiety and enthusiasm, Commander Ross gave in
and allowed the men to rest, perhaps more so to allow himself to make
further observations. By this time, he had given up almost all faith in his

horizontal compass, which kept binding on its bearings and rarely pointed reliably. He worked with his dipping needle the whole day while his men rested. At nine in the evening they were on the move again, "rendered unusually labourious by the inefficiency of two of the men."

The thermometer fell to zero shortly after midnight. A sharp northwest wind snapped at the men's faces. Although he was hell-bent on reaching the pole, James Ross insisted that they explore every little inlet, bay, point, and cape along the coastline. Up and down the winding indentations they trudged. After eleven hours, they had advanced just twelve miles. Again, the men rested during the daytime and Ross took to his magnetical observations. They were on their way again at 9:30 P.M.

A thick haze settled in. Snow fell, and the snow-blinded men lost their way. Commander Ross, apparently not blinded by the sun's glare, led the troupe along the undulating coastline. Finally, the haze lifted around midnight and they marched on for another thirteen miles until eight in the morning. According to Ross's calculation, he was within fourteen miles of the North Magnetic Pole. "[M]y anxiety, therefore, did not permit me to do or endure anything which might delay my arrival at the long wished-for spot," wrote Commander James Ross in his journal.

Anxious that bad weather or an accident might prevent him from reaching his goal, Commander Ross ordered that they leave behind everything but their most essential provisions and, thus lightened, immediately moved onward in a rapid march. "Persevering with all our might, we reached the calculated place at eight in the morning." The date was the first of June 1831. Commander Ross was at a loss to describe his feelings,

> *I believe I must leave it to others to imagine the elation of mind with which we found ourselves . . . it almost seemed as if we had accomplished everything we had come so far to see and to do . . . and nothing now remained for us but to return home and be happy for the rest of our days.*

The men were fortunate to find abandoned igloos to set up camp about a half-mile from the magical spot. All that day and the greater part of the next, Ross made his magnetical observations. He set up the dipping needle, anxiously waited for it to settle, then recorded the value in his journal. Then he purposely disturbed it with a small magnet and again waited for it to settle before taking a new reading. And then again. And again. After nearly two days of repeating the same tedious process, James Ross's observations gave an average reading of 89° 59' 28"; for all purposes, the needle pointed straight down. Conventional compasses further confirmed the truth of the location. No matter how much he tapped their cases, their horizontal needles had no inclination to point in any one direction over another. Commander James Ross's feet stood on the North Magnetic Pole.

Observations with his sextant and chronometer showed the location to be 70° 5' 17" north latitude and 96° 46' 45" west longitude—about forty miles from the spot predicted by the leading experts back in London. (Today, the North Magnetic Pole has wandered about 580 miles farther to the north.)

As soon as Ross had satisfied himself that they had reached the coveted spot, he and his companions erected the British flag and took possession of the pole and the surrounding area. After the formalities, they buried a record of their proceedings in a canister under a cairn of limestone rocks.

The North Magnetic Pole was situated on a low beach on the west coast of Boothia Peninsula immediately across a channel (later named James Ross Strait) from King William Island. The surrounding countryside is bleak and barren: a rock-strewn beach with low hills slowly rising from the shore to a height of just sixty feet a mile away. James Ross wrote,

> *It was scarcely censurable to regret that there was not a mountain to indicate a spot to which so much of interest must ever be attached; and I could even have pardoned any one among us who had been so romantic or absurd as to expect that the magnetic pole was an object as conspicuous and mysterious as the fabled mountain of Sinbad, that it even was a mountain of iron, of a magnet as large as Mont Blanc. But nature had here erected no monument to denote the spot she had chosen as the center of one of her great and dark powers.*

Commander Ross's relentless drive to reach the North Magnetic Pole had brought him and his companions to the pole sooner than he had planned. With a little extra time on hand, therefore, he and Thomas Blanky hiked along the shoreline toward the north until three in the morning. There, they erected another cairn to mark their furthest point and then turned back. Ross wished he could have explored further and lamented, "Oh that men could live without food!"

He and Blanky arrived back at the igloos just in time before a snowstorm with gale-force winds blew out of the south. The hungry men spent a miserable, soggy time in the igloo as it melted under the relatively warm, southerly winds. As soon as the storm let up, they headed back to where they had left their provisions three days earlier. Luckily, all were intact.

For the next several days, the journey was difficult and painful for the six explorers, several of whom were quite lame by this time. Even though the month was June, the temperature dropped to four degrees. Rugged, hummocky ice blocked their passage across an inlet. For ten hours they climbed up and down the jagged, slippery mounds, slowly making their way across the frozen waterway. When they reached the other side, they met a party of Inuit who sold them some fish. After a rest of just two hours, they were on the march again until a dense fog forced a halt. In spite of the hardships of the journey, Ross found the energy and time to make more magnetical observations. He was determined to present his discovery to the Royal Society, and he knew his data had to be unimpeachable.

On June 12, just ten miles from *Victory*, another powerful snowstorm erupted. Gale winds up to force 9 on the Beaufort Scale raced down the hills and across the ice. Snow fell so heavily and violently in the fifty-mile-per-hour wind that it cut visibility to zero. For fifteen hours, the men huddled together in the whiteout. At last, the storm eased enough that they could see their way. At five in the morning on June 13, after an absence of twenty-eight days, the six fatigued and snow-covered men stumbled aboard *Victory*. "[E]xcepting petty grievances, we were all in good health," wrote the indomitable—and perhaps callous—Commander James Ross.

Three years later, Captain John Ross's detractors—mainly Sir John Barrow—falsely accused Ross of trying to usurp from his nephew the credit for locating the North Magnetic Pole. As we shall see, John Ross merely claimed his role in the discovery as commander of the expedition and not the man who reached the pole. Recalling Lord Nelson's motto, Captain Ross wrote in his journal, *"Palmam qui meruit ferat"*—let him bear the palm who has deserved it.

# CHAPTER SEVEN

# Abandon Ship

### (June 1831–July 1832)

*S*HERIFF'S *Harbor, June 21, 1831—the Summer Solstice.* Vast flocks of Canada geese honked overhead on their northbound commute. King and eider ducks added to the cacophony. Ptarmigan and plovers scurried along the shore. Yet *Victory* remained motionless. In spite of the twenty-four-hour sunshine, not one day had passed when the temperature did not drop below the freezing point, and, more often than not, an inch-thick layer of ice formed overnight on any pools that might have thawed around *Victory.* "A winter solstice in England is very rarely indeed what the summer one was in this most miserable region and most abominable climate," wrote Captain Ross.

Nonetheless, preparations got underway for *Victory*'s release... release that must come, else the men would be forced to abandon her and take to the *Fury's* three whaleboats—old open boats—to sail for home, 3,000 miles away. The men tore down the canvas housing, greased the masts, filled the water casks, stowed them in the hold, picked oakum from old ropes, and rammed caulk into the topside seams. By the end of June, they had completed her re-rigging. With her flagstaff positioned on high, *Victory* was ready. "It was somewhat dispiriting to find that we should be ready so long before the weather," wrote a frustrated Captain Ross in his journal.

The first week of July saw more snow squalls, daytime temperatures only a degree or two above the freezing point, and the air penetratingly damp and bone-chilling. With the exception of the mate George Taylor, whose amputated foot was healing slowly, the crew were in good health, thanks to both the returning waterfowl and an abundance of fish supplied by their Inuit friends.

July's monotony and the crew's frustration with *Victory's* entrapment eased when five Inuit families, who had not previously visited the ship, showed up. They were heading north when they heard about the strangers and the ship. The usual exchange of presents and showing off *Victory* was a welcomed relief.

For several weeks, the new visitors fished and hunted seal with *Victory's* crew. The sailors taught the Inuit to fish with nets and even gave instruction in net-making, although where the Inuit—who were eager to learn the new technology—were to obtain fiber to make their nets was an open question.

The natives and sailors caught 1,600 salmon in one haul of their nets, 500 in another, and a whopping 3,378 on July 27 alone. The average fish weighed just over three pounds. As Commander Ross and crew dragged load upon load of fish to *Victory*, those aboard ship sorted, cleaned, washed, and packed. Some 2,800 fish were pickled in brine, pickled in vinegar, salted on the rocks, dried in the sun, and packed in jars and casks.

Always looking for something to gripe about, William Light complained heavily that Captain Ross's insistence that the men eat fish—"such a weak and watery aliment . . . which, as an article of human food, is . . . the least nutritive matter"—was unpardonable. How could the captain persevere in forcing his men to eat food so "injurious to their health, and totally unfit to support the physical strength, which they were daily and hourly called upon to exercise?" fomented Light, who was not only a habitual complainer, but also a slacker and looked for any excuse to be relieved of duty. He spent an inordinate amount of time on the sick list with nebulous complaints and begged to be excused from the heavier work. Ross, frustrated and disgusted, threw up his hands and assigned Light to "wash linen and mend stockings." The order insulted Light, and he felt he should be paid extra for the "drudgery of washing . . . Yet not a farthing did Capt. Ross pay him for the labour," whined Light in his published narrative.

Notwithstanding Light's allegation, Ross was correct to order a diet of the highly nutritive fish, and the near total absence of scurvy to that point is a direct testament to Ross's wisdom in encouraging, if not insisting, that his men eat fish. Indeed, the remarkable survival of most of *Victory*'s crew is a tribute to Ross's knowledge of nutrition.

The Inuit kept 3,000 fish for themselves—an unheard-of bounty for a people whose usual method of fishing was to wade through the water and drive the running salmon into small pools where they could spear them, or, with luck, drive the flopping, jumping salmon onto the shore.

While the sailors taught the Inuit to fish with nets, the Inuit taught the sailors to hunt seal on the open ice. Instead of finding the seal through breathing holes as they had done in the winter, the Inuit hunted seals in the summer months as they lay on the ice, basking in the sun. In single file—to create as small a presence as possible—the hunters sneaked up to the dozing animal. Slowly they crept, alternating between a stoop and a crawl; and moved forward only when the seal looked away. After nearly an hour of stooping, creeping, and crawling, the natives reached within striking distance while the crewmen watched in silence from afar. In a flash, they speared the seal and the hunt was over.

On one of the last days of fishing, Seaman Anthony Buck was seized with an epileptic fit. His companions dragged the stricken man on a sledge seventeen miles back to the ship. Because this was the first anyone aboard had seen Buck experience a fit, Ross hoped that he would quickly recover. But two days later, he suffered three more fits in just six hours. These left him blind in his left eye and greatly weakened. From that day on, the twenty-four-year-old sailor's very survival was in serious doubt. As Captain Ross later found out, Buck had been hospitalized in Malta for epilepsy. Ross was furious that Buck had not mentioned this when he signed on and wrote that Buck's joining the *Victory* expedition was "an act of folly to himself and a cruelty to us, which was as unaccountable as inexcusable . . . and [he] was very near being numbered among the dead."

As the weather warmed and open pools formed around *Victory* and her release appeared imminent, Captain Ross reflected on his crew's relationship with the Inuit of Boothia Peninsula,

*One consolation . . . [w]e had sold them no rum, we had introduced no diseases among them, nor had we, in anything, done aught to corrupt their morals or injure their health, to render them less virtuous or less happy than we had*

*found them. Nor had they learned anything from us to make them discontented with their present and almost inevitable condition. On the contrary, while we soon hoped to leave them as happy as we had found them, we had reason to believe that they would hereafter so far profit by our example, and by the displays of knowledge and ingenuity which they had seen with us, as well as by the various useful things we had distributed among them, as to augment their own ingenuity and resources, and thus improve their condition of life as far as that was capable of improvement. That we could not instruct or improve them in religion or morals, we might regret . . . but . . . [this] was rendered impracticable by the limited nature of our communication.*

Indeed, Captain Ross had attempted religious instruction. One stormy night in mid-June, with the temperature at 20 degrees and the wind howling at fifty miles per hour, a party of snow-covered natives appeared out of the tempest with a load of fish for sale. While they thawed themselves in Captain Ross's cabin, he pulled from his library shelf Hans Egede's 1745 *Description of Greenland* from which he read aloud Egede's Inuit translation of The Lord's Prayer,

> *Attavut killangmepotit, akkit usorolirsuk;*
> *Nallegavet aggerle;*
> *pekorset Killangme nunam etog tamaikile;*
> *Tunnisigun ullume nekiksautivnik;*
> *pissarauneta aketsorauta, pisingilaguttog akectsortivut;*
> *Ursennartomut pisitsaraunata;*
> *ajortomin annautigut:*
> *Nallegauet, Pisarlo, unsornartorlo pigangaukit isukangithomun.*
> *Amen.*

Ross was not sure if his guests had understood his purpose, but he remarked that they listened politely and corrected his pronunciation. Thus far for religious instruction.

*Sheriff's Harbor, August 1, 1831.* The men completed cutting the ice from around *Victory*, which corrected her "inconvenient" starboard list. The next day, a disruption in the ice shoved *Victory* forward about half her length—the first time the ice-bound ship had budged in 275 days. As she floated free, her crew moored her to an iceberg that looked solidly grounded. The wet ice of the berg glistened in the mid-summer sun. Rivulets streamed down the ice mountain.

Five days later, the iceberg split and rolled with an explosive splash. Had not every one of *Victory's* hawsers snapped, almost certainly she would have capsized and been dragged under by the overturning berg. The loose ship bobbed out of control. The crew hurried hawsers to another iceberg and held their breath that this one would endure.

Dangerous as the collapsing berg had been, it was clear proof that the twenty-four-hour sunlight had at last had an effect. A shore party observed great movement of the ice to the northeast—the homeward route down Prince Regent Inlet.

Ross put all hands on alert. Last-minute repairs to the sails were made. Water casks topped. Gunpowder brought on board. Whaleboat hoisted. All was a bustle. Then, a sudden shift in the wind choked the canal with ice from the north. The crew remained undismayed, however, as a wind shift in another direction could just as quickly open the escape route. Captain Ross ordered a twenty-four-hour watch.

In the meantime, the crew spotted a group of about twenty Inuit waving and shouting on the shore. With *Victory* moored to an iceberg and a broad expanse of water separating the natives from the ship, Ross dispatched a boat to bring his friends aboard. As the crew ferried the natives, a young Inuk woman took a fancy to Joseph Curtis, the blue-eyed, dark-complexioned, twenty-six-year-old harpooner who rowed the boat. In her enthusiasm to *kunik* him, she nearly upset the boat and had to be restrained by one of Curtis's mates. Everyone was delighted to find that Tulluahiu and his relatives were among the crowd. They had brought skins and clothing for sale, which they wished to trade for iron hoops and a dinner of fish and fat.

Captain Ross observed,

*[W]e found a relief from the self-converse of our minds and the society of each other, from the eternal wearisome iteration of trigonometrical registers and winds, and tides, and ice, and boats, and riggings, and eating, in the converse of these greasy gormandizing specimens of humanity, whose language we could scarcely comprehend.*

That evening, the sailors celebrated the welcomed company with a dance. Light, who enlivened the festivities with his fiddle, wrote,

*[T]he ladies . . . began to display their grace and agility in the dance, catching hold of the first sailor who came within their reach, no matter whether an officer or a foremast man, and hugging him to their affectionate bosom, which imparted to the favored being some idea of what his feelings would be if he should perchance happen to fall within the embraces of a shaggy bear.*

The festivities lasted well into the night with dancing, eating, hugging, and *kunikking*. "In some of the females, the sailors recognized their former sweethearts, in consequence of which, many a nose came into affectionate collision," wrote Light. Around and around the deck the sailors, in their worn and tattered clothing, whirled the ladies in their fresh, summer outfits. Light fiddled madly on his violin. Even Tulluahiu tried to play a few strains on the violin. With each new medley of songs, the cacophony increased. Everyone sang or shouted. Vocal cords strained, and throats grew hoarse. Every so often the boom of Captain Ross's deep, sonorous voice was heard above the ruckus, but no one knew what he was trying to say, nor did anyone pay much attention. Whether he was enjoying the party or protesting the racket shall forever be a mystery.

The Inuit loved to jump in the air to the music. Even the children took part and threw themselves about as if "bitten by a tarantula." In the midst of a particularly wild jump, one unfortunate young woman lost the entire top of her outfit. A gallant sailor scooped it up and handed it back to her. "*Koyenna! Koyenna!*" "Thanks! Thanks!" shouted the comely Inuk as she tossed the deerskin over her shoulders without missing a beat.

At last the music died down, and after a feast of baked seal and blubber, the officers rowed the exhausted but happy guests to shore. The crew extinguished the oil lamps and retired to their hammocks, while Captain Ross repaired to his solitary cabin for a nightcap of Booth's Gin.

The next day, Captain Ross and Chimham Thomas paid Tulluahiu a visit so the carpenter might repair the wooden leg, which had split again. Not only did the "carpenter-doctor . . . who . . . always displayed abundance of good nature . . . ," as Ross described him, repair the broken leg, but he gave Tulluahiu several spares, "which excited new demonstrations of . . . gratitude and regard." Ross noted that his Inuit companions "were not only kind, but ... they were the cause of kindness in those around them, including ourselves; and perhaps, among ourselves, in one or two, who, with a different people, would have displayed a far other character than they did."

On the fifteenth of August 1831, the Inuit of Boothia Peninsula prepared to leave for the fishing waters to the west. Amid promises to bring venison in the winter, and after an array of presents and warm farewells were exchanged, the dear friends parted ... they never met again.

The last two weeks of August saw much shifting of ice, opening of pools of water, rain, fog, and even snow. Although the signs continued to point toward *Victory's* release, the situation was far from positive. On August 26, the moving ice crushed the whaleboat between an iceberg and the side of the ship, breaking the boat's timbers and five thwarts. Disheartened, Captain Ross remarked,

> *"Till the rocks melt with the sun" is held that impossible event ... to which some swain compares the durability of his affection for his beloved; and I believe we began at last to think that it would never melt these rocks which ... continued to beset us in every shape which their beautiful, yet hateful crystal could assume.*

Nonetheless, the whaleboat was not a total loss. Carpenters Thomas and Shreeve salvaged the pieces and built a four-oared boat from one originally designed to carry six oars. Two days later, the carpenters faced a far more critical task.

A lead opened through the ice. Laying out hawsers and trudging 'round and 'round the capstan, the crew managed to warp *Victory* a quarter-mile to an open pool to await the next lead. A passage soon opened. The moment for freedom had finally arrived, but the ice anchor of the port side hawser jammed under a piece of grounded ice and prevented *Victory's* escape. "Cut the hawser!" shouted the mate. "All hands aboard!" *Victory* was under sail at last.

Directly into their path loomed a slowly moving iceberg. "Tack to leeward," shouted Commander Ross. "Windward!" ordered the captain, as he and his nephew broke into another of their quarrels. In the confusion, and with the ship in stays (headed into the wind), the crew were unable to bring about the slow, but steadily moving 150-ton schooner. She collided with the berg on her portside bow, lost her mizzen boom, and, failing to weather a second iceberg, careened off the mountain of ice and headed toward shore. Her bow drove up on the rocks, and her stern dropped down and grounded with an explosion of splintering wood. The men uncoiled the hawsers and hove her off the bottom and alongside the shore. Although her hull was undamaged, the rudder was in a dreadful state, with its lower gudgeon and pintle assembly (hinge) smashed.

Thomas and Shreeve labored at the damaged rudder throughout the night—the scene dimly lit by lanterns. While one carpenter hung over the side of the ship to reach the rudder and the other stood in the shallow water, their mates stretched hawsers to shore to hold *Victory* steady against the changing tide and surf, which threatened to pound her to bits against the rocks. Not only that, but the water was so shallow that she was in imminent danger of falling on her broadside.

By early morning, the two carpenters had completed their repairs and reshipped the rudder. Immediately, all available hands worked the capstan to haul *Victory* off the shore and into deeper water. The hawsers creaked with the strain. *Victory* held fast, stuck on the rocks. The capstan was not enough. They brought out extra hawsers and wrapped them around a windlass. The men applied all their weight and even hung from the handspikes of the windlass. The capstan groaned. The windlass ratchets clacked. The hawsers creaked and popped. "England, or a miserable residence ... in a country of desolation ... depended on the strength and goodness of the hawser," exclaimed William Light. He recorded the moment of freedom,

"Yo ho! My lads!" exclaimed Commander Ross.

"Yo ho!" echoed the seamen.

"Off she goes!" cried Commander Ross.

"Helm-a-lee," shouted Captain Ross.

"Steady, my lads," cried Commander Ross. "She is right!"

*Victory* was under sail again, only to have her headway slowed by a sudden wind from the northwest. The breeze quickly built to a violent gale, estimated at force 7 on the Beaufort Scale—nearly forty miles per hour. Soon, heavy snow cut visibility to almost nothing. At 5 P.M., the jib tore in two and the wind carried away the lug boom. The crew immediately bent a new jib and set the gaff-topsail and fore-topgallant sail. *Victory* worked hard to windward. She entered a small bay, and in the poor visibility she came so close to the shore that the sailors "could spit their quids on the rocks," wrote Light. *Victory* tacked safely away from the shoreline, where she dropped anchor in twenty-three fathoms of water to wait out the storm.

Overnight the weather improved, and the crew weighed anchor and warped the ship to the head of her newfound harbor. She had progressed a mere four miles from Sheriff's Harbor.

The next morning, the sea was clear to the north, their route to freedom, but the wind, too, was from the north. Ross went ashore and scrambled up a hill to have a look. Just beyond some open water immediately to the north, ice blocked Prince Regent Inlet as far as he could see. Mountainous ridges and buckles in the ice produced a formidable scene of violence and solidity. It was clear to Ross that *Victory* had reached the safety of her harbor just in time. He named their new home Victory Harbor. (After returning to England, he changed the harbor's name to Victoria, "by permission of their Royal Highnesses the Duchess of Kent and Princess Victoria.")

Prospects for further sailing did not look good. Nevertheless, Captain John Ross and his crew held onto a glimmer of hope. What choice did they have? If the ice did not break up in the next week or so, they would be trapped in Prince Regent Inlet for a third winter. If that were not depressing enough, their stock of provisions was sufficient to last only until May. Furthermore, because the sea had not thawed significantly until late August the previous two summers, come May, they must abandon *Victory* and somehow make their way to Fury Beach, with the uncertain hope that *Fury's* remaining provisions were still intact.

The wrecked *Fury's* stores were already four years old when *Victory* had reached them in 1829. In the forthcoming May, they would have moldered for another three years. And how to get home from Fury Beach? Take to the whaleboats and either row and sail to Greenland or, if lucky, be rescued by a whaler—which were rarely known to enter Lancaster Sound?

Captain Ross took stock of their situation. Although the men's health was diminished, in that they had lost much of their stamina, scurvy had not appeared and, with the two exceptions of Taylor, whose amputation was still healing, and Buck, who was almost totally blind following his epileptic fits, none were laid up. Ross looked around,

*On the land there was nothing of picturesque to admit of description: the hills displayed no character, the rocks were rarely possessed of any, and the lakes and rivers were without beauty. Vegetation there was hardly any, and trees there were none; while, had there even existed a beauty of scenery, everything was suffocated and deformed by the endless, wearisome, heart-sinking, uniform, cold load of ice and snow. On the sea, there was no variety; for here, equally, all was ice during the far greater part of the year, and it was thus indifferent what was water and what land.*

The first day of September, the ice set in and carried away one of *Victory*'s warping lines, obliging them to drop anchor until a new line was stretched to shore. The wind blew from the north. Snow fell, then rain. Their passage to freedom cleared of ice the next day, but the tide was out, which made the channel too shallow, as had happened so many times before. *Victory* and her crew waited. With the flow of the tide, the ice moved back in. The carpenter caulked the whaleboat. The others picked oakum. A twenty-four-hour watch kept a lookout for a break in the ice.

From the third of September through the sixth, another Arctic storm rocked *Victory*. Winds raked across her deck at sixty miles per hour. The driving snows and wind made it impossible to stand. The men retreated to their hammocks. Boulders of ice boomed against *Victory*'s hull, a tumult that was "calculated to instill the feeling of terror and of awe in the stoutest heart," wrote the steward as the little schooner strained at her mooring lines and rocked back and forth. Ever harder, the ice pressed against her. She careened over. For several hours the ship hung dangerously close to capsizing. Captain Ross called all hands. After the most strenuous exertions, the crew cleared away the ice and got her righted and safely moored between the rocks and an iceberg. The men returned to their hammocks, but spent a sleepless night as the storm continued its rage.

Come morning, the storm passed. A week later found the idle men ice-skating; "an amusement we would gladly have dispensed with," wrote Captain Ross. And then,

> *Hyde Park is doubtless a great regale to those who can exhibit their attitudes to the fair crowds who flock to see that which the sex is reputed to admire. . . . Could we have skated the whole country over, it would not have been an amusement; for there was no object to gain, no society to contend with in the race of fame, no one to admire us, no rivalry, no encouragement, no object.*

From a high hill, Ross gazed over the sea but saw no open water. Then, on the twenty-third day of September, the harbor ice slackened and offered a hint of hope. The crew warped *Victory* to the edge of the channel ice in the event that a fortunate shift in the winds and tide freed up the main channel. No such luck. "The harbour was safe; much too safe indeed; since, for all motion, not less than for hazard of injury, we might as well have been walled in with masonry on dry land," wrote a depressed Captain Ross in his journal the last day of September 1831.

By then, no one aboard *Victory* held any hope that she would ever ply the open seas again.

*Perilous Situation of the Isabella and Alexander. Aug.t 7.th 1818.*

While trapped in rapidly moving ice, HMS *Isabella* and HMS *Alexander* narrowly avoid a violent collision. As the ships sweep past one another, the anchors entangle and stretch between the two ships. Unable to withstand the strain, the cables snapped in a violent explosion that fired a deadly whip back at the men standing on the decks.

*Photo by Joe Pellingra, from the author's private collection.*

The *Victory* settles safely in Felix Harbor for the winter of 1829–30.

*Photo by Joe Pellingra, from the author's private collection.*

Captain John Ross pays his first visit to the homes of the natives of Boothia Peninsula. "They had the appearance of inverted basins, and were placed without any order; each of them having a long crooked appendage, in which was the passage, at the entrance of which were the women, with the female children and infants."

*Photo by Joe Pellingra, from the author's private collection.*

Seated at a table in the cabin aboard *Victory*, Ikmallik draws a map for his British visitors while his wife, Apellagliu, proudly watches.

*Photo by Joe Pellingra, from the author's private collection.*

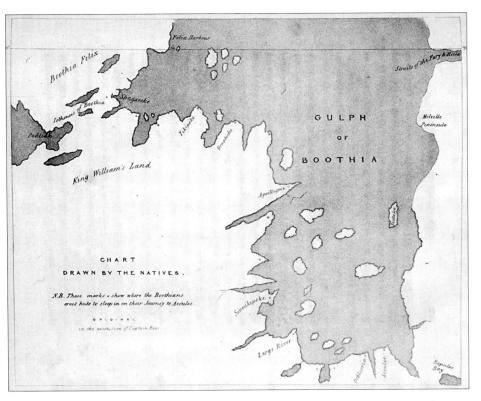

This chart, drawn by Tulluahiu and Ikmallik, correctly shows that Prince Regent Inlet terminates in the Gulf of Boothia with no waterways to the west.

*Photo by Joe Pellingra, from the author's private collection.*

Tulluahiu shows off his wooden leg made by the ship's carpenter, Chimham Thomas, and carved with "Victory June 1831." Tulluahiu's wife, Tirikshiu, stands to his left. Behind her back she hides a piece of wood that she stole from *Victory*. Shullanina, the couple's daughter, holds a knife and small bucket.

*Photo by Joe Pellingra, from the author's private collection.*

On Stone by J. Brandard from the original Drawing by Captain Ross

UMÍNGMAK

Commander James Ross takes shelter behind a rock to fire at a charging musk ox while the dogs and Poyettak run to catch up.

*Photo by Joe Pellingra, from the author's private collection.*

Crewmen shove blocks of ice aside to make way for *Victory's* escape from Sheriff's Harbor. It was her last time under sail. She made just four miles to Victoria Harbor where the men abandoned her the following spring.

*Photo by Joe Pellingra, from the author's private collection.*

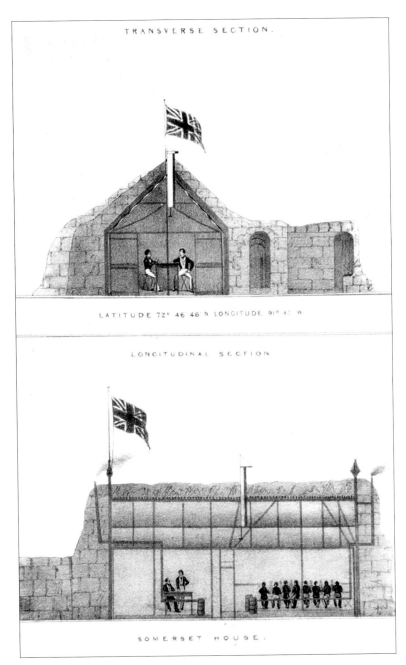

TRANSVERSE SECTION.

LATITUDE 72° 46' 48" N LONGITUDE 91° 47' W

LONGITUDINAL SECTION

SOMERSET HOUSE.

Somerset House on Fury Beach, where the officers and crew of *Victory* spent their last Arctic winter, was built from canvas and spars from the abandoned HMS *Fury* and banked with blocks of snow to insulate against the cold and wind. The four officers shared quarters separate from the men.

*Photo by Joe Pellingra, from the author's private collection.*

Crewman of the whale ship *Isabella* climb the masts and shrouds to cheer *Victory*'s survivors who approach the ship in three old and battered whaleboats—saved at last.

*Photo by Joe Pellingra, from the author's private collection.*

Sir John Ross

*Photo by Joe Pellingra, from the author's private collection.*

Old Alictu and his wife, Kanguagiu, pose outside an igloo for their portraits.

*Photo by Joe Pellingra, from the author's private collection.*

ALICTU* AND KANGUAGIU.

On Stone by J.Brandard from the original Drawing by Captain Ross.

KAWALUA.    TIAGASHU.    ADLURAK.

Tiagashu, one of Ross's favorite Inuit, is flanked by his pretty, pigtailed wife, Adlurak, and Ikmallik's nephew, Kawalua. The jackets of the women of Boothia Peninsula had flaps that hung down in both the front and rear. The men's outfits had only rear flaps.

*Photo by Joe Pellingra, from the author's private collection.*

On Stone by J. Brandard from the Original Drawing by Captain Ross

ILLICTU.                                        OOTOOGIA.

Commander James Ross's young guide Illictu stands next to Otoogiu, the tribe *Angekok* or physician. Otoogiu holds a knife and the magnifying lens that he stole from Captain Ross's cabin. The small piles of stones are to prevent reindeer from escaping along the shore when the natives drive them into the water to be slaughtered.

*Photo by Joe Pellingra, from the author's private collection.*

For the third time, they took to preparing *Victory* for wintering. Unbend the sails, take down the masts, unship the rudder. Unrig and stow goods on shore. Boats turned upward on the ice. Anchors carried ashore. "It would have been keeping up the farce of hope much too idly to have delayed this longer," summarized Ross.

Then, the collecting instinct of John Ross raised its curious head. In that the *Victory*'s abandonment in the spring had become inevitable, he ordered a large chain passed twice around her amidships. Ross believed that this chain would aid salvagers if the sunken ship were ever found in the future. In truth, he fully realized the hopelessness of ever again seeing *Victory* raised, and he was unsure why he bothered to order the crew to encircle the ship with the chain, "but it is probably our nursery education . . . which induces us to do all that we can in prevention of waste, or, like our grandmothers, to preserve old rags, or what not, because their turn of service will come 'round at some indefinite future."

A late October storm with winds up to force 11 on the Beaufort Scale tore the ship's canvas housing to shreds. Not until four days later did Captain Ross order his weakened men out in the 50-below-zero windchill to repair the tent, only to have it shredded by another gale a few days later. They repaired it a second time, although by then the threadbare canvas barely held a stitch.

The forthcoming winter augured worse than the past two. The sea ice had already grown to nineteen inches thick. Yet the men's preparedness and their states of mind were undoubtedly of a more serious concern than the weather. The novelty of wintering in the Arctic had long since dissipated. Classes were no longer conducted. The daily diet was far less varied and hardly substantial: mostly preserved meats, broth, bread, cocoa, and dried or pickled salmon. Again, Light complained bitterly in his published narrative about the difference between the crew and the officers' fare. "The convicts onboard the hulks, are, in a certain degree, better fed than were the crew of *Victory*." Although, by Light's own account, the difference was primarily that the officers had sugar with their cocoa at breakfast plus occasional preserved meats, which the crew had not, and, at dinnertime, the officers enjoyed the addition of a meat pie. Nonetheless, Light ranted for nearly 3,000 words about the inequality of the two diets. Although his criticism had merit, Ross's ways were not exceptional and even the crews of Light's hallowed Edward Parry suffered bouts of scurvy, while Parry and his officers stayed healthy. But Light's contempt for Ross was so strong that he singled out the captain for any criticism he could muster, real or imagined.

The dispirited, bored men trod the deck 'round and 'round. To add to the ship's gloom, the last of the sledge dogs died, apparently from licking lead-soldered pipes that remained from the extinct steam engine. "If the provisions were not still remaining on Fury Beach, a death by actual starvation threatened to be [our] lot," wrote Light in his private journal.

At the end of November, the temperature plummeted to 42 degrees below zero, the ice grew to thirty-three inches thick, and signs of incipient scurvy made an appearance in one of the men . . . and then a few days later, six men: lethargy, aching limbs, spongy flesh. MacDiarmid quickly brought it under control with a prescription of lemon juice. Having observed that the natives never suffered from scurvy, Ross was convinced (and rightly so) that fish oil was antiscorbutic, but in spite of his insistence, he was unable to convince his crew to drink the vile liquid. Instead, they continued with the usual extended walks (excruciating to a scorbutic man with weakened muscles and ulcerated lesions), restriction on alcohol consumption, and insistence to not brood or sink into despair—a ridiculous request for a man painfully ill, let alone trapped thousands of miles from home.

*Victoria Harbor, Christmas Day, 1831.* The ice around the ship measured four feet thick. The thermometer registered 15 below zero. Light winds, snow flurries, and an overcast sky opened the day. An extra allotment of grog, eight-year-old beef from *Fury's* stores ("as good as the day on which it was cooked"), some veal, and a few vegetables marked the extent of the celebration. The day passed slowly and sadly. The men's imaginations carried them home to their families and friends who "heard in their fancy the jovial song, the merry laugh, and last of all they heard the toast go 'round to those, who were 'far away on the billow.'"

New Year's Day passed without celebration. Light took the midnight watch and paced the quiet deck in solitude. The only sounds from without the ship were the distant rumbles and booms of colliding floes and icebergs. Wind whistled around the lower masts and flapped the tattered canvas. Thoughts of abandoning *Victory* haunted him. Her "noble structure" had been the sailors' home for three years. How could they forsake her, their "dear and valued friend"? Leave her, to fall to pieces in so desolate a land? Oh, how he wanted to furl her sails in her home port, drop anchor in friendly waters, walk ashore, look back, and give three hearty cheers and a wave of his hat.

In spite of their depressed spirits, most of the men, though feeble, were in moderately good health. Scurvy had apparently been checked, and even Taylor and Buck were doing well. Nevertheless, a new addition to the sick list was engine stoker James Dixon.

Dixon, a hand on the *John* until the mutiny, was not a sailor and had joined Ross's expedition as a stoker for the steam engine. Before signing on the *John*, he swept the flue pipes of steam vessels. In late October, he had fallen in the water while fishing, and since that time suffered pain and tightness in his abdomen. Toward the close of the year, his conditioned worsened. Surgeon MacDiarmid administered laxatives, diuretics, and mercurials, but the young man's illness only increased. When his abdomen swelled to the point of insufferable agony, the surgeon drained fluid. But that provided only temporary relief; he died on January 10, 1832, at the age of twenty-four. MacDiarmid gave the cause of death as congestive heart failure aggravated by ascites—a dropsical condition in which fluids accumulate in the abdominal cavity.

Dixon's mates labored for a week to dig a shallow grave in the frozen ground. "Not a murmur was heard amongst the crew, as it was the last office which they would have to perform for one of their companions, who had shared with them their dangers and their sufferings," wrote William Light.

On the first day of February, an old wound in Captain Ross's side split open and bled. The odd incident was no puzzle to Ross. He knew very well it was a clear sign that he had been touched by the scurvy.

Scurvy, caused by a deficiency in vitamin C (ascorbic acid), is a devastating disease. Early symptoms are fatigue, aching in the limbs, and complaints of a vague malaise. Old wounds reappear. New wounds are slow to heal, if they heal at all. As the disease progresses, the sufferer develops spots on the legs, which are actually small hemorrhages beneath the skin. The skin loses its elasticity. Indentations made with a finger are slow to spring back. Gums redden, bleed, blacken, turn putrid, and recede to the edges of the sockets of the teeth. Teeth loosen. Salivary glands and tear ducts dry up. Hemorrhaging spreads to the eyes, muscles, and intestines. Pain in the arms and legs is excruciating. The victim can barely stand. Legs swell as water builds up. Urine output declines. Without timely restoration of the deficient vitamin, a slow, painful death is inevitable.

The disease was particularly well known to sailors, forced to live for long periods on a diet lacking in fresh meat, vegetables, and fruit. In 1740, British Admiral George Anson set out to sail around the world with a six-ship squadron and crew of 961 men. Within a year, scurvy had killed half his crew. In 1753, the Scottish physician James Lind published *A Treatise on Scurvy*, in which he described experiments that showed strong evidence that fresh citrus fruit was a preventative of scurvy. The British Admiralty was slow to adapt Lind's recommendations, but by 1804, had enforced regulations that required shipboard diets to contain antiscorbutic foods. Preserving freshness—that is, antiscorbutic potency—continued to be a problem right up through Ross's time, however, and as a consequence of sailors still becoming scorbutic, doubts persisted as to the cause and the best means for prevention of the dreaded disease.

As the days progressed, the horrible malady affected every crewman in one way or another. Anxiety and melancholy depressed everyone. Their reduced provisions offered no remedy. Where were the Inuit, who had clearly helped ward off the disease during the previous two years by selling *Victory*'s crew fresh game? The answer, Ross knew, was that the Inuit had migrated to where the game was plentiful, and he held no hope for their return that winter.

Ross, believing that exercise might help, ordered the men to dig a hole in which to hide supplies in the God-forbidden event that they were forced to return to the ship after her abandonment. They dug the excavation whenever the wind was light—even though the temperature at times reached 48 degrees below zero. The only persons excused were Taylor, who could walk only a short distance, and Buck, who had suffered another violent series of epileptic fits that left him totally blind.

Throughout March, the men worked at the hole, weather permitting. And when the weather was foul, they busied themselves sewing sleeping bags of animal skins for their upcoming journey. All the while, the carpenters built sledges to haul the boats, supplies, food, arms, ammunition, tools, fuel, instruments, clothing, and personal belongings. Every activity pointed toward *Victory*'s abandonment and the escape to Fury Beach, nearly 200 miles to the north. Even so, Thomas Blanky faithfully kept up his hourly magnetical and meteorological logs until March 31, a day with clear blue sky, drifting snow, temperature at 20 below zero, and the sea ice seven feet thick, as he noted in his final entry. When possible, he continued to record the daily temperature for the duration of the adventure.

Preparations for the retreat continued into the first two weeks of April. On April 19, the men loaded the boats onto the sledges and made a preliminary run. The sledges "were found to answer as well as we had expected," wrote Captain Ross. One boat was advanced about four miles, the other six. Ross planned to head out again the next day, but snow, high winds, and the temperature at 28 below zero forced a three-day delay.

In that it was impossible for the men to haul everything at once,

Ross's plan was to advance the bulk of the provisions and the boats a certain distance and then return to the ship for the remainder, which would then be brought up to where the first was cached. They would repeat this two-steps-forward, one-step-backward process until they reached Fury Beach. Once established at Fury Beach, where, they prayed, the provisions were still intact, they planned to spend a little time to refresh themselves and then take to the boats for the long sail and row home—with hopes of meeting a whaler en route.

*London, Spring of 1832.* Not having received any news from Ross for more than two years, concern for the well-being of the *Victory* expedition began to circulate around England. Ross's friend, the noted naturalist and Arctic explorer Sir John Richardson, wrote a letter to the Geographical Society proposing an overland search-and-rescue mission. He offered up himself to head the risky endeavor. Unfortunately for Ross and his crew, however, none other than Ross's nemesis, John Barrow, was chairman of the Geographical Society. As chairman, Barrow held a powerful sway over the society. Indeed, one of the society members complained that he "could not submit to the harsh dictatorial language of Barrow" and wondered how the other members could. "Barrow's" Geographical Society quickly rejected Richardson's proposal—the government would not expend resources to rescue a private venture.

Shortly thereafter, George Ross—brother to the captain and father of James—put another plan in motion for a rescue mission. George Back, another veteran of the Arctic, offered to lead the effort. This time, George Ross petitioned William IV, who responded with a recommendation

*. . . to the Lords Commissioners of the Treasury to grant the sum of £2,000 in aid of the expenses of the expedition . . . it being understood that the Hudson's Bay Company will furnish supplies and canoes free of charge, and that the remainder of the expense, which is estimated at £3,000, will be contributed by Captain Ross's friends.*

With the support of the king in hand, George Ross formed a committee to manage the expedition and solicit contributions. Perhaps wishing to appear sympathetic to the cause, even John Barrow sat on the new committee. Contributions rolled in from all over Great Britain. Ultimately, about a thousand contributors donated more than £4,500. By early February 1833, the expedition was financed, organized, outfitted, and on its way.

*Victoria Harbor, April 23, 1832, 9 A.M.* Captain Ross and George MacDiarmid set out with two sledge parties on the first major leg to Fury Beach. Fourteen men made up the contingent. The seventeen others who remained aboard *Victory* repaired sledges, brought supplies up from the hold, put them in order, baked biscuits, cooked meat, packed bags, and secured the ship. Taylor and Buck helped where they could.

The shoreline ice along the route was horrendously rough. Neither team could haul its sledge without help from the other. After struggling for an hour, they gave up trying to advance both sledges and concentrated on just the one. Ice hummocks towered as high as fifty feet in some places. They chopped footholds and handholds in the ice, climbed to the top, and dragged the sledge up the jagged, slippery wall with ropes, then climbed back down to haul up the boat. Down the other side they lowered the goods, put the boat back on the sledge, and moved to the next obstruction. They chopped passageways through the buckled ice, crawled over the lower obstacles, and sometimes unloaded the sledges and brought the supplies forward piece by piece. The sledges tipped over. The men slipped. They fell. They bruised their scurvy-wracked limbs. For a solid hour, they dragged forward the one sledge and its boat. Then they went back and worked the second sledge forward. Then they advanced the first for another hour. Then the second. Again. And again. After five hours' labor, they had gained one mile.

Toward evening, the temperature dropped to 30 below zero. The wind came up. Snow fell and formed great drifts. The snail-pace progress stopped altogether.

Unskilled in igloo construction, they built a four-walled hut of snow. While one man cut the snow blocks with a spade, another used a cutlass. Slowly, the walls went up until they were about five or six feet high. Then they laid oars across the top and covered them with sails to make a roof. Lumps of snow weighted down the sails to keep them from blowing away. Within their little hovel they huddled in silent misery inside their damp, deerskin sleeping bags.

Although the effort to advance the sledges was killing and progress was absurdly slow, at least they had been advancing. The thought that each step took them a few feet closer to Fury Beach gave the men a modicum of cheer. Now, trapped and immobilized by the weather, all agreed that they preferred the labor to the wait—but to survive in the tempest that raged outside was impossible.

The cook stove and the men's body heat raised the temperature in the hut by 15 degrees—to 15 below zero. This compared pitifully to the Inuit's marvelous igloos, which even on the coldest nights could be oppressively hot. "How did we continue to sleep, how can men sleep in such a temperature? I must leave it to the all-informed physiologists," wrote Captain Ross.

The next morning, frost from the men's breaths coated everything. When they attempted to fold the sleeping bags, more than one bag snapped in two.

They were on their way again at noon. After four hours of difficult travel, they reached the sea, where a smooth terrace of ice along the shore made travel comparatively easy. By 6 P.M., they had completed another seven miles. There, they left the first sledge and headed back to their sleeping quarters to spend another night before they brought up the second boat and sledge. That night, some of the sleeping bags were still frozen solid, which forced their owners to sleep on, rather than in, the bags.

On the third day, in spite of high winds and drifting snow, they made good progress and advanced the second sledge up to the first and even advanced the first one a little beyond that. At this new location, they built another snow house. By this time, their meat was frozen so hard that the only recourse was to cut it with a saw. To add to their exasperation, they did not have enough fuel both to warm their cocoa and thaw the meat. With no choice, they heated their cocoa and thawed the meat by soaking it in the hot drink.

Overnight yet another storm buried the hut in snow and then continued to rage for twenty-four hours. Ross tried to look at the brighter side: "We were imprisoned . . . but it gave an advantageous rest to the men."

After the storm broke, the men dug themselves out, only to discover that the route was more rugged than ever. For two hours, they plowed through knee-deep snow. Their labor gained them a mere three hundred yards. At last, they reached another shelf of smooth ice along the shore. However, to stick with that easier route required them to follow every indentation, point, bay, nook, and cranny of the coast. But follow it they did, dragging both sledges and boats along at a good clip for about two miles to where the smooth shelf ended at a cape. From that point, the rugged and impassable ice extended all the way to the horizon. There was no option but to drag the sledges ashore and find an inland route.

After climbing up, over, and down three formidable hills, all the while dragging just one sledge at a time, the fourteen men reached a frozen creek bed that promised to be a good route. By this time, everyone was so exhausted that all they could do was build their snow hut and collapse in their sleeping bags for the night. Again, as if nature had not dealt enough punishment, another storm buried the hut and trapped them inside.

The storm worsened on the third day. This time the idleness was too much. They secured the boats and, with the wind mercifully at their backs, headed back to Victoria Harbor and the comfort of the ship. They reached their first hut by evening and the ship by noon the following day.

Ross figured that to advance the two boats and sledges just eighteen miles they had walked a total of 110 miles. He further estimated that to advance the whole crew and all the supplies to that same point would require them to walk the route three more times.

In consideration of the men's deteriorating health, the prospects were far from encouraging. George Taylor was lame. Anthony Buck was blind. Henry Eyre, the fifty-three-year-old cook, was considered an old sailor and "fit for the caboose," according to the steward. Moreover, Captain John Ross, at age fifty-five and scorbutic, was barely holding his own. Everyone else, too, suffered from scurvy in varying degrees and was exhausted and weakened from the poor diet, the cold and damp, and the strenuous work. Yet there was nothing to do but push onward.

Ross's goal over the next two weeks was to advance five weeks' worth of provisions to Eclipse Harbor, about thirty miles north of Victoria Harbor. Once that had been accomplished, they would abandon *Victory* and move on to Elizabeth Harbor, about ten miles beyond Eclipse Harbor, where they would establish a new base. From Elizabeth Harbor they would take half the provisions (the other half would be cached in case they needed to retreat to *Victory*) and advance the entire crew another thirty miles north. From that point, an advance party would rapidly proceed to Fury Beach to ascertain the state of *Fury*'s provisions and boats and then hurry back with the good or grim news. In the meantime, the main party would follow. If word came back that all was well at Fury Beach, everyone would advance. If not . . . Ross did not want to think about it. With their provisions almost gone, there was literally nothing he could do. To return to *Victory* might provide shelter, but with so little food . . . then what? Or to take to sea in the boats with almost no provisions . . . what was the point?

Captain Ross, Commander Ross, and ten men set out on May 4 on the second major advance. This time they hoped to travel faster because they did not have to deal with the two boats and the route was already established. Indeed, progress the first day out was better until a sledge broke while trying to traverse some hummocks. Continuing with just the one sledge, they came to the first hut by nightfall, where they rested for eight hours before Ross sent a couple men back to the ship to repair the damaged sledge. By the end of the second day, the men had advanced the supplies to the depot eighteen miles from the ship; a much-improved rate over the first time out, which had occupied five days.

The next day they advanced the first load, including the boats, another fourteen miles. Back and forth they shuttled. Two miles with one sledge. Seven miles with two. Back again. Forward with another load. Back again. "We could not help feeling that our travelling resembled that of a person in the algebraic equation, whose business it is to convey eggs to a point by one at a time," cracked Captain Ross.

High winds and a heavy snowfall on the fourth day sent everyone scurrying to one of the huts, which was "so cramped that it was impossible to change positions." The foul weather kept the twelve men cooped inside for three days. When the storm finally broke, the shuttle took up right where it had left off . . . after first digging the sledges and boats out from under a mountain of snow.

At last, after seventeen days on the road, Ross and his men were safely back at *Victory.* They had met his goal of advancing the two boats and five weeks' of full provisions thirty miles toward Fury Beach. To move the supplies just thirty miles, Ross and his crew had spent nearly a month and walked 329 miles.

They spent the next week repairing the sledges and burying items in the excavation: chronometers, astronomical instruments, and gunpowder. Ross hid the instruments because he just could not bring himself to think of the Inuit dismantling the exquisitely engraved, precision, brass devices, no matter how useful the pieces might be to the natives. Besides, he reckoned, who knew that they would not be forced to return to that "wretched spot"? Captain Ross then ordered the crew to remove anything from *Victory* that might be useful to the Inuit—masts, sails, rigging . . . everything—and stow it on the shore for them rather than let it go down with the doomed ship, which by then leaked ominously.

The day before the planned abandonment, Captain Ross mustered the crew to inform them what they might bring and that they would be on half-rations until they reached Fury Beach, nearly 200 miles to the north. The daily half-ration amounted to about eight ounces of meat and eleven ounces of bread. He went on to say that each was allowed to bring ten pounds of personal belongings sewed up in a blanket, which was to include three pairs of hose, two pairs of drawers, and two pairs of trousers. In addition, everyone would wear two shirts, a jacket, and waistcoat. The 200-mile journey, he told his officers and men, would take about a month.

Although they had advanced five weeks' worth of provisions thirty miles, Ross had several reasons to place the men on half-rations. He had no way to know what the traveling conditions would be farther to the north and whether they could actually make the trek in a month's time. Or perhaps they would have to return to Victoria Harbor. And although the situation would be hopeless if the stores at Fury Beach had been destroyed (perhaps spread afar by high winds, washed away by the sea, devoured by polar bears, or moldy and spoiled), Ross insisted on an ace up his sleeve, no matter how insignificant. Thus, if after a month of travel they found Fury Beach barren of provisions, another month's half rations was his ace . . . at least they would live that much longer.

*Victoria Harbor, May 29, 1832, 7 A.M.* The day to abandon their ship had come. A sailor hoisted *Victory's* colors and nailed the flag to the mast. Officers and crew assembled on the shore, and Captain Ross handed around glasses of Booth's Gin to everyone. With a wave of their hats and three hearty cheers of "Good-bye, *Victory!*" the men bade farewell to their "old friend . . . which had deserved a better fate." Tears rolled down more than a few cavernous cheeks.

With ten days' provisions and their personal belongings loaded on sledges, the procession slowly drew from *Victory*. Looking over their shoulders, views of the empty ship came and went as they worked their way along the meandering coastline.

To Captain John Ross, leaving behind *Victory* was the first time he had ever had to abandon a ship in forty-two years at sea. He recorded his feelings as she slipped from sight,

> *I did not pass the point where she ceased to be visible without stopping to take a sketch of this melancholy desert, rendered more melancholy by the solitary, abandoned, helpless home of our past years, fixed in immovable ice, till time should perform on her his usual work.*

Although the snow was hard packed and the well-traveled route was smooth, the sledges were so heavily laden that it took five hours to reach the first hut, twelve miles away. There, they rested until I A.M., when they started again, because Ross had determined to travel by night to minimize the threat of snow blindness.

The next post, only eight miles farther, took ten hours. Ofttimes, ten men worked together to drag just one sledge up a hill. Even Taylor and Buck got in line and pushed and pulled. The next two days were comparatively uneventful: on the road at 8 P.M., quit at 7 A.M., distance traveled . . . maybe eight miles.

On June 3, they reached their fourth station on the trail. There, the exhausted men conferred with First Mate Thomas Blanky and urged him to propose a plan to the captain. Their strategy was to abandon the boats and all the provisions except enough for the immediate journey and proceed directly to Fury Beach. To Ross, the epitome of an authoritative nineteenth-century Royal Navy officer, this seemingly innocent, and probably not unreasonable, suggestion smacked of mutiny. Did the men think the expedition was a democracy? In a pamphlet published in 1819, the no-nonsense Ross had written,

> *[T]he commander of a British ship neither requires nor asks the advice which he, or anyone in his situation, might imagine himself capable of giving. If he required it, he would be unworthy of his trust; if he asked it, he would deserve reprobation, for introducing into the British navy a practice that must ultimately be subversive of discipline, and would, in the meantime, introduce discussion and dissensions, perhaps mutiny, where the wise policy of the Government has properly judged that one opinion alone should rule.*

Captain Ross was livid. He not only refused to accept their proposal, but also ordered them "in a manner not easily misunderstood" (Ross's own words) to gather up everything and proceed immediately. Furthermore, he severely reprimanded First Mate Blanky for the "extreme impropriety of his conduct."

In his eyes, Ross felt that he had closely averted a mutiny. Yet he did understand how the hardship had worn down his half-starved men, and for that reason he never mentioned the "near-mutiny" in his official report to the Lord's Commissioners of the Admiralty. He did, however, record the incident in his published journal twenty-two months after his return to England.

Notwithstanding his perception of Blanky's insubordination, Ross continued to think highly of the thirty-two-year-old first mate. Thomas Blanky, a well-seasoned sailor, had been at sea since the age of eleven and had accompanied Sir Edward Parry in his 1827 attempt to reach the North Pole. He was a valuable man and a diligent student of navigation in Ross's evening classes. Moreover, Ross had not forgotten how Blanky had saved *Victory* from being thrown into the breakers of the heavy pack of ice when they sailed down Prince Regent Inlet in August 1829. Upon their return to England, Captain Ross unhesitatingly gave Blanky a strong recommendation, which ultimately led to the first mate's command of a merchant ship.

On June 9, six days after the attempted "mutiny," everyone and all their belongings had been forwarded to Elizabeth Harbor—about forty miles from the *Victory*—where Ross had planned to cache half the provisions and then advance another thirty miles. To reach this point, every leg of the route had required two journeys—the men simply could not haul everything at once. Half-rations and the mountainous, rugged ice had taken its toll.

Ross climbed a hill to check the prospects. The ice ahead was so rough that he decided to leave the boats at Elizabeth Harbor and proceed with just three sledges, heavily laden with three weeks' worth of provisions, ammunition, arms, tools, instruments, clothing, and tents. Other valuables, for which there was no room, they hid beneath an overturned boat. They were on their way again at 1:30 the following morning.

After two days of continuous toil, they set up camp and prepared to send the advance team to reconnoiter Fury Beach—still 150 miles away. Commander James Ross, Second Mate Thomas Abernethy, and John Park made up the advance team.

Park was a twenty-nine-year-old sailor who had been to sea for eleven years. His father had apprenticed him as a hairdresser, but unhappy with the trade, he went to sea as soon as he completed his apprenticeship. When signing on the *Victory*, Ross asked Park what had been the most remarkable event in his life. Park stated that it was when he had shaved the Duke of Devonshire in a gale onboard the *Glasgow*. Puzzled, Ross asked, "Were you not on board her at the Battle of Navarino?" "Oh, yes, but that was nothing," replied Park. (The Battle of Navarino took place off the coast of Greece on October 20, 1827. A combined fleet of British, French, and Russian ships, in support of Greek independence, waged battle with the Ottoman and Egyptian fleet, which was decidedly defeated with upward of 4,000 casualties.) Thus, Park had endeared himself to Ross.

With a send-off of three hearty cheers from the whole crew, Commander Ross, Abernethy, and Park left for Fury Beach, hauling a sledge loaded with a tent and fifteen days' worth of provisions. Ross estimated that they would take about seven days to reach their goal, whereas the remainder of the crew, now short three of the best men, would take at least twice as much time to reach Fury Beach. The advance team was soon out of sight.

The main body moved slowly onward. Lack of water made their suffering even more extreme. Although the calendar showed mid-June, everything was frozen solid. Crevices in the ice, normally filled with pools of water, had refrozen days ago. "All was rock: It seemed as if there was never to be water again," wrote Ross. Fuel to melt snow and ice for drinking was nearly gone, and what little remained had to be conserved to prepare dinner. The men sucked on icicles or scooped handfuls of snow to their parched mouths—admittedly risky deals that they well knew could lower body temperatures to dangerous levels. Ducks and other fowl often flew overhead and tantalized the starving men. Without fuel to cook the birds, however, there was no point in firing at them. The irony of laboring bodies soaked in sweat with the temperature at just 24 degrees, coupled with agonizing thirst, near drove them mad.

A snowstorm detained the whole party for two days on June 14 and 15. Afterward, they set out again in the freshly fallen snow that hid treacherous ice. Many experienced severe falls. Progress was slow but steady. Nine miles one day. Eleven miles the next. Then eight.

Every few days they found a note left behind by the advance party. On one occasion the note informed Captain Ross that the three men had been slowed by lameness and snow blindness, but as they were nowhere to be seen, Ross concluded that they must have recovered and moved onward.

On June 22, Captain Ross and the others reached the point of land where he had taken possession three years previously. Nearby, he found a cairn with a note from Commander Ross informing his uncle that all was well with the advance team. Ross estimated that by the time he had reached the cairn, the advance party should already have been at Fury Beach for two days—if all had continued well. Because Commander Ross was to come back to look for the rest of the party after refreshing at Fury Beach, Captain Ross left a new note at the cairn informing his nephew that they, too, had reached that point.

The next day, the men spotted what appeared to be a Union Jack fluttering on the northwest horizon. Sure enough, it was Commander Ross, Abernethy, and Park, dashing across the ice, a flag flying from a boarding pike attached to the sledge. Moments later, the three men reached the main party and quickly told the great news that the stores at Fury Beach were intact. "It would be difficult to describe the joy and exultation which pervaded the whole of the crew, on the receipt of this glorious intelligence," wrote William Light in his journal.

Commander Ross reported that, although the sea had carried off *Fury's* three boats and quite a number of things, the boats and most of the goods had washed ashore a short distance northward. One of the boats had been seriously damaged, but everything else was just as they had left it nearly three years ago. Even the bread was in good condition—and an abundant supply it was.

When the advance team had reached Fury Beach, they packed up forty pounds of meat to carry back to their companions. At the sight of the extra food, the hunger-wracked men who "could have devoured the flippers of a seal" were in near ecstasy, reported Light.

The welcomed knowledge that the provisions at Fury Beach were intact prompted Ross to put the men back on full-allowance, paltry as it was for the half-starved, heavy-laboring men. After a day of refreshment, they were on the move again at Captain Ross's bark, "It is life or death with us, therefore haul away."

For the next four days, a thaw forced them to trudge through cold, wet snow and to wade water above their knees. By that time, George Taylor's injured foot pained him so greatly that his mates were compelled to carry him along with all the rest of their load. The temperature rose to 47 degrees and made their misery all the greater as sweat soaked their clothing and then chilled them to their very soul with the inevitable night-time drop in temperature. Water spurted like geysers from cracks in the ice. Torrents gushed from ravines in the hillsides. Soddenness pervaded everywhere and everything. Open water forced them to walk around bays on which a week or even a few days earlier they might have walked across as solid ice. Often the route around these bays or inlets was so protracted that, with each passing hour, objects in the distance seemed to recede rather than draw closer.

At last, at 10 P.M. on July 1, the little band of twenty-one weary travelers reached Fury Beach. The men's "hearts ... were light as a feather; nor could they, comparatively speaking, have felt much happier, had they set foot on their own native land," recorded William Light. The distance from Victoria Harbor to Fury Beach, as the crow flies, was about 180 miles. Nevertheless, the total distance walked, with all the detours and undulation of the coastline, could not have been less than 250 miles.

Upon their arrival, Ross ordered the men to bed for the night to bring their waking hours back to daytime. He furthermore advised them not to stuff themselves on the sudden abundance of food. But the hungry men scattered in every direction and, once out of Ross's sight, many filled their stomachs for the first time in a month—only to pay for it shortly thereafter as their empty bowels reacted painfully to the sudden influx.

After a day of rest, Ross assigned everyone a task. His plan was to build a house in which to recuperate for about a month while at the same time making preparations to depart for home. Besides building the house, much needed to be done, such as gathering together the *Fury*'s dispersed stores, taking an account of the provisions, repairing the boats, and putting in order the spars, sails, and cordage. Yet even if they were ready to depart Fury Beach at the moment of their arrival, to do so was impossible: Ice still blocked the sea.

In a few days, the men completed construction of the house, dubbed Somerset House, because Parry had previously named the region North Somerset in honor of his native county. The posts of the building were fashioned from the *Fury*'s spars. The lost ship's sails formed the coverings for the roof and walls. The house, which measured sixteen by thirty-one feet in plan and seven feet in height, was divided into one large room for the crew and four private rooms for the officers: Captain Ross, Commander Ross, Surgeon MacDiarmid, and William Thom, the purser.

On July 21, Captain Ross climbed a bluff about 1,000 feet high and looked out over Prince Regent Inlet. From Fury Beach far below his feet to the distant horizon, the sea was one solid mass of ice without the slightest hint of motion. Eight days later: unexpected great news—the ice showed signs of moving off Fury Beach. The following day—the last day of July—the sheet of ice covering Prince Regent Inlet suddenly broke up in a spectacular rumble.

With the breakup of the ice and the men's health greatly improved, there was no time to linger. The crew loaded each of three boats with bedding and sufficient provisions to carry them to the first of October. Captain Ross and his nephew exchanged copies of their charts and each other's journal in case of their separation. A bottle with a short account of the expedition's proceedings was buried at Somerset House.

At four in the afternoon of the first day of August 1832, the whaleboats pushed off Fury Beach to the whoop of three hearty cheers.

CHAPTER EIGHT

# Cold, Hunger, and Misery at Fury Beach

### (August 1832–October 1833)

*F*URY *Beach, August 1, 1832. Victory's* twenty-one surviving crewmen,
packed in three whaleboats, pushed off from Fury Beach in high
spirits with strong hopes to encounter a ship in Baffin Bay before the
close of the whaling season. In spite of their jubilation over the breakup
of the ice in Prince Regent Inlet the previous day—which finally
allowed them to depart—thousands of pieces of ice, large and small,
greatly impeded their progress. Using boarding pikes to shove the ice
aside, the men worked the whaleboats down narrow, crooked channels—so narrow that in most cases it was impossible to manipulate the
oars. At the end of the day, they unloaded the boats and hauled them
across the ice to the shore. That first day, after nine hours of effort, they
had made just eight miles.

During the night, two giant ice floes crashed together, broke apart, and formed a ridge of hummocks along the shoreline. With the advancing tide, the hummocks moved en masse against the shore and threatened to crush the boats. The men hauled the boats higher up the beach, only to be threatened by boulders, loosened by the thaw and rain, that crashed down from the limestone cliffs towering five hundred feet above the narrow beach. Stopped by the ice and harassed by sleet, rain, and falling rocks, the men huddled in their tents. "It was a position of the utmost danger ... the brains of any individual among us might have been 'knocked out' before he could have suspected any accident. But ... we were fully tried by hazards and had become somewhat careless ..." Nonetheless, when a boulder hit the mainmast of one of the boats, Ross decided it was time to move a couple miles farther down the shore to where the beach was somewhat wider. Yet even at the new location, the men were afraid to fire their guns at the myriad gulls and dovekies that circled overhead, for fear of launching an avalanche of boulders and mud.

Openings in the ice appeared over the next few days, but progress was excruciatingly slow. The leads through the floes widened and narrowed, opened and closed. After advancing as little as forty yards at times, the closing channels brought the boats to a halt. The exhausted crew unloaded each boat of hundreds of pounds of supplies, including stoves weighing eighty pounds each. Then, with the assistance of a block and tackle, they heaved the thirty-foot whaleboats onto the ice. Across the ice they slid the boats and supplies to the next lead. Then, down into the water went the boats. Reloaded, they rowed onward for another hundred or so yards, only to repeat the process of hauling everything up onto the ice again.

Progress was so poor that after just two weeks of effort, it was obvious that they would run short of food before reaching Baffin Bay. Ross sent William Thom and six others sixteen miles back to Fury Beach for more supplies. The seven men reached Fury Beach in an astonishing three hours because the water to the south was almost free of ice. Thom and his men loaded the boat with fresh provisions and sailed partway back to Ross before resting for the night. The next day, they were horrified to find that they were unable to shove the heavily laden boat off the beach. Thom sent one of the men to Ross for help. But even with two extra hands, the boat remained stuck. It was hopeless. The boat was stuck fast. Even after they removed the sacks and casks of food, the whaleboat refused to budge. With no choice, they abandoned the boat and dragged the supplies along the shore to their companions. Finally, with the help of a nine-foot spring tide and even more hands, they relaunched the boat.

By the end of August, the three whaleboats had reached the mouth of Prince Regent Inlet, about seventy miles north of Fury Beach, only to discover that ice completely blocked Lancaster Sound, the passage to Baffin Bay and home. The mass of ice was so thick that it reached above the gunwales of the boats and made it impossible to see beyond.

Sailing east along the edge of the ice, *Victory's* crew set up camp at the foot of the headland that marked the northeast limit of Prince Regent Inlet. There, the men built a lookout shack at the top of a cliff from which to watch for changes in the ice in Lancaster Sound— hoped-for changes that never came. The only changes were higher winds, dropping temperatures, occasional snow, and worsening depression. After twenty-four days of wearisome, anxious waiting, everyone agreed that the ice would never break up that season. They must return to their refuge at Fury Beach and try again next year.

To Ross, there was a bittersweet satisfaction when he saw Lancaster Sound blocked with ice. Recalling his 1818 voyage and the vicious attacks he had undergone from John Barrow for not proceeding down Lancaster Sound, Ross now felt more than ever that he had been right to turn back in 1818. There was no doubt that at certain times, ice totally blocked Lancaster Sound.

> *The fact, indeed, was but too surely proved for our safety or hopes: It would have been far better for us at present, had that been false which I had asserted to have been true; had [Lancaster Sound] been incapable of freezing, had it never been, and never was to be, frozen over; as had been most confidently asserted of late. It was now frozen, or at least had hitherto been so, during the preceding winter and the present summer, even up to this time, into a solid sea . . . and this is precisely what I found it to be in 1818.*

Sick with reluctance, Ross ordered his men to turn about—launch the three whaleboats and return to Fury Beach.

Sailing back across the wide mouth of Prince Regent Inlet, they reached the western shore and located a passage southward through the ice along the shoreline. Although the opening was so narrow that the boats had to move in single file, at least they were underway, and Ross set aside his fear that they might have to abandon the boats and walk the seventy or so miles back to Fury Beach.

Six days later, however, Ross's fear became reality: The channel through the ice narrowed to a jagged crack and vanished. Solid ice stood between them and Fury Beach, still a distant forty miles away. Worse yet, they were two miles from shore. The men unloaded the boats and then dragged and carried the supplies across the ice to shore. Despite the cold, perspiration soaked the laboring men's outfits. Barnard Laughy, the stoker who had replaced William Hardy when Hardy lost his arm to the steam engine, removed his mittens as he rolled a cask of bread across the ice. The sweaty labor, however, had deceived Laughy. The thermometer stood at zero degrees, and before he reached shore his fingers froze solid. Two of Laughy's fingertips never regained their feeling. Instead, at first rock hard and opalescent, they soon turned gangrenous, blackened, and ultimately fell to Surgeon MacDiarmid's instruments.

With the boats unloaded and all the provisions stowed safely on the beach, the men set to getting the boats ashore. Using a block and tackle, they raised the first boat out of the water and commenced to drag and shove it over the hummocks. About halfway to shore the boat crashed through the ice. "[S]he lay as snug as if she were in a cradle," wrote William Light.

The men hauled on cables and pried with oars and pike poles, but the ponderous, solid mahogany boat refused to rise. Just when it seemed she might come free of her cradle, the ice crumbled around her and down she went again. By putting a mast crosswise under her bow, they finally rolled the boat onto the ice and forward...only to have her break through again. Again, they hauled her out. Again, she broke through. Repeatedly, through the ice, out of the ice, down into the water, up onto the ice, they worked her closer to the shore. Fortunately, the ice grew thicker as they neared the land, and the heavy boat broke through less often. The crew finally got the boat ashore and stowed on the beach about thirty feet above the high waterline. The situation was the same with the remaining two boats. After a full day's effort, they at last had all three whaleboats safely on shore.

There, at Batty Bay, about thirty-six miles north of Fury Beach and the longed-for comfort of Somerset House, the men slept in trenches dug in the snow: seven men in each of three trenches, huddled together for warmth; their only protection from the below-zero temperature, the howling wind, and the drifting snow was a blanket of canvas thrown over each trench.

The next day, carpenters Thomas and Shreeve built sledges from barrel staves for the journey to Fury Beach. Others greedily gathered up the wood chips from the carpenters' handiwork to use for cooking fuel. Captain Ross cut the daily allowance to half-rations: a quarter-pound of meat and a half-pint of cocoa per man, along with whatever foxes might be shot along the way. Just four miles were gained that first day.

The lame Taylor tried to keep up, but working his crutches through the deep snow and over jagged, slippery hummocks was impossible. He fell by the wayside. His companions tried to drag him on a sledge with the provisions, but the same forces that tripped his crutches upset the sledge and he fell off. By the end of the day, the sledge was broken and useless.

The next day, Ross ordered the broken sledge abandoned along with the supplies it carried. And there was no choice—Taylor must be left behind, too. William Light made a great deal of this in his published book, in which he accused Ross of abandoning Taylor for dead. But as paralyzing as it must have been for poor Taylor—watching his companions disappear into the swirling snow as he sat helpless, propped up on the broken sledge—Captain Ross's orders were essential to the group's survival and the crippled third mate was brought forward at the close of each day.

Two days later, the main party, frostbitten and cut and bruised by tumbles over the jagged ice, reached Fury Beach and Somerset House.

"Our labors at an end, and ourselves once more at home," wrote Captain Ross in his journal.

Somerset House, with flimsy walls and ceilings made from the *Fury's* sails, was more of a tent than a house. Even so, it provided some degree of shelter, and luckily so. Three days after their arrival, a blizzard descended on Fury Beach. For six days, the storm raged. The canvas walls of the house snapped loudly in the hurricane. Snow piled deep on the roof. The canvas stretched taut under the weight. Suddenly, without warning, the roof collapsed and dumped mounds of snow in the beds. Snow and frost coated everything inside. The men huddled around the stove, waited, and prayed the storm to moderate.

Even under those grim circumstances Ross saw good fortune,

> [H]ad we been obliged to walk all the way from our farthest position, the journey would have been fatal to some, if not all of us, since we should have been overtaken by the storm of the ninth. We, therefore, felt very thankful that we had been so mercifully permitted to reach even this cold and dreary spot in safety. Having constructed our house previously was also a very providential circumstance; for, defective as it was, it could not have been nearly so well done at this season; and indeed before it could have been done at all, we must have suffered severely.

When the storm finally blew itself out, the crew set to repair the building. They strengthened the roof with spars and ropes and covered it with a thick layer of snow for insulation. To insulate and fortify the walls, they built a wall of snow four feet thick and nine feet high. Unfortunately, however, with the temperature at 10 degrees below zero and fuel critically short, it was impossible to make the usual "mortar" of snow and water to fill the interstices between the snow blocks. Nonetheless, the desperate men completed the construction using mortar made from snow and their own urine.

By the end of October, the work was completed—and just in time, too, as another blizzard pounded the walls and drove the outside temperature to 18 below zero. "We however now felt the advantage of the snow wall and had no reason to complain within doors," wrote Ross as he watched the inside thermometer hold steady at 50 degrees.

As usual, William Light found reason to complain, however. Somerset House had two stoves—one in the officers' quarters and the second in the men's quarters. According to Light, although the officers' quarters might be comfortable, "the cold was at times so intense in the seamen's berth, that they could not rest in their blankets, but were obliged to walk about the whole of the night, to keep life within them." His complaint seems to have been that the four officers had a stove all their own, whereas just one other stove had to suffice for the sixteen other crewmembers. Yet the sizes of the two rooms heated by each stove were not greatly different, so that both the officers' and men's quarters were most likely at similar room temperatures. If anything, the temperature was higher in the men's quarters because of the greater contribution of body heat. Light, himself, remarked that "there being no scarcity of funneling . . . that the warm air might be diffused through every part of the house."

In the first week of November, the sick list jumped alarmingly. Besides George Taylor, Anthony Buck, and Barnard Laughy, lingering scurvy devastated Chimham Thomas and Seaman John Wood. Both men were gravely stricken and appeared on the brink of death. MacDiarmid wrote that Wood's "gums were absorbed almost to the edge of the sockets of the teeth, and had become black and putrid, livid patches appeared on the limbs, the legs became edematous, and the powers of life were prostrated even to repeated faintings." Thomas, who had just completed making frames for the bunks and had started to floor the house with barrel staves when he came down with the illness, not only agonized with similar symptoms, but was "debilitated by recurrent hæmorrhage from the nose." Every passing day Thomas grew weaker. Yet somehow in his torture, he managed to carve a complete set of chessmen for his mates. It was his last work of craftsmanship.

On a Saturday morning in September, Chimham Thomas, the "carpenter-doctor" of Tulluahiu's wooden legs—his wasted body blotched with purplish discoloration and oozing, bloody extravasations—succumbed to scurvy. He was thirty-nine years old. Somehow, his crewmates gathered the strength to swing their pickaxes and dig him a grave. Red sparks glinted against the midnight-blue snow as the axes clanked on the frozen gravel. Blow after blow. Pebble by pebble. Inch by inch the men hacked, and dug, and chiseled. After six days' labor, it was obvious that a grave just one foot deep must suffice. At the first real lull in the wind, Thomas's crewmates—those well enough to walk—formed a dark funeral procession to the gravesite. Captain John Ross conducted the service but had to improvise the ending when the 45-below-zero cold frosted over his eyeglasses and prevented his reading the remainder of the liturgy. The men placed Thomas's frozen body in the shallow grave, covered him with a layer of gravel, and marked the site with a headboard of wood. Nailed to the board was a copper plaque on which Engineer Brunton had engraved Thomas's name, age, and trade. Ross looked down at the headboard and shook his head—Thomas had married the year before *Victory* set sail and had had a daughter.

The conditions of Anthony Buck and John Wood steadily deteriorated, and every day their messmates expected either of them to join Thomas. Henry Eyre suffered not only from scurvy, but also from an aggravated case of rheumatism. Purser William Thom was next to join the list with his scurvy-ridden mates. And Captain Ross's scurvy, although not disabling him, opened old wounds to such a hideous extent that he feared he would be unable to lead his men to safety if the bloody eruptions did not heal in time.

Perhaps even worse than the illness were the interminable boredom and confinement. Captain Ross captured the feeling,

> [T]he inevitable lowness of spirits produced by the unbroken sight of this dull, melancholy, uniform, waste of snow and ice, combined to reduce us all to a very indifferent health. Even the storms were without variety, amid this eternal sameness of snow and ice: There was nothing to see out of doors, even when we could face the sky; and within, it was to look, equally, for variety and employment, to find neither. Those among us who had the enviable talent of sleeping at all times, whether they were anxious or not, fared best.

To add to the pastime provided by Thomas's chess set, William Light made a deck of playing cards from scraps of tin from the meat canisters. Not surprisingly, though, the metal edges cut their hands. Undaunted, Light ventured outdoors with a pickax and chopped through the ice and snow to retrieve boxes of candles from *Fury's* stores. He then made his playing cards by pasting together multiple layers of the tissue paper in which the candles had been wrapped. To print the pips on the cards, Alexander Brunton carved little stamps in the shape of a heart, club, diamond, and spade. Black was the only color at hand. "Nevertheless, the sailors contrived to beguile away many a wearisome hour at cribbage or put [an old game of cards in which each player is dealt three cards and then calls the number of tricks he expects to take]," wrote William Light in his journal.

About the first of April, the weather moderated sufficiently enough to begin preparations for evacuation—still months away. Literally tons of food and supplies had to be forwarded about thirty-six miles north to Batty Bay, where the whaleboats had been left the previous September. Since its abandonment eight years ago, much of the *Fury*'s bread had turned soggy and moldy. To salvage what remained, the men spread a sail on the ground, dumped the contents of the bread casks, and sorted through it. They charred the inside of the barrels to kill off the mold and then repacked them with the best of the bread. The effort yielded nearly 2,600 pounds of edible bread. Other provisions included 1,400 pounds of preserved meats and 20 gallons of lime juice (which long ago had lost its antiscorbutic properties). Along with the provisions, the men also had to transport a half-ton of coal for the stoves. They estimated the total load at seven tons. Seven tons to haul to Batty Bay. Fourteen sledge loads. Thirty-six miles.

Yet only thirteen of the twenty survivors were well enough to drag the sledges . . . and it took half that many to drag just one sledge. The plan, then, was to advance two sledges eight miles, unload the contents, drag the empty sledges back for another load, and repeat the process until all the supplies were forwarded to the first cache. This first leg—at times impeded by extreme cold, other times by snow blindness—took twelve days to complete. By the first day of June, everything had been brought eight miles north of Fury Beach.

Ross also dispatched a party to travel directly to Batty Bay to check on the condition of the boats. When the advance party arrived at the site, however, the boats were nowhere to be seen. Only after probing and digging the whole afternoon in the deep snow were the three boats located. Fortunately, they were in good condition with the sole exception of some damage by a family of foxes, which had made the overturned boats their winter home. The furry creatures had eaten the tarpaulins, the tops of seaboots, and the leather wrappings of the thole pins (a pin affixed to the gunwale, which acts as a fulcrum for an oar—analogous to an oarlock). "In fact, nothing appeared to have come amiss to their rapacious appetites," wrote the steward. That night the men, exhausted from their twenty-eight-mile hike to Batty Bay and an afternoon of digging out the boats, spent the night camped under the boats. In their dark hole, lit only by a candle, a small creature crept out of the shadows and pounced on Brunton's sou'wester hat. The engineer hurled a wooden candlestick at the hat thief, but the reynard escaped with his odd delicacy.

*Fury Beach, Monday, July 8, 1833.* Warmer days brought game birds to the region, including ptarmigans, gulls, geese, and ducks. The fresh meat had a marked effect at reducing scurvy, and by mid-summer just three men were incapacitated with the disease: John Wood, Anthony Buck, and Henry Eyre. Most of the others still showed signs but were well enough to get about. Even George Taylor, with his amputated foot, managed to hobble alongside his shipmates.

"The roof was repaired and strengthened, in case we should be obliged to return to it for the ensuing winter; though somewhat at a loss to know how we were to subsist under such an unfortunate event." With that understatement, Captain Ross ordered Somerset House abandoned and, "in parting from our miserable winter house of timber and wood, we left nothing behind us but misery and the recollection of misery." Also left behind were the three invalids, who were brought forward at the end of each day in canvas hammocks slung from uprights on specially built sledges.

Progress was good that first day: ten miles. Similar progress was had over the next four days, which brought the troupe to Batty Bay—only to find that, not only had the foxes returned, but bears had wreaked considerable havoc on the stores, opening casks of bread, oil, and sugar and even gnawing at every shoe and boot they could find. The men shooed away the foxes and immediately set to gathering the scattered provisions and repairing and caulking the whaleboats.

The three sick men flourished on a lucky find of sorrel, a dwarfish plant that grows on rocks in the highest Arctic regions. The tart, kidney-shaped leaves of the plant were well known, even in the 1830s, to be an effective antiscorbutic. Anthony Buck, however, continued to suffer from epileptic fits. In one twenty-four-hour period, he underwent an incredible thirty-two attacks, which prompted the surgeon to assign two sailors to watch over the sick man. Yet for each violent episode, all they could do to try to ease the poor seaman's spasms was apply a cool, wet cloth to his forehead. Miraculously, this appeared to help, and his attacks subsided after the grueling all-day bout.

Through July and early August, the weather continued to moderate. Hundreds of dovekies nesting in cliff-side nooks offered a welcomed addition to the men's diet. Yet as if to counteract that small offering, nature poured rain from the cinerous sky, which again loosened boulders from the cliffs. Rocks and mud showered down as relentlessly as the rain. Two men suffered severe concussions. Then, as if in atonement, the sea ice grew honeycombed and gave encouraging signs of breaking up. For the first time in months, the ice undulated with the flow of the tide. Not a day passed when a sailor did not climb to the top of the cliffs with the hope of seeing clear water to the north.

Then, on August 14, Second Mate Thomas Abernethy reported the joyful news that a clear channel stretched northward and across Prince Regent Inlet as far as he could see. Not a man slept that night, so anxious were they of what the next day might bring and whether the ice would coalesce again. Conditions changed even more favorably through the night. At four o'clock in the morning, all hands turned out to load the boats and to saw the ice that still obstructed the shoreline. At 8 A.M., as soon as the tide flowed, the three boats shoved off. As Captain John Ross recorded,

*We were really underway at last; and it was our business to forget that we had been in the same circumstances, the year before, in the same place; to feel that the time for exertion was now come, and those exertions to be at length rewarded; to exchange hope for certainty, and to see, in the mind's eye, the whole strait open before us, and our little sailing fleet with a fair wind through that bay which was now, in our view, England and home.*

The farther they went, the wider the lane of water. A southerly breeze sprang up, and they ran quickly along the shore. "It was at times scarcely to be believed, and he who dozed to wake again, had for a moment to renew the conviction that he was at length a seaman on his own element, that his boat once more rose on the waves beneath him, and that when the winds blew, it obeyed his will and his hand," wrote

Captain Ross. That first three days, with the aid of a stiff breeze and occasional near gale, they made 112 miles.

On the fourth day, the winds ceased and the men took to the oars. After twenty hours of rowing, the exhausted sailors pulled to shore, pitched their tents, and rested. A stiff easterly wind, however, threatened the exposed boats so they were forced to move onward and eventually came to an excellent harbor just west of Navy Board Inlet, a fjord about 170 miles to the east of Prince Regent Inlet. Rain, snow, fog, high winds, rough seas, and the temperature hovering around 30 degrees stranded them in their safe harbor for six days. At length, when the wind abated and the seas settled, they again launched the boats.

*August 26, 4 A.M. South coast of Lancaster Sound, twenty miles east of Navy Board Inlet.* Everyone was asleep with the exception of David Wood, who had the early morning watch. Wood thought he saw a sail on the horizon. He shook Commander Ross awake, who confirmed Wood's suspicion with his spyglass. A ship! All hands were immediately awakened. And although some were convinced it was only an iceberg, everyone jumped to work. Some launched boats. Others ignited wet gunpowder to create smoke signals. They fired rockets. Muscles strained at oars. A contrary wind, however, impeded their progress, and the ship, oblivious to the smoke and rockets, left the frantic rowers far astern.

Six hours later another sail was espied. This time, everyone took to the boats. This ship, too, appeared to sail beyond their reach. The men rowed hard and sailed with all their skill. "Every muscle seemed to be animated with fresh strength, as [we] pulled away, for now it was in reality life or death," wrote Light. The ship appeared to be lying in wait for her whaleboats. Surely, thought Ross, they had been spotted. But in the next moment, she bore up under all sail and soon left *Victory*'s survivors in the mist. Onward they rowed. From time to time, Ross assured his men, "We are coming up with her," although it was only too evident to him that "although we were near to no less than two ships . . . we should probably reach neither." After about an hour at the oars, the wind calmed and the three whaleboats made significant gains on the mystery ship. And then, "We saw her heave to with all sails aback and lower down a boat, which rowed immediately toward our own," rejoiced Ross. Harder and harder his men pulled at the oars. When at last the strange boat was alongside, *Victory*'s crew dropped their oars and wept.

The boat's mate called out whether they had met some misfortune and lost their ship. Ross replied that, indeed they had and he requested the name of the ship. To Ross's utter astonishment, the mate replied, "The *Isabella* of Hull, once commanded by Captain Ross." When Ross replied that he was that very man, the mate responded, "with the usual blunderheadedness of men on such occasions," that Ross had been dead for two years. Captain Ross then "easily convinced him, however, that what ought to have been true, according to his estimate, was a somewhat premature conclusion." After a hearty congratulation, the *Isabella*'s mate steered his boat back to the ship to inform his commander of the incredible news.

*Victory*'s men cheered as they dashed their oars in the water, each boat striving to be the first to reach the *Isabella*. The *Isabella*'s mate scampered up the side of his ship, and in a moment the ship's crew crowded her rigging and sang out three hearty cheers. *Victory*'s rowers roared back, "Hip hip hooray!" and clambered aboard the *Isabella*.

As Captain Ross shook hands with Captain John Humphreys, he grew conscious of his and his men's ludicrous and motley appearance,

*[N]ever was seen a more miserable-looking set of wretches . . . that we were a set of repulsive-looking people, none of us could doubt. Unshaven since I know not when, dirty, dressed in the rags of wild beasts instead of the tatters of civilization, and starved to the very bones, our gaunt and grim looks, when contrasted with those of the well-dressed and well-fed men around us, made us feel, I believe for the first time, what we really were, as well as what we seemed to others. Every man was hungry and was to be fed, all were ragged and were to be clothed, there was not one to whom washing was not indispensable, nor one whom his beard did not deprive of all English semblance.*

Following washings, a change into clean clothing, and a fine meal, the crew of *Victory* spent the day regaling their rescuers with tales of *Victory's* trials and their adventures with the Inuit. In turn, *Isabella's* men related news on the politics of England and other items, much of it four years old by then. They also explained that the *Isabella* had been in company with another whaler, the *William Lee*, and that, when first spotted, *Isabella's* lookout thought the whaleboats belonged to the *William Lee*. Hence, they had not paid much attention and almost sailed out of sight when the wind calmed and it became evident that the three whaleboats were trying to reach the *Isabella*.

With nightfall, the weary men were each assigned a place to rest. "Long accustomed, however, to a cold bed on the hard snow or the bare rock, few could sleep amid the comfort of our new accommodations. I was myself compelled to leave the bed . . . and take my abode in a chair for the night," wrote Captain John Ross.

The next morning, Captain Humphreys disappointed Ross and *Victory's* crew with the news that, although the *Isabella* had taken twenty-seven whales, her hold was only about two-thirds full and he, therefore, intended to continue whaling in the Arctic waters for some time to come. The disappointment in *Victory's* men can hardly be imagined. Captain Ross took advantage of the time to get his journal in order and to write a letter to George Elliot, First Secretary of the Admiralty, to document the happenings on the voyage of the *Victory*. In his letter, Ross praised the purser William Thom ("My steady and faithful friend . . . to [whose] suggestions must be attributed the uncommon degree of health which our crew enjoyed"), Surgeon MacDiarmid ("an ornament to His Majesty's service"), and, especially, his nephew, whose labors in the "departments of Astronomy, Natural History, and Surveying, will speak for themselves in language beyond the ability of my pen. . . ." He also remarked on the valuable information attained from the published journals of Sir Edward Parry and Sir John Franklin. The letter was handed off to a homeward-bound whaler and made it to England well ahead of Ross.

About a month after Humphreys gave out the disappointing news that he intended to remain at sea, the weather turned unusually severe and, to the great joy of *Victory's* survivors, the *Isabella* turned about and set sail for home. After some delays with the weather, she reached the Humber on the North Sea coast of England. From there, Ross proceeded to Hull on the Rotterdam steamship *Gazelle*.

In that other whalers had already brought word of the rescue to Hull by the time Ross arrived, welcomers thronged to the waterside to see their hero. They crowded the pier so densely that it was only with difficulty that the weather-beaten captain, dressed in sealskin trousers and his faded naval uniform, reached the Vittoria Hotel, where he was greeted by the mayor, elders of Trinity House (administrator over England's lighthouses), prominent merchants of the town, and the president of the Philosophical Society. The old seaport rang with the sound of bells. Nearly every ship in port displayed her colors. The *Hull Advertiser* wrote, "We stop the press to announce the arrival at Hull of Captain Ross, who is onboard the *Gazelle* steamer, from Rotterdam. We had the pleasure of bidding Captain Ross welcome to his native land and were happy to see that he appeared in excellent health."

The following morning, Ross boarded a London-bound steamboat. A couple hours later, after an absence of four years and 149 days, Captain John Ross strode up the steps between the majestic Ionic columns that flank the entrance to the Admiralty building.

CHAPTER NINE

# Recognition, Rewards, and Rancor

(October 1833–May 1850)

$W$*INDSOR Castle, October 20, 1833.* Just hours after Ross made his report to the Admiralty, he received word that His Majesty King William IV wished to see both Ross and his nephew. One can only imagine the feelings welling up within the breasts of the crusty sea captain and his handsome nephew as they strolled the quadrangle of the Romantic medieval edifice and walked past the statues of Edward III and the Black Prince that stare down from the square tower of the entryway *porte-cochère.* After more than four years with nothing to discern but bleak whiteness blotted by the occasional sombrous rock, the emblazonry of the castle was surely staggering. Suits of armor and medieval weaponry stood sentinel between towering gothic windows, through which sunlight, filtered by delicate stone tracery, cast dark shadows across the red carpet; heraldic arms of Knights of the Garter,

dating back to 1348, honored the vaulted, ribbed ceiling; sensuous ivory and gold rococo swirls and acanthus leaves complemented the French wainscoting; tapestries, paintings, sculptures, cabinets, vases, busts, marble fireplaces, and gilt columns graced the passage of the two sailors.

King William IV, ensconced on his throne—not of ice but of intricately carved and gold-leafed wood overhung with blue velvet, tassels, and floral needlework—welcomed his guests. The uncle and nephew bowed to His Majesty and spread at his feet the flag that Commander James Ross had flown over the North Magnetic Pole. The king was pleased. Capitalizing on the moment, John Ross requested permission to dedicate his journal to his lordship, and he also asked if he might inscribe "Magnetic Pole of William IVth" on his published chart—a silly notion in that the pole is constantly on the move. Nonetheless, William IV granted both requests. When the *Edinburgh Review* later heard that the pole had been named for the monarch, they quipped, "Some Russian or French navigator may next year find it a degree to the east or west . . . and will be equally entitled to give this *new place* the name of the magnetic pole of Nicholas, or of Louis Philippe."

As a testament to the impression Captain Ross must have made on the king, fourteen months later, Ross was again invited to Windsor Castle to receive the accolade of knighthood and to be made a Companion of the Order of the Bath—just in time for him to add "Sir" before his name on the title page of his forthcoming book.

The day after his audience with the king, Ross turned to address a critical concern: His crew were clamoring for their back pay. What with being away from home for more than four years, the men had bills to pay and families to feed and many were financially stretched to the limit.

They milled around London to await their due. Yet English maritime law did not require that sailors be paid for time following abandonment of a ship. That meant that Captain Ross legally owed wages only through October 1831, which would still leave the men two years without pay. (Although *Victory* was not vacated until May 1832, the official date of her abandonment was in October, when it was clear that she was hopelessly lost.) However, that was not the greatest problem. Ross had calculated on a voyage of just fifteen months—not four and a half years. He had lost a sizable fortune with the ship and its scientific instruments. In addition, like the others, he had been without income for four years, aside from his standard half-pay as an idle navy captain. Captain John Ross was broke, with no way to pay his crew.

Straightaway, he sat down in his London hotel and drafted a letter to George Elliot, First Secretary of the Admiralty. Ross turned to the Admiralty with the hope that, although *Victory* was a private venture, the Admiralty might consider that the voyage had served a public service in the name of science and, thus, might allocate funds to pay his crew. In his letter, Ross requested Elliot to bring his case before the Lords Commissioners of the Admiralty, and he asked that, in light of the public nature of the undertaking and that the crew, "whose constancy was never shaken under the most appalling prospects, and to whose fidelity and obedience" he owed so much, be paid accordingly. Ross was proud of his crew's exemplary behavior and steadfast courage throughout their suffering, and he felt it would be unfair if they were not paid from the moment of *Victory*'s loss right up to their arrival in England. By "accordingly," Ross requested that his men not only be paid double wages (standard for Arctic service) up to the abandonment of *Victory*, but also that they receive full pay for the period from the loss of the ship until they reached home. Ross figured that because he did not have the money himself, he might as well ask the Admiralty for all he might get.

Within four days, Ross received a verbal reply from the Lords Commissioners that he should submit a list of claims to Second Secretary John Barrow for their review. He immediately did so, and over the upcoming weekend, the Lords Commissioners granted his request to the very last pence. So it happened that just nine days after Ross's arrival in London, a tight-lipped John Barrow penned the following to Ross,

> *I am commanded by their Lordships to acquaint you in reply, that although these men have no claim on His Majesty's Government, inasmuch as the expedition was not sent out by the Board of the Admiralty, yet, in consideration of its having been undertaken for the benefit of science, of the sufferings these men have undergone, the perilous situation in which they were placed for so long protracted a period, and their uniform good conduct under circumstances the most trying to which British seamen were perhaps exposed . . . their Lordships have, therefore, directed the Accountant-General of the Navy to advance to you the sum of 4580£. 12s. 3d. as the amount which by your statement you feel yourself under an engagement to pay.*

The tone of Barrow's letter speaks for itself: "I am commanded . . . these men have no claim." Outraged and left with no choice but to release the funds, the embittered John Barrow vented his anger through the *Quarterly Review*. Ross, he said,

> *had no claim whatever on the public for an ill-prepared, ill-concerted, and (we may add) ill-executed undertaking, wholly of a private nature. The wealthy*

*individual at whose expense the ship was fitted out, and who made or sanc-
tioned the 'sacred' engagements with the men, was the proper quarter to which
application should have been made.*

To add to Barrow's ire, not only had the Lords Commissioners's
largesse removed Ross's financial burden, but also the grant had the effect
of stamping Ross's private venture with the unofficial approval of the
Lords of the Admiralty. Now, after weathering fifteen years of Barrow's
sardonic scorn, the impenetrably dull—as Barrow had called him—Captain John Ross had pulled a coup. Nevertheless, the caustic pen of the
Second Secretary would not be idle for long. Barrow fumed and watched
and waited for just the right opportunity, which he knew the proud and
stubborn captain would grant him eventually. Meanwhile, Ross basked in
glory and fame.

And fame it was. More than 4,000 pieces of fan mail flooded the
captain's post box. The most fashionable drawing rooms of London
sought his burly, scarred presence. There were dinner parties to attend.
Soirees to go to. And evening conversazioni at which to recount stories
of the *Victory*, the Inuit, the Hydrographer, sledges of crystal, mountains
of ice, the discoveries, the cold, starvation, suffering, death, and rescue.
Overweight and imposing, yet always gallant, the heroic sea captain cut
an impressive figure in his officer's regalia: his magnificent double-
breasted blue coat studded with sixteen brass buttons, red striping, gold
epaulets and accents; his long, shaggy, red hair, grayed by age and the
Arctic sun, curling over his ears; his pudgy cheeks and bushy eyebrows;
the white gloves; the medals; the bejeweled sword and scabbard; and the
cumbrous, ever-present, sealskin fur cape. Every head turned, every eye
gazed, every ear listened at the announcement of the arrival of Captain

John Ross. Beautiful women flocked to his side. Others wrote poems
and love letters.

It was probably at one of these socials that Ross met Mary Jones.
Miss Jones, the daughter of a navy commander, was without doubt
charmed by the rugged captain and relished the attention she gained at
his side. The London society scene was surely a heady experience for the
young woman of twenty-three. And Captain Ross, then fifty-seven,
undoubtedly enjoyed her youthful company. The two married that
October—a marriage that was sadly doomed.

To the public, Ross's feat of bringing most of his crew safely
home after four winters in the Arctic, if not an outright miracle, was
an act of incredible heroism. His popularity increased daily. He was car-
icatured in magazines and lauded at gala affairs. Titles and honors of
state were heaped upon the man: Commander of the Sword of Sweden;
Knight of the Second Class of St. Anne of Prussia; Second Class of the
Legion of Honor; Second Class of the Red Eagle of Prussia; Second
Class of Leopold of Belgium; Gold Medals from the Geographical
Society of London, the Geographical Institute of Paris, and the Royal
Societies of Sweden, Austria, Denmark; the Freedom of the cities of
London, Liverpool, Bristol, Hull; and even gold snuffboxes from the
sovereigns of Russia, Holland, Denmark, and Austria.

In addition to the bounty of acclamations to Captain Ross, the voyage of the *Victory* resulted in a baronetcy conferred on Felix Booth. And
James Ross's presentation of his scientific paper to the Royal Society
was met with great praise, not only for his discussion on the North
Magnetic Pole, but also for his detailed descriptions of the natural history of Boothia Peninsula. (To this day, James Ross is memorialized
through the names of two Arctic birds: Ross's Gull [*Rhodostethia rosea*]

and Ross's Goose [*Anser rossii*].) Shortly thereafter, the Admiralty placed Commander James Ross on full pay and appointed him a position on HMS *Victory* (the former flagship of Lord Nelson), which quickly led to his promotion to post-captain. Most other crewmembers were also promoted or found good positions because of the voyage.

Captain Ross's fame and the public's fascination with the voyage of the *Victory* spread. By mid-March, upward of 15,000 persons had paid a shilling each to view dioramas at the Oxford Street Queen's Bazaar, which depicted Ross's interview with the Inuit and a view of Fury Beach. Another exhibit was the Panorama at Leicester Square. There, William Light was the chief narrator and actor, but the manager eventually fired him for fabricating pernicious tales against Captain Ross. As popular as those exhibits were, they paled in comparison to the display that opened at Vauxhall Gardens on Friday, May 30, 1834.

Vauxhall Gardens, on the south bank of the Thames, had been a fashionable gathering place since the middle of the eighteenth century. Promenades, bandstands, dancing, refreshments, quiet alcoves, statues, and gardens added to the romantic allure of the waterside park. At the time of Ross's voyage, stage plays and elaborate presentations, such as the reenactment of the Battle of Waterloo with 1,000 soldiers, were regular occurrences. Vauxhall Gardens was the perfect place to capitalize on Ross's adventure. The excitement over his miraculous return grew to such a fever that Vauxhall Gardens opened two weeks early that season. And what a show!

The scale of the display—occupying 60,000 square feet—exceeded anything ever before attempted at the gardens. The scenery included masses of rocks and ice that towered seventy feet in height. "The undulation of the waves is excellently contrived," gushed the *Times* as the reporter described how *Victory* steered her way amidst floating fragments of ice. "She does not, in the usual method of theatrical navigation, merely pass from side to side of the stage . . . but she performs what may be supposed to be the evolutions of a ship in a dangerous predicament to which she is exposed, and displays at times every part of her rigging and hull," continued the newspaper article. Groups of polar bears, "or at least living representations of them," scrambled over the rocks and ice, and "their doleful howling [increased] the wildness of the scene." The meeting between the Inuit and the crew was "very cleverly depicted." Perhaps most ingenious was the aurora borealis produced by "a very skillful foreign chymist" who used chemical reactions and different colored gases to create the beautiful phenomenon. A spectacular display of fireworks concluded the show each evening. Ross, who provided drawings and oversaw much of the three-scene production, pronounced the extravaganza as surpassing his greatest expectations.

Still, as famous as Captain John Ross had become, the loss of the ship and his personal belongings and valuable scientific instruments, together with no real income for more than four years, had left him in a troubled financial situation. Although, thanks to Ross's bidding, the Admiralty had moved swiftly to recompense his crew, Ross knew that obtaining compensation for himself was an entirely different matter, especially with Barrow lurking on the scene. Yet hope brewed. Not only was the public flocking to see the shows at Vauxhall Gardens and others, but also sentiment grew among the populace that something should be done to reward the captain for having "done more than any [expedition] that preceded it, and Captain Ross and his nephew were volunteers, serving without pay, for the attainment of a great national object, in prosecuting which they have lost their all," editorialized the *Times*.

Before long, the citizens of Hull and Liverpool had signed petitions urging that Ross should be rewarded. The petitions quickly brought the desired effect. In late March, the Honorable Cutlar Ferguson, M.P., made the motion in the House of Commons "that a sum of £5,000 be granted to His Majesty to enable him to reward the great services of Captain Ross." Ferguson emphasized the extent and importance of Ross's voyage, especially because it had established that the Northwest Passage would not be found at a latitude practical for commercial use, and, thus, presumably halt the waste of resources and lives in the pursuit—a supposition proved only too false by the fatal Franklin expedition twelve years later.

The motion did not go unopposed, however. One member objected on the grounds that Ross had undertaken the expedition, not for the sake of science and discovery, but for the sole purpose of redeeming his reputation. A member countered that, although the voyage may very well have been undertaken to redeem Ross's reputation, it had not been undertaken "with the view of private emolument." Cheers of "Hear! Hear!" interrupted the speaker. Not only that, went on the M.P. when the cheers subsided, but he felt that "considering the feeling of the country on this subject, the house would be justified in voting a moderate sum of money as a remuneration for the gallantry and successful enterprise of Captain Ross." Again, cheers filled the hall. At that point, a third M.P. voiced that he considered the sum of £5,000 a "most stingy and inadequate one" for the "great exertions of the gallant captain." Another added that it would be a most "invidious distinction to leave [Commander James] Ross . . . without receiving some mark of the favorable notice of the house." He proposed that the award be increased to £7,000 so that Ross's nephew might receive £2,000. "Hear! Hear!"

reverberated throughout the chamber. Passions were clearly on the side of the Rosses. Nonetheless, after more pronouncements and debate, Parliament decided that it was only right that they appoint a select committee to consider the issue further.

The committee, with a membership of twenty-six, met three times over a period of two months and heard testimony from Ross, his nephew, Felix Booth, and Francis Beaufort, among others. Toward the end of April, Lord Viscount Sandon issued the committee's findings. The report stated that the select committee had "no hesitation in reporting, that a great public service has been performed." It went on to describe how the officers of the *Victory* had been promoted as a result of the voyage and that even Captain Humphreys of the *Isabella* had been compensated for his role in the rescue. Yet, noted the committee, Captain John Ross, "who had the anxious and painful responsibility of the health and discipline of the party for above four years, under circumstances of unparalleled difficulty and hardship," had received nothing. The committee estimated that the losses that Ross incurred amounted to about £3,000. In consideration of this and the great importance of the scientific discoveries—especially the Magnetic North Pole, of such importance to a maritime nation—the committee recommended that Ross be awarded the full £5,000. The select committee did not recommend compensation for Commander James Ross, with the stated reason that he had received a commission aboard HMS *Victory*, which would, most assuredly, lead to promotion to post-captain, which it did. Their one regret was that they did not have the power to propose a token of public acknowledgment for Sir Felix Booth.

Although the outcome was a great financial boon to Ross, Barrow would later use Ross's testimony before the committee to disparage and embarrass the captain. Furthermore, the investigation widened the nagging rift between Ross and his nephew.

In a routine opening question, the committee asked James Ross if he had signed on as second in command. Oddly, young Ross answered, "Not precisely as second in command, but in a great measure sharing with him the chief command; that is to say, I had the entire direction of the navigation of the ship, without being under Captain Ross's command." Yet this made no sense. Why would John Ross, after years of planning, outfitting the ship, and arranging financing, give command to his nephew? Besides, a ship can have only one commander.

Catching the paradox, the committee asked the young commander, "With your experience of naval matters in cases of danger, do you consider it possible there should be two officers of coequal power?" "No," replied James Ross, "the command must devolve on one person . . . [i]n all cases it devolved upon me." This made even less sense. The committee challenged further: "The question [of command] did not arise between you and Captain Ross?" "No, it was quite understood between us before we sailed. I should conduct everything myself. Captain Ross might have said if he chose, 'I do not approve of this or that,' and then I could only have said, 'you must conduct it yourself, both cannot do so.'" James Ross had clearly implied that Captain John Ross wanted to sit back and go along for the ride, while he did all the work.

To the further astonishment of the committee, Commander Ross testified that Felix Booth had told him that if he (James) chose not to sail with the *Victory*, that Booth would withdraw his backing. In an effort to resolve the issue, the committee called Felix Booth to the stand.

"To whom did you give command of the expedition?"

"To Captain Ross."

"Captain Ross was the sole commander?"

"Yes, he was the sole commander, with liberty to appoint whom he pleased under him. I only said, let them be men who will be of great service. I left the command entirely to him."

"Did you make any stipulation that Commander Ross should accompany him?"

"No, it was the wish of his uncle, which I thought a very natural one; his uncle said, he was not doing anything, was a clever young man, and if I had no objection, he should like him to accompany him as it might obtain his promotion."

"Had Commander Ross refused to go, would you have sent the expedition?"

"Certainly I should."

While there is no doubt that James Ross conducted the great majority of overland sorties, there is also no doubt that the command of the entire expedition rested solely in the hands of Captain John Ross. That the captain stayed aboard ship while his nephew, twenty-three years his junior, conducted overland missions should be no surprise— just as a ship's captain does not climb the ratlines to furl the sails. Indeed, it is likely that, if Captain Ross had not assigned his nephew command of most of the overland excursions, an even greater clash might have developed between the two egos. James Ross's peculiar testimony is a puzzle. Perhaps he was jealous over the great attention his uncle received when they returned home. Yet James received his fair share of fame—his name would forever be connected with the North Magnetic Pole—and he later capitalized on his experience with the *Victory* to win appointment to command perhaps the most renowned expedition to the Antarctic. There is further evidence that the young commander had become a puppet of John Barrow, as we shall see, and he may have been trying to disparage his uncle at Barrow's dictate.

In making its recommendation that Captain Ross be awarded, the committee made it clear that it was wholly satisfied that Ross was the true commander of the expedition. Perhaps their refusal to grant compensation to James Ross was a result of the young commander's strange assertion that he was the leader. More likely, though, the committee overlooked the absurdity of his claim and merely considered that James Ross had not experienced great financial loss as his uncle had and that, simply, James was the subordinate. In addition, as mentioned, they took into account his appointment on His Majesty's Flagship *Victory*.

John Barrow soon got wind of the findings. As if the Admiralty's ordering Barrow to release funds to pay Ross's crew had not sufficiently outraged him, he was livid when he heard that Parliament had awarded the man £5,000. He accused Parliament of "inaccuracy" when it reported that Ross had performed a great public service, and he charged that the motion in the House of Commons had been brought about by a "puffing parade of Captain Ross's countrymen." "No public service, that we can discover, has been brought about," he shouted through his favorite medium, the *Quarterly Review*.

Captain Ross held his tongue.

At about the same time, a series of weekly installments of a narrative of the voyage began to appear on the newsstands. Although the publications appeared under the authorship of a writer named Robert Huish, it was obvious to all that William Light was behind the work. Yet even when the narrative came out as a bound book in 1835, the cowardly steward remained disassociated. The following year, he finally emerged from hiding when an issue came out with "transmitted by

William Light" on the title page. Robert Huish was a well-known writer who had authored a series of lengthy "memoirs" of Queen Consort Caroline, George IV, and Princess Charlotte. His highly vitriolic biography on George IV is approvingly quoted to this day.

*The Last Voyage of Capt. Sir John Ross,* as that was the title of the Light and Huish collaboration, was laced with vicious attacks on Ross's personality, his treatment of the crew, and the management of the ship. Hardly a page is free of a silly or sarcastic attack on the captain. Huish enjoyed tabloidlike reporting and took advantage of the opportunity Light had given him to write embroidered, swollen prose, peppered with Latin expressions, references to mythology, and sentences that ran on for upward of a full page.

Through Huish, Light damned Ross every chance he had . . . or, rather, invented. The work was rife with inaccuracies, digressions, petty grievances, and outright fantasies. Light's most disgraceful tale was that Captain Ross had urged the crew to abandon and leave for dead the crippled third mate, George Taylor. On the drive to reach Fury Beach, said Huish and Light, "a very different plan was suggested by Capt. Ross, and that was, *to leave the poor fellow behind them!!!*" (Italics in original.) The writer raged in melodramatic prose: "horrid suggestion . . . the blood chills along our veins . . . deliberate cruelty, staggers our belief . . . few acts which will bear a parallel . . . the murder of Abel." After rambling in a like manner for about 500 words, the passage concluded with, "[O]ur motive in the discussing of it has not been to impute the commission of so barbarous an act to Capt. Ross, but to give him an opportunity of purifying his character from a stigma, which will otherwise cling to his name forever."

Captain Ross did not rebut. He did not have to. The accusations in the Huish and Light tale were so transparent that virtually no one gave it credence. An Admiral Sir Robert Stopford wrote, "This attack should be positively repelled, as it strikes at the root of all the commendable parts of Ross's conduct." The vicious allegation—never supported by any other crewmember—was simply unfounded and made no sense. Indeed, when Ross signed on Taylor, who had been master of the *Victory* before Ross bought the ship, he was so fond of Taylor that he arranged for Felix Booth to support the man's family during his absence.

Light probably had nothing against Captain Ross, per se. The steward was nothing more than an insignificant malcontent, who harbored a strong disrespect for authority. He had come to Ross with apparently good recommendations—having had fourteen years of experience at sea and, better still, he had sailed with Parry on two voyages to the Arctic. Ross later learned, however, that on another ship, Light had been caught stealing and "was to have been punished, but deserted in Rio in the night leaving his clothes behind him to escape a flogging." Moreover, *Victory's* third mate caught Light taking provisions from the ship's stores, which led Ross to dismiss him as steward and assign him to the laundry.

While all this was going on, Captain Ross was hard at work on his own book about the voyage. James collaborated with his uncle—the apparent disaccord between the two Rosses notwithstanding—and contributed six chapters' worth of narratives on the overland excursions, including an extensive chapter on the discovery of the North Magnetic Pole.

Yet even the discovery of the magnetic pole provided fodder for tension between the two Rosses. Captain Ross had the irritating habit of using the pronoun "we" whenever he spoke about the discovery. As work on the book progressed, James wrote to his uncle for assurances that he (James) would be given sole credit for finding the pole and he reminded Ross of troubling testimony his uncle had given to the Parliamentary committee; namely, "by our observations we had determined that we were in a measured distance, where the ship was from the Magnetic Pole and by continuing these observations we arrived at the spot."

Without a doubt, the world knew that James Ross was the sole discoverer, but the young man was concerned—and rightfully so—of the wording he thought his uncle might use. As it turned out, Captain Ross made it perfectly clear in the book that his nephew was the discoverer. Nevertheless, John Ross could not restrain himself from claiming credit through his role as captain:

> *Heaven forbid that I should attempt to rob them of such honours as they are entitled to on this ground, or to claim credit of having planted the British flag on this long desired spot with my own hand. If I myself consent to award that palm to him who commanded this successful party . . . it must not be forgotten that in this I surrender those personal claims which are never abandoned by the commander. . . . It must be hereafter remembered in history, and will so be recorded, that it was the ship Victory, under command of Captain John Ross, which assigned the north-west Magnetic Pole.*

Irritating to James Ross? Yes. Nevertheless, everyone knew who actually found the pole, and the actions of his proud and stubborn uncle looked petty, if not pathetic. On the other hand, rightly or wrongly, a leader taking undeserved credit for a discovery was and is far from unusual.

In those days, the House of John Murray—"publisher to the Admiralty, and Board of Longitude"—handled most publications on voyages of discovery. These had included the narratives of Edward Parry, John Franklin, and even Ross's 1818 voyage. John Murray had also published books by John Barrow. Not only that, but Murray was the publisher of the *Quarterly Review,* Barrow's favorite vehicle for his anonymous and vitriolic attacks on Ross. Hence, in view of John Murray's cozy relationship with Barrow and the Admiralty and that Ross's voyage had been a private undertaking, Ross chose to publish his narrative through subscriptions rather than the usual route of John Murray.

Word quickly reached Barrow that Ross had decided to publish the narrative himself. Unthinkable! Here was a captain of the navy, who took "the command of a merchant-ship, without commission, without official instructions, and without any authority but such as is given to the skipper of a trading vessel," and now he had the gall to self-publish a book, grumbled Barrow. "While we admit that everyone has an undoubted right to make the most of his labours," continued Barrow, "something is also due to situation in life, and to character. The public had more than remunerated Captain Ross for any damage that his pocket might have sustained." It was plain to Barrow that Ross's motive was a simple "lust for lucre," as the irate Second Secretary of the Admiralty worded it. Using again the *Quarterly Review,* Barrow spluttered at Ross's having opened a storefront to take subscriptions and "the sending of a set of fellows, usually called *trampers,* but who call themselves *agents,* to knock at every gentleman's door in town and country, not humbly to solicit, but with pertinacious importunity almost to force, subscriptions." Barrow, clearly jealous over Ross's fame, even sniffed in the *Review* at the spectacle at Vauxhall Gardens as "not worth detailing."

While there is little doubt that Ross wished to make money on his book, and it is true that some of his fellow officers considered that ignoble, he did have the right, as even Barrow admitted in his left-handed way. And the list of subscribers grew—much to Barrow's chagrin, no doubt—so that by the time of the release of the book, more than 7,000 had signed up. In addition, Ross had the extra satisfaction of adding to the opening leaves,

TO

HIS MOST EXCELLENT MAJESTY,

WILLIAM IV.

KING OF GREAT BRITAIN, IRELAND, &C.

THIS NARRATIVE

OF THE

DISCOVERIES MADE IN THE ARCTIC REGIONS,

IN THE YEARS

1829, 1830, 1831, 1832, AND 1833,

IS DEDICATED WITH HIS MAJESTY'S GRACIOUS PERMISSION

The ponderous, 740-page tome finally came out in the spring of 1835. It was a handsome volume, with twenty-eight finely detailed lithographs and engravings—several hand-colored—plus a large foldout map that measured 21 by 24 inches. In the fall, Ross followed up with an appendix made even more colorful by a dozen hand-colored lithographs. Engaging illustrations of Ross's Inuit friends complemented the two volumes: Old Alictu, supporting himself with a staff; Tiagashu, with a worried expression; the smiling Adlurak; the alluring Kakikagiu, flanked by her two husbands; Tulluahiu and his wooden leg; the Hydrographer, drawing a map while seated at the captain's table; Ikmallik's son

Ooblooria brandishing a dog whip. The elegant books sold for £2 12s 6d, almost as much as an able seaman's monthly pay.

Most newspapers and magazines gave the books favorable reviews. The *Times* wrote, "Never did we read a history of almost unexampled disappointment, labour, suffering, and peril, written in a tone so free from querulousness... an expedition which... attests the skill and capacity of the commander and his officers, and exhibits in a strong point of view the sterling qualities of British seaman."

Others commented similarly:

The *Observer*, "The volume abounds with interesting detail... written with much simplicity, but in a very pleasing manner."

*Leeds Mercury*, "most deeply interesting... riveting. The Captain certainly displayed a cool seamanlike heroism."

*Sheffield Mercury*, "a monument of maritime devotion and success... this splendid quarto volume should be immediately placed in every respectable library."

*Edinburgh Review*, "one of the most remarkable voyages which has been recorded in the annals of maritime discovery."

John Murray's *Quarterly Review*, on the other hand, was not so admiring. The *Review* allocated to John Barrow thirty-eight pages to foment and rant; thirty-eight pages—nearly 20,000 words—of searing sarcasm, ridicule, and sneer. Anyone unaware of Barrow's campaign against Ross would have thought that Barrow had read a different book. To Barrow, Ross had done nothing right, nothing useful, nothing noteworthy. And foolishly for Ross, he set himself up for some of Barrow's ridicule. The never-say-die captain had not been able to contain himself—he just *had* to use his book to revisit his 1818 voyage to Lancaster Sound and try to weasel an explanation for his Croker's Mountains.

While on retreat from Fury Beach, Ross had seen a mountain on the south coast of Lancaster Sound. In his book, he claimed it as coincident with Croker's Mountains: "The mountain . . . lies between the latitudes of 73° 53' and 74° north; and as its longitude is 90° west, it occupies the place at which I had marked Croker's Mountain, in 1818." Nice try, except for a couple details. In 1818, Ross had written, "I distinctly saw the land, round the bottom of the bay, forming a connected chain of mountains . . . The mountains, which occupied the centre . . . were named Croker's Mountains." But wait . . . that was a *chain* of mountains, not a single mountain like the one with which he tried to replace them. Furthermore, Ross's 1818 map depicted Croker's Mountains at about 84 degrees west longitude, not at 90 degrees—a difference of 110 miles. Ross's attempt to recreate Croker's Mountains was so obvious that it seemed the sad rationalization of a dotty old man.

Barrow licked his lips and dove in for the kill . . . or so he thought. "Captain Ross having thought fit to throw down the gauntlet, he will find us prepared for the combat . . . we [anticipate] an easy conquest over such an antagonist."

If Barrow had restricted himself to addressing Ross's silliness over Croker's Mountains, his points may have been worthy of remark. However, like Ross, he, too, could not contain himself. "Notwithstanding the bulk of the knight's [Barrow loved to scoff at Ross's accolades] book, a summary of his voyage need not cost us many pages; for though its duration was long, the incidents were few, and the results next to nothing." Then he continued for another thirty-five pages. Word after word, paragraph after paragraph, Barrow's anonymous, petty, acid pen flashed through the pages of the *Quarterly Review*. He disparaged everything:

The ship: "The *Victory*, fitted as a steamer—the very worst description of vessel to navigate among the ice."

Felix Booth: "his worthy, though not wise patron."

The Inuit: "A very large portion of the book is taken up with the traffic and transactions of the voyagers with these dismal savages."

Pleasures of Christmas dinner: "While Ross and his party were feasting on salmon and venison—with mince-pies and cherry-brandy—Franklin ... was left alone to waste away by famine." (Barrow referred to a disastrous overland expedition by Franklin that had taken place *ten years before* Ross's *Victory*.)

Ross's artwork: "Captain Ross's original drawings ... would have disgraced the fingers of a schoolboy of twelve."

Names of landmarks: "Then comes a whole host of foreigners, who, we conceive, have no business there:—Louis Philip (*sic*),—Capes Nicholas, Carl XIV...."

Barrow even latched on to William Light's claim that Ross abandoned Taylor: "Sir John may affect to treat it with what is called silent contempt, which is but too frequently resorted to when it may not be quite convenient to answer a charge of delinquency.

"We are much mistaken if the account of the voyage ... does not disappoint every one that may take the trouble to toil through it," scoffed Barrow. "The first reflection to which the perusal gives rise, is the cold and heartless manner in which the bulk of the narrative is drawn up," he continued as he accused Ross of "unwillingness to give praise or make acknowledgment" of the contributions of James Ross. To bolster his case, Barrow harped on Ross's use of the word "we" in his testimony before the Parliamentary committee and chose to ignore the chapters written by Commander Ross and the multitude of credits and references to his nephew that Captain Ross broadcast throughout the book.

Barrow's sarcasm reached its apex when he came to Croker's Mountains. "We are, indeed, utterly at a loss to comprehend what evil genius could have urged on the gallant Captain to stumble, once more, on those fatal mountains on which he suffered shipwreck in the year 1818. Had he no friend at his elbow?" With that opening volley, Barrow tore into Ross for no less than five pages. Although that section of his critique was mostly well founded, his mean-spiritedness was pointless and invited backlash. "Barrow's criticism is unnecessarily cruel and harsh," wrote a senior naval officer.

At the conclusion of his tirade, Barrow pronounced Ross,

> . . . *utterly incompetent to conduct an arduous naval enterprise for discovery to a successful termination.* . . . *John Ross had proved himself to be wanting in the high qualifications for . . . deciding such a question as that of a passage from the Atlantic to the Pacific; a passage which, baffled from incompetence, and prejudiced from spite, he now,* ex cathedra, *pronounces to be impracticable.*

That Ross was stubborn and blinded by his determination to prove that Croker's Mountains existed in one form or another, no one will argue. But "incompetent" was clearly not the correct moniker for a captain who brought most of his men safely through four Arctic winters, charted miles of new coastline, lived peacefully among the Inuit, and oversaw the discovery of the North Magnetic Pole. If anyone were prejudiced from spite, it was John Barrow. Indeed, history has proved Barrow wrong and Ross correct—the Northwest Passage *is* impracticable.

Again, Captain John Ross chose to ignore Secretary John Barrow.

Another fallout from the publication of Ross's book was an eighteen-page pamphlet by John Braithwaite, of Braithwaite and Ericsson, boiler manufacturers and installers of *Victory's* steam engine. In his pamphlet, Braithwaite defended the machinery and laid the blame for any failures on Ross because, among other things, he had kept secret the intended purpose of the ship. (In that Booth originally had wished his philanthropy anonymous, Ross did not tell Braithwaite and Ericsson that the ship was headed for the Arctic.) Braithwaite was especially offended that Ross had called his steam engine "execrable." What *was* execrable, complained Braithwaite, was "telling the makers of the engines that they were intended to propel a vessel constructed for 'war purposes.'" Three months later, Ross countered with his own pamphlet. "The machinery was execrable," squawked Ross. "[It was] an utter failure." The two pamphlets were nothing more than a "he said, she said" affair, and that was the end of it.

*London. January 1846.* Twelve years had passed since the miraculous return of *Victory's* crew. In the intervening years, Sir James Ross, now a captain and knighted, had completed an extraordinarily successful four-year voyage to Antarctica. John Barrow (now Sir John) had sent HMSs *Erebus* and *Terror*, under the command of Sir John Franklin, to discover, once and for all times, the Northwest Passage. Captain Sir John Ross had busied himself with an appointment as Consul to Sweden; expanded North West Castle, his home in Scotland; had made a bid for Parliament (and lost); and dabbled in a money-losing railway venture with his brother George (the father of James). Ross's wife, Mary, meanwhile, showed signs of discontent with the marriage. She disliked the cold of Sweden, the damp of Scotland, the lack of London society, and the uncertainty of her husband's solvency despite the £5,000 award from Parliament.

With the passage of time, Fury Beach, the Inuit, and the *Victory* had slipped from the forefront of the public mind. In one mind, however, the story continued to ferment.

"Mr. Murray's List of New Works Now Ready," read the January advertisement from the publishing house of John Murray. The third book on the list was *Voyages of Discovery and Adventure, Within the Arctic Regions; From 1818 to the Present Time,* by Sir John Barrow, Baronet. Price: 15 shillings. "Abridged and arranged from the official narrative, with occasional remarks," continued the advertisement copy.

Based solely on published journals, Barrow's book related the story of every British voyage and journey to the Arctic from 1818 to 1845, as the title asserted. With the exception of a single expedition, Barrow granted each its own chapter title: "Commander Parry's Second Voyage," "Franklin and Richardson," "Back's Journey," to cite several. Barrow even granted Ross's 1818 voyage to Baffin Bay a chapter title, "Commander John Ross." But for one exception, Barrow told the tale of each expedition by simply digesting and abridging the published narratives—with occasional remarks. That one exception to Barrow's scheme was Ross's voyage in the *Victory.* Rather than merely insult Ross by excluding mention in his book, the crotchety Barrow, then eighty-two years old, chose to relegate Ross and his *Victory* to a chapter that he titled, "Miscellaneous." Even so, Barrow barely touched on the voyage itself. He gave it less than three pages. Instead, Barrow spent his printer's ink on nearly twenty pages of "occasional remarks," reharping on selected testimony before the Parliamentary committee and the "absurd nonsense" that Ross's voyage proved that a passage does not exist between the bottom of Prince Regent Inlet and the Polar Sea. It was in this chapter that James Ross's kowtowing to Barrow is especially evident. Barrow asserted,

> *It will be seen from the chart that Sir James Ross thinks it not improbable . . . that the space . . . may be a wide channel, opening into the lower part of Prince Regent's Inlet: Should this be so, it will form the continuation of his own* Strait, *through which not only a single ship and boats, but whole fleets, may pass.*

Although James Ross could hardly have believed in his heart that a strait existed from the southern end of Prince Regent Inlet, it appears that he pandered to Barrow's conviction, perhaps because the all-powerful Barrow controlled appointment of the command of exploratory missions, such as James Ross's voyage to the Antarctic. When Barrow wrote approvingly and defensively of Ross's nephew as, "the officer who did all that was done, or could be done, and appears not to have been treated on this Committee as he ought to have been," his favoritism toward the younger Ross was obvious.

Not content with his "occasional remarks" about the voyage of the *Victory,* Barrow repeated, *ad nauseam,* his worn-out attacks on the character of Captain Ross, the fabled Croker's Mountains, and the 1818 voyage. He concluded,

> *In taking leave of Ross, it may be stated that the observations made on his strange conduct have relation only to his situation for conducting the voyage of discovery, where science and accuracy were indispensable. In practical seamanship it is understood and admitted that he is sufficiently skilled.*

Even this last sentence was a sarcastic swipe from the pen of Barrow. It referred to an earlier remark in his book, "The ordinary duties of a good seaman are well known; that he can hand, reef, steer, and heave the lead, keep the dead reckoning, and take and work an observation for the latitude," and implied that that was the extent of Ross's talents.

John Ross kept his silence no longer. In that Barrow's previous attacks on Ross were published anonymously through the *Quarterly Review*, this new publication with Barrow's name affixed handed Ross the right and the obligation to strike back. He grasped the opportunity and immediately brought forth a sixty-two-page *Refutation of the Numerous Misrepresentations* in Barrow's *Voyages of Discovery and Research*. "The main object of Sir John Barrow's work," wrote Ross, "is to traduce the professional character of a brother officer, and to destroy the reputation of one who, for upwards of fifty years, has laboured assiduously to serve his Sovereign and to maintain the glory of his country." Although Barrow's book professes to be an abridgment of Arctic voyages, continued Ross, the first and last chapters "are filled with little else than charges and insinuations against my personal conduct and character.... The spirit in which everything relating to myself is written is so transparent, the personal animosity which breaks out in every page so obvious, and the gross unfairness of the narrative so palpable."

Even Ross admits that he is at a loss to explain Barrow's long-lived campaign of hatred:

> *The only explanation I can give of the absence of truth and fairness exhibited by Sir J. Barrow, when referring to me or my services ... is that immediately after my first Voyage of Discovery, circumstances occurred which caused a personal altercation, and a rupture of our former friendly relations. Although*

*twenty-seven years have elapsed, Sir John Barrow still cherishes the feelings then excited, and either in his own person, or through those organs of the press over which he has any influence, incessantly seeks to depreciate my professional character and services.*

The "personal altercation" Ross referred to was an embarrassing moment Barrow had experienced during an after-dinner conversation with Ross and Lord and Lady Melville (Lord Melville was First Lord of the Admiralty, who was essentially Barrow's boss). During the conversation, Barrow told a story of his having sailed on a whaler to Greenland when he was a boy. When Ross shook his head and raised his eyebrows at the tale, Lady Melville asked Barrow the name of the ship. Barrow stammered that he could not remember, nor could he recall the captain's name, but he stated that the ship sailed from Whitehaven Harbor. Hearing the name of the harbor, Ross chuckled that whalers never sailed from the small and shallow harbor. From that moment onward, Ross felt that Barrow was his most bitter enemy.

In his pamphlet, Ross argued elegantly against the libel within Barrow's book. His writing was clear-eyed and well constructed, and although he refused to join Barrow in a venom-spitting contest, he does not let Barrow off lightly just because of the retired Second Secretary's advanced age:

*At his age we generally expect to find the passions and animosities of former life allayed, whilst a desire to live in peace with all men is the becoming and paramount sentiment: the exhibition of such feelings commands alike our veneration and forbearance, and had I found them in Sir John Barrow's work, I would have endured any amount of misrepresentation rather than uttered one*

*word calculated in any degree to embitter his declining years. But his language
is so imbued with bitterness, the spirit he manifests is so alien to everything like
kindness and generosity, and his attacks are so gratuitous and unprovoked, that
he himself sets aside the considerations which under other circumstances would
have imposed silence upon me . . . when I looked for an historian I found a
calumniator.*

Toward the end of his pamphlet, John Ross reflected on his relationship with his nephew. He expressed hurt and puzzlement over James's testimony before the Parliamentary committee. "Since that day," wrote Ross,

> *. . . my enemies received their warmest ally; in private and in public, in every
> club and in every society—the Royal, the Astronomical, the Geographical—
> did I hear of efforts to depreciate my talents, my acquirements, and my ser-
> vices; but I have borne all in silence, because I knew the quarter from whence
> these efforts emanated, and grief subdued my indignation.*

He lamented James's alliance with Barrow, "To all the calumnies in Sir John Barrow's works, Sir James Clark Ross has affixed his signature." Ross correctly called the charts showing a strait at the southern end of Prince Regent Inlet "hydrographical curiosities, and nothing more. . . . They represent the arctic regions as Sir John Barrow *thinks* they *ought* to be, or as Commander Ross, anxious to second Sir John Barrow in all his views, *thinks* they *may* be." Indeed, Commander Ross had previously produced accurate charts that showed no strait. Sir John Ross, made bitter and wounded by his nephew's betrayal, could only wonder.

Barrow never publicly responded to Ross's pamphlet. Less than two years later, he was dead at the age of eighty-three.

The year 1848 not only saw Ross's nemesis forever removed from his life, it also saw another person forever removed. After enduring fourteen years of an apparently unsatisfying relationship, Ross's thirty-seven-year-old wife, Mary, suddenly left her aging husband and went into hiding.

"My own dearest Mary," wrote Ross to the vanished woman, "Return to your husband who has given no just cause for the rash step you have taken. On the anniversary of our marriage I shall add a few lines, but unless I receive a favourable answer they must be the last! God Bless you my still beloved wife, says your fondly affectionate husband John Ross." She never answered his letter.

As it turned out, Mary had accused her seventy-one-year-old husband of having sexual relations with two of their servants. The events were purported to have taken place about a month before Mary left and had resulted in the pregnancy of one of the maids. Ross vehemently denied any such thing and ultimately obtained from the women affidavits that supported his claim of innocence. The pregnant woman's child was said to have been fathered by her brother and that the accusations against Ross were intended to draw suspicions away from the incestuous affair. Nonetheless, Mary was forever gone from Ross's life. He never saw her again.


Abandoned by Mary, John Ross sat alone in his North West Castle in Scotland and lost himself in thoughts about his first love—the sea—

and thoughts about his friend, Sir John Franklin. Under the direction of Barrow, Franklin had sailed in the spring of 1845 in command of a two-ship squadron tasked with finding the Northwest Passage. Ross had promised to come to Franklin's rescue if he did not hear from him in two years. It was now nearly three years since Franklin had sailed, and no one had heard a single word. Consensus had it that the expedition was lost or trapped somewhere in the mysterious Arctic.

Besides Ross's friend Franklin, Thomas Blanky, *Victory*'s first mate, was also a member of the missing expedition. Prized for his skillful navigation of the treacherous ice in the *Victory*, Blanky was signed on by Franklin as the expedition's ice master. Because he had made a miraculous return with Ross after having been given up for dead for more than four years, some hoped that Blanky would bring the same luck to the Franklin expedition. Ross, however, feared the worst. Despite repeated appeals to send him to the aid of his comrades, the Admiralty turned Ross down. Younger officers, and even his nephew, had joined the Franklin hunt, while the aging captain was left behind.

Unwilling or unable to sit idle at home, Ross turned to his old friend and sponsor, Sir Felix Booth, and received assurance that Booth would fund a private search. Tragically, however, Booth died before the arrangements came through. The tenacious Ross then successfully obtained the sponsorship of the Hudson's Bay Company. With the company's help and additional private subscriptions, Ross, by then seventy-three years old, launched his expedition to search for his missing friend.

*Loch Ryan, Scotland. May 23, 1850.* The schooner *Felix* pushed off from her mooring at North West Castle. She towed the tender *Mary*, crammed with extra provisions for the long Arctic nights. As the two vessels reached the open water, an aged sea captain stood solidly on the rolling deck of the *Felix* and hummed his favorite sea song,

> *The sea, the sea, the open sea!*
> *The blue, the fresh, the ever free!*
> *Without a mark, without a bound,*
> *It runneth the earth's wide regions round;*
> *It plays with the clouds, it mocks the skies,*
> *Or like a cradled creature lies.*
> *I'm on the sea! I'm on the sea!*
> *I am where I would ever be,*
> *With the blue above, and the blue below,*
> *And silence wheresoe'er I go.*
> *If a storm should come and awake the deep,*
> *What matter, what matter? I shall ride and sleep.*

A stiff breeze ruffled his gray locks, but a fur sealskin cape draped over his broad shoulders kept out the chill. Captain Sir John Ross breathed deeply the salty air and fixed his gaze toward the frozen waters of Fury Beach.

# Epilogue

JOHN Ross did not find the missing Franklin, nor did any of the other half-dozen or so search-and-rescue missions launched in 1850. Franklin's fate was not learned until 1858, two years after Ross's death.

Nonetheless, Ross relished his return to the Arctic sea. As he sailed down Lancaster Sound, he encountered an American search expedition sponsored by the philanthropic New York merchant Henry Grinnell. American surgeon, Elisha Kent Kane, captured the moment as the two ships of his expedition bounded through the rough waters and approached Ross's schooner *Felix*:

> *We were nearly up to her, for we had shaken out our reefs, and were driving before the wind, shipping seas at every roll. The little schooner was under a single close-reefed top-sail, and seemed fluttering over the waves like a crippled bird. Presently, an old fellow, with a cloak tossed over his night gear appeared,*

*in the lee gangway, and saluted with a voice that rose above the winds. I shall
never forget the heartiness with which the hailing officer sang out, "You and I
are ahead of them all." It was so indeed . . . the* Felix *and the* Advance *were
on the lead.*

The thirty-year-old Kane, awestruck by the venerable old captain,
described Ross as "apparently very little stricken in years and well able
to bear his part in the toils and hazards of life." And there he was, in a
"flimsy cockle-shell," embarked in the crusade of search for a lost com-
rade.

Not only was the *Felix* flimsy, but the men's health was poor. In just
three months, scurvy had wracked the crew as their diet of preserved
vegetables lost its antiscorbutic potency. By the onset of winter, the horrid affliction disabled eight men. Fortunately, other search vessels wintering in the region offered Ross's crew fresh potatoes and carrots,
which brought the scorbutic attacks under control.

Moreover, Ross welcomed the company of the other ships and
often attended their plays and musicals. "Nothing was more common
than to see the Arctic admiral keeping time to the music with both feet
and hands, and at the conclusion of a piece, uttering a few words of
approbation," wrote George M'Dougall, a surgeon on one of the ships
of the squadron.

Despite no less than seven ships and a tremendous effort sledging
hundreds of miles of coastline, the search accomplished virtually nothing more than ruling out regions in which not to find Franklin. Discovery of Franklin's 1845–46 wintering site and the graves of three of his
crewmen were the sole findings; no clues to the fate of Franklin or his
ships were unearthed.

When Ross and his men returned home the following October, he brought a rumor from Greenland that Franklin's ships had been wrecked in Lancaster Sound and that all were lost to cold, starvation, or murder by the natives. The rumor was without substance, and although most everyone gave it little credence, oddly, Ross stood by the Inuit guide from whom he had heard it and insisted on its accuracy. His conclusion that Franklin was dead infuriated Lady Franklin, who feared that it might bring rescue efforts to a halt. She said that if her name were not already printed on the list of sponsors of Ross's expedition, she would have asked the printer to add after her name, "with a deep sense of gratitude to Sir John Ross for murdering her husband." She need not have worried; the Admiralty launched a five-ship search mission the following year, although it, too, proved fruitless.

During his absence, the Admiralty had promoted Ross to the rank of Rear Admiral. He remained active as a consultant to the government and was valued as the only officer who could speak both Swedish and Danish—an important asset, as war with Russia loomed on the horizon.

In the ensuing years, he busied himself with his writing, which included a tract titled *On Temperance in the Royal Navy* and a book that expressed his opinion regarding the failings of the missions in search of Franklin. Still disunited from his nephew, Ross criticized the ships James Ross had used in his campaign to rescue Franklin as too large and with too great a draft—a pointless criticism in that James Ross, like everyone else, was looking for Franklin in the wrong place, but this was unknown at the time of Ross's critique. Even so, John Ross's criticism had some merit; the ship that carried the crew who eventually discovered Franklin's fate was a small steam yacht with a shallow draft that allowed it to successfully navigate the narrow, ice- and rock-strewn Arctic channels.

Ross spent his final years at his beloved North West Castle with occasional commutes to London to participate in meetings of the Astronomical, Geological, and Meteorological societies. It was for one of these meetings that he traveled to London in August 1856. The rail trip left him exhausted, and he was unable to attend the gathering. On August 30, 1856, five days after his arrival in London, Rear Admiral Sir John Ross, worn out by seventy years of naval service, died at the age of seventy-nine.

James Ross was the first to be notified of Ross's death and, despite their estrangement, it was he who arranged for his uncle's funeral. A large assembly of shipmates, admirals, captains of the Royal Navy, and old friends, including John Ross's brother-in-law Thomas Rymer Jones, attended the burial at London's Kensal Green Cemetery. His body rests in company with such greats as Trollope, Thackeray, and Wilkie Collins.

Ross's will, drafted in 1847, had provided that his estate pass to his wife for the remainder of her life and then to his son, Andrew. The estate was small, however, and North West Castle was soon sold. The fate and fortunes of Lady Mary Ross remain a mystery. Today, North West Castle is one of Scotland's four-star hotels. The room that Ross built to replicate his cabin on the *Victory* is called "The Ross Bar" and commands a captivating view of Loch Ryan below.

In the aftermath of his voyage to Boothia Peninsula, James Ross's career as an explorer and scientific investigator soared. In 1834, he was selected to lead an expedition to make a magnetical survey of the British Isles, but a call to aid eleven whalers trapped by the ice in Davis Strait interrupted the survey. Ironically, the crew of the *Isabella*, which was lost to the crushing ice, was among the six hundred stranded men. Most of the whalers escaped unaided so, instead of commanding a rescue mission, James Ross turned his attention to set up a hospital at Stromness, Orkney Islands, for the half-frozen and scurvy-ridden survivors. Curiously, Ross turned down the knighthood he was offered for his humanitarian work.

If James Ross were not already famous enough through the voyage of the *Victory*, developments occurred in 1837 that would forever establish him as one of the greatest scientific navigators. In that year, plans were underway to send an expedition to the Antarctic to make another series of magnetical observations. Although it was not known at that time that a continent exists at the South Pole—only a scattering of islands had been spotted—the location of the South Magnetic Pole had been predicted, and finding its exact location was an important goal. Naturally, Barrow's choice for the man to command the expedition was James Ross.

Young Ross set sail in 1839 aboard HMS *Erebus* accompanied by HMS *Terror*, two ships that would later achieve notoriety as those of Franklin's lost expedition. Thomas Abernethy, James Ross's good friend and the man who was with him for the discovery of the North Magnetic Pole, accompanied him. Ultimately, the voyage lasted four years, but the severe climate and ice conditions prevented their reaching the South Magnetic Pole. Even so, James Ross and his men made considerable discoveries. The two ships circumnavigated Antarctica and proved that it was a continent and, among other achievements, discovered both the Ross Sea and the Ross Ice Shelf, and established the record for reaching the farthest south, which would stand for fifty years. When he returned home in the spring of 1843, James Ross was again offered knighthood, which this time he accepted.

Although the exploratory and scientific accomplishments were impressive, they did not capture the public interest to the degree that the voyage of the *Victory* had. Still, James Clark Ross had won lasting fame.

Ironically, he named a range of mountains that did not exist—just like his uncle's Croker's Mountains. The tricky, frigid polar atmosphere had created another mirage, and James Ross's "Parry Mountains" were later found to be merely a series of rolling hills on a few low-lying islands. Fortunately for the younger Ross, the error was of no real significance, and he did not have to undergo Barrow's caustic ridicule.

James Ross had one more voyage to make before his polar exploits were over. By 1848, with still no word from John Franklin, a worried Admiralty at last commissioned an expedition to look for the missing Franklin and gave James Ross command of one of the ships. The search vessels sailed to Lancaster Sound, overwintered, and dispatched land parties to fan out over the region. One of the parties even reached Fury Beach and noted that the *Fury's* remaining provisions were still largely intact. The mission failed, however, in its quest for Franklin and returned to England in 1849 having accomplished nothing.

By this time, although James Ross was but forty-nine years old, he was an old forty-nine and was exhausted and mentally drained. Nevertheless, he continued his magnetical work, but spent much of his time at home and never again returned to sea. In 1856, the Royal Navy honored him with promotion to the rank of Rear Admiral.

When his wife, Anne, died of pneumonia in 1857 at the age of forty, James Ross was crushed. By his own description, he lived as a near recluse from that point onward and is said to have begun drinking heavily. A heartbroken and worn-out man, Rear Admiral Sir James Clark Ross died in April 1862, two weeks short of his sixty-second birthday. He was buried beside his wife in Aston Abbotts, Buckinghamshire.

## The Officers and Crew of the *Victory*

*William Thom, Purser*

Before sailing with Ross on the *Victory*, William Thom was purser to HMS *Isabella* on Ross's Arctic voyage of 1818. Upon arriving home after that notorious voyage, Thom wrote a letter to Ross in which he asserted that the *Isabella*'s officers, with few exceptions, had agreed among themselves that Lancaster Sound was *not* an opening to the Northwest Passage. This letter no doubt helped cement the friendship between the purser and his captain, and Ross eagerly sought Thom's service aboard the *Victory*. Like Commander James Ross, Thom volunteered to serve aboard the *Victory* without pay. Upon his return home, he was appointed to the "lucrative situation of purser," according to Ross, aboard HMS *Canopus*, an eighty-four-gun ship of the line.

*George MacDiarmid, Ship's Surgeon*

With receipt of his back pay of more than £818, MacDiarmid was the highest-paid officer on the *Victory* in that both James Ross and William Thom served without pay. MacDiarmid's role in the extraordinary survival rate of the crew no doubt led to his appointment to the rank of full Surgeon in the Royal Navy.

*Thomas Blanky, First Mate*

The Lords Commissioners of the Admiralty approved £349 9s 4d back pay for Blanky for his efforts on the voyage of the *Victory*. His sailing skills, his presence of mind, and his decision-making repeatedly impressed John Ross throughout the voyage. Even though Blanky was the spokesman for the crew's discontent during the struggle back to Fury Beach, Ross admired the man and overlooked the act of insubordination, as Ross put it, and gave the first mate a strong recommendation to his friend and M.P., the Honorable A. Chapman. Chapman owned a fleet of merchant ships and appointed Blanky mate, which led to his obtaining full command of a vessel. However, Blanky yearned to return to the Arctic. In 1845, he signed on as ice master of HMS *Terror,* one of the two ships of Franklin's ill-fated expedition. Tragically, along with Franklin and 127 others, Thomas Blanky perished in the Arctic.

### Thomas Abernethy, Second Mate

Abernethy received slightly over £329 for his participation on the *Victory*. Ross thought highly of Abernethy and described him as "the most steady and active, as well as the most powerful man in the ship." With Ross's recommendation, Thomas Abernethy was appointed gunner of HMS *Seringapatam*. Yet, like Blanky, he could not stay away from the polar regions. As already mentioned, he joined James Ross's expedition to the Antarctic as gunner aboard HMS *Erebus*. In 1848, he returned to the Arctic as ice master with James Ross on HMS *Enterprise* to search for Franklin. After completing the *Enterprise* voyage, he still had not had his fill of the Arctic and returned two more times to look for Franklin: in 1850 as ice master on John Ross's *Felix* and in 1852 aboard the *Isabel,* a search expedition privately financed by Lady Franklin. None of these expeditions located the missing Franklin.

Much to Ross's surprise and displeasure, Abernethy was repeatedly drunk aboard the *Felix*. When they returned home, Ross said, "We parted good friends at last. Abernethy and the Mate Mr. Sivewright 'shewed their teeth' but were soon obliged to 'shut their mouths.' "

*George Taylor, Third Mate*

Before his jaunt with the *Victory,* Third Mate George Taylor had completed a five-year apprenticeship in the trade of a ship carpenter. After the voyage, Ross located him a carpenter's position in the navy dockyard. Nevertheless, Taylor, who had lost much of his foot to frostbite, declined the favor and returned to his family in Liverpool. His back pay amounted to almost £330.

*Alexander Brunton, First Engineer*

Alexander Brunton worked hard aboard *Victory* up until the total failure of the steam engine. From that moment onward, Ross put the "excellent but very slow workman" to work at making tin pots, which, taking his wage into consideration, cost £1 apiece, noted Captain Ross with sarcasm. When he arrived home, Brunton had the gall to sign a petition (along with Light, Shreeve, and Macinnes) for payment of lost clothing even though Booth had supplied the clothes free of charge. His petition failed. He married a widow and used his back pay to open a pub called the Crown and Cushion.

*Allan Macinnes, Second Engineer*

Macinnes, left with little to do after the steam engine was dismantled, used his skills earned in former days as an apprentice baker to keep his mates well supplied at Fury Beach with steaming, baked bread. Ross, who had put in a good word for a position for the engineer when they returned home, was taken aback by Macinnes's ingratitude in filing the petition with Brunton, Light, and Shreeve. Ultimately, Macinnes sought Ross's forgiveness, which the captain granted.

*Robert Shreeve, Carpenter's Mate*

Shreeve met Ross while he was employed doing odd jobs with the firm of Braithwaite and Ericsson. Although he had never been to sea before, he signed on with the *Victory* but was soon overwhelmed with the strenuous duties. Ross liked him, nonetheless, and considered him "a useful person" but "not well calculated for such service." Upon their return to England, Ross sought a position in the navy for Shreeve, but the twenty-eight-year-old Shreeve declined the offer and instead used his earnings of £166 9s 4d to set himself up as a carpenter and undertaker.

*William Light, Steward*

It is hardly necessary to say that Ross made no effort to find William Light employment upon their return to England. Ross considered Light as "decidedly the most useless person in the ship, as well as the most discontented . . . and I was compelled, conscientiously, to except him from my recommendation of the crew to Government for future employment."

Light squealed in his published account that he was owed additional pay for the "extra" duty of washing and mending. He was paid, however, according to the same schedule as the others and received £172 14s 8d.

In his published narrative, Light championed James Ross as the savior of the expedition and a great friend of the crew. His contrasting Commander Ross with his uncle, however, has every indication of a ploy for his attacks on the captain. Indeed, Light's contempt for the younger Ross was exposed when he scoffed at James Ross's discovery of the North Magnetic Pole, which he called a sham that most likely never took place. Apparently, any level of authority was fair game for

Light's vituperation—even Royalty, for whom "twenty-one charges of gunpowder had been wasted" at Felix Harbor to celebrate the king's birthday.

As mentioned above, Light conspired with Shreeve, Brunton, and Macinnes to petition the Admiralty for more money to cover lost clothing. The Admiralty, however, was satisfied with Captain Ross's assertion that payment enough had been made and dismissed the appeal.

After his arrival in England, Light reported via his book with Huish that, "Through the interest of Commander Ross, Mr. Light obtained a situation near Leamington, in Hampshire." James Ross did not acknowledge such, and Light did not disclose the nature of the supposed position. He soon dropped into obscurity.

*Henry Eyre, Cook*

Next to Captain Ross, Henry Eyre, born in 1779, was the eldest man on the voyage. The voyage took its toll on Eyre and, although he was sickly and weak upon his arrival home, he nonetheless established a pub, which he named The North Pole. Unfortunately, he was robbed of his earnings shortly after the pub opened and, unable to pay his bills, the establishment closed. Tired and broke, Eyre fell to drinking and soon succumbed to intoxication. His pallbearers were his former crewmates from the *Victory*, who also took up a collection to buy a small monument for the likable old cook.

*Richard Wall, Harpooner*

Richard Wall, born in North Shields, an important seaport on the River Tyne, was the son of a career sailor. He had been at sea since his childhood and, to Ross, he was one of the best aboard the *Victory*. His experience and hard work earned him £171 16s. Ross was pleased to note that the harpooner obtained a "good situation in his Majesty's Dockyard at Deptford."

### Joseph Curtis, Harpooner

We remember the handsome harpooner for having been the catalyst that nearly upset a whaleboat when an affectionate Inuk maiden, thrilled to see him again, scrambled across the thwarts to *kunik* him. Although only thirty years old when he returned home with *Victory*'s crew, Curtis by then had twenty years of service at sea, and Ross gave him a strong recommendation to enroll aboard HMS *Excellent*, His Majesty's gunnery training establishment at Portsmouth.

### Anthony Buck, Able Seaman

As an able seaman, Buck's share of the Admiralty's largesse was £127 9s. He, too, appealed to the Admiralty for more money, but received none. The epileptic sufferer partially regained his eyesight after returning to England, but otherwise Ross heard no more of him.

### John Park, Able Seaman

Park, whose facetious remark that the excitement at the Battle of Navarino was nothing compared to that of shaving the Duke of Devonshire in a gale, was a "good seaman" who always "conducted himself well," and Ross gave him a strong recommendation, like his shipmate Joseph Curtis, which enabled him to enroll aboard HMS *Excellent* for gunnery training.

### David Wood, Able Seaman

David Wood, who was the first to spot a rescue ship in Lancaster Sound, was one of three crewmen from the *John* who had joined the *Victory* following the mutiny. He defied the mutineers "in a very handsome manner," remarked Ross. Ross's ubiquitous measuring tape tells us that Wood was barely five feet two inches tall. He was blue-eyed with a fair and freckled complexion. After his cruise with the *Victory*, Seaman Wood headed back to his native Midlothian, the county of Edinburgh, and Ross lost track of him.

### John Wood, Able Seaman

John Wood, no relation to David, was also from the Edinburgh region: Fifeshire. Early on in the voyage, Wood broke his leg in a jump from the stern of *Victory* to the launch, which was under tow. As a consequence, Wood was somewhat inactive throughout the voyage. He was gravely ill with scurvy at Fury Beach but fully recovered, and Ross wrote that, "he retired, after receiving his wages, for which he had done so little, to his friends in the North."

### Barnard Laughy, Stoker and Ordinary Seaman

Laughy recovered from the loss of his fingertips to frostbite. Ross wrote that, although Laughy's constitution was "not calculated for such a voyage, and he was one of those who generally gave out soonest. His conduct was, nevertheless, good; and I procured him a situation in the Coast-guard, which was very acceptable to him, as he managed to lose the whole of his money before he got the length of his father's house." In that Laughy had never been to sea before the voyage, his inexperience brought him the lowest pay at £121 15s.

*George Baxter, Stoker and Ordinary Seaman*

George Baxter receives no mention in this volume simply because Captain Ross never mentioned him in his narrative other than to say that the sailor was ill one day. Like Shreeve and Dixon, Baxter was originally with the *John* and joined *Victory* after the mutiny. He had never before been at sea, but despite the green hand's inexperience, Ross thought well of him and would have been pleased to give him a good recommendation. Four winters in the Arctic were enough for Baxter, however, and he never asked Ross for any help, but instead returned to his friends and family in Scotland.

## THE GEORGE BACK OVERLAND RESCUE MISSION

George Back left England to find Ross in February 1833. He reached his planned staging area deep in the Canadian Arctic that August. The season was too late to do much exploring, so Back spent the winter of 1833–34 holed up in the Arctic with plans to begin the search and rescue in earnest the following spring. Unbeknownst to Back, however, Ross had, of course, already returned to England in October 1833. Word of Ross's miraculous return reached Back in April 1834, just in time to stop him before he recommenced his search. Much to Back's delight, the sponsors of the search expedition directed him to continue exploring with the goal of "completing the coastline of the northeastern extremity of America." As a result of his discoveries, the Back River has been named for him. Severe ice conditions, however, prevented Back from traveling to Ross's farthest westward reach—thus, he, too, failed to complete the Northwest Passage. He returned safely to England in September 1835.

## THE FATE OF SIR JOHN FRANKLIN

After the government conducted a series of unsuccessful expeditions between 1848 and 1854 to find the missing Franklin, interest in launching another government-sponsored search waned. While Parliament debated the issue in early 1857, a frustrated and heartsick Lady Franklin sponsored another expedition out of her own purse. She outfitted a small yacht named the *Fox*, which she placed under the command of Sir Leopold M'Clintock, a well-experienced veteran of one of the government searches. After months of trials, M'Clintock and his men discovered that the ice had crushed and sunk Franklin's ships off King William Island just across James Ross Strait from Boothia Peninsula. The starving and freezing men had tried to drag themselves over the ice to a Hudson's Bay Company outpost hundreds of miles down the Back River, but they never made it. Franklin, at age sixty-one, had died aboard ship a year earlier in June 1847. The cause of his death remains unknown. Thus, thirteen years after the expedition had set sail, Lady Franklin's anguish finally found closure.

## THE INUIT OF BOOTHIA PENINSULA

Very little is known of the natives of Boothia Peninsula after Ross and company departed in the summer of 1831. The first paltry news came sixteen years later when Dr. John Rae, an employee of the Hudson's Bay Company, was on an extensive overland search for the lost Sir John Franklin. Rae encountered a group of Inuit who personally knew

Ikmallik, Ooblooria, and Tulluahiu. They told Rae that the Hydrographer and his son were both alive and well at the time. Tulluahiu, on the other hand, had died (he would have been about sixty years old if still alive) but, sadly, Rae was unable to learn the cause of the one-legged man's death or how long ago he had died.

The next encounter was in 1869, twenty-one years later. Charles Francis Hall, an eccentric American explorer of the Arctic, was also searching the region for Franklin relics when he came across Poyettak, Commander Ross's former guide. Poyettak, by then nearly seventy years old, told Hall that years ago he had found an awning-covered boat that contained the remains of more than thirty men along with a number of European items, including a keg of gunpowder. Unaware of the danger, Poyettak's young son blew up their igloo while playing with the gunpowder. Fortunately, no one was killed, but the explosion destroyed the igloo and severely burned the faces of the boy and his playmate. Poyettak provided Hall with valuable information that added considerable insight into the ultimate fate of Franklin's crew.

Today, Boothia Peninsula is part of the Kitikmeot Region of the Canadian territory of Nunavut. Nunavut was formed in 1999 as a self-governed Inuit territory from parts of Canada's Northwest Territories and the Canadian Arctic archipelago, which includes Baffin Island, Ellesmere Island, the islands of Hudson Bay, Queen Elizabeth Islands, and adjoining regions. The present-day community of Taloyoak, located on the western side of the isthmus of Boothia Peninsula, is about sixty miles southwest of Ross's Felix Harbor and is the closest settlement to where the *Victory* harbored. Both Rosses visited the location of Taloyoak, which they had marked on their chart as Spence Bay. The 1996 census lists the population of this northernmost community of the Canadian mainland as 639 persons of which 92 percent are Inuit.

## THE NORTHWEST PASSAGE

During its investigation into whether Ross should be compensated for his losses with the *Victory*, the select Parliamentary committee asked Captain Ross, "Do you conceive that any further attempt to discover the North-West Passage would be attended with great danger?"

"I do," answered Ross.

"And if successful, would it be attended with any public benefit?"

"I believe it would be utterly useless."

Ross was correct on both accounts. The tragedy of Franklin and his 128 men and officers grimly testifies to the veracity of his answers. Indeed, no ship sailed through the passage until Roald Amundsen completed it in the *Gjöa* in 1903–05; and at that, it took Amundsen two years of uncertain and dangerous labor.

Although various small ships and boats have made the passage since Amundsen, the utility of the Northwest Passage is nil. When great reserves of oil were discovered in Alaska in the late 1960s, the Esso Corporation conducted an experiment to determine the practicality of shipping the oil via tankers through the Northwest Passage. The company commissioned the *Manhattan*, a specially strengthened 155,000-ton supertanker more than 1,000 feet in length, for the voyage. In August 1969, she set out from the Delaware River and headed north toward Baffin Bay, where she picked up the assistance of aerial reconnaissance and two icebreakers. She steamed down Lancaster Sound with her escorts and high hopes of traversing the Northwest Passage.

Yet, despite 155,000 tons of ship and 43,000 horsepower, mountains of buckled ice, up to fourteen feet thick, damaged the *Manhattan's* hull and repeatedly brought the ship to a dead stop. Although she eventually made Prudhoe Bay, the ice prevented her completing the passage to the Pacific.

The *Manhattan* suffered such extensive damage en route to Prudhoe Bay and back (with a symbolic barrel of crude oil) that it showed beyond doubt the peril of the passage and directly led to building the Alaskan pipeline. One hundred and seventy years after the voyage of the *Victory*, the commercial practicality of the Northwest Passage remains precisely as Captain John Ross had claimed: "utterly useless."

# Select Bibliography

## (a list of sources consulted)

PERIODICALS

*Blackwood's Edinburgh Magazine*. Vol. 4, December 1818, pp. 338–344.

*Edinburgh Review*. Vol. 31, Art. V. March 1819, pp. 336–368.

*Edinburgh Review*. Vol. 61, Art. VII. March 1835, pp. 417–453.

*Fraser's Magazine for Town and Country*. Vol. IX, No. XLIX, January 1834, pp. 64–65.

*Quarterly Review*. Vol. 21, Art. XI, January 1819, pp. 213–262.

*Quarterly Review*. Vol. 30, Art. XI, October 1823, pp. 231–272.

*Quarterly Review*. Vol. 34, Art. III, September 1826, pp. 378–399.

*Quarterly Review*. Vol. 54, Art. I, July 1835, pp. 1–39.

*Times*. 10 April 1819. "Northern Voyage of Discovery."

*Times*. 21 October 1833. "Captain Ross's Arctic Expedition: Arrival of Captain Ross."

*Times.* 22 October 1833. "Captain Ross's Arctic Expedition."

*Times.* 17 March 1834. "Captain Ross's Diorama of his Interview with the Natives in Felix Harbour."

*Times.* 18 March 1834. "Parliamentary Intelligence: Captain Ross."

*Times.* 31 May 1834. "Vauxhall Gardens."

*Times.* 13 May 1835. "Sir John Ross's Narrative of His Arctic Expedition."


BOOKS

Back, George. *Narrative of the Arctic Land Expedition to the Mouth of the Great Fish River, and Along the Shores of the Arctic Ocean, in the Years 1833, 1834, and 1835.* London: John Murray, 1836.

Barrow, John. *A Chronological History of Voyages into the Arctic Regions; Undertaken Chiefly for the Purpose of Discovering a North-East, North-West, or Polar Passage Between the Atlantic and Pacific: From the Earliest Periods of Scandinavian Navigation, to the Departure of the Recent Expeditions, Under the Orders of Captains Ross and Buchan.* London: John Murray, 1818.

Barrow, John. *Voyages of Discovery and Research within the Arctic Regions, from the Year 1818 to the Present Time: Under the Command of the Several Naval Officers Employed by Sea and Land in Search of a North-West Passage from the Atlantic to the Pacific; with Two Attempts to Reach the North Pole.* London: John Murray, 1846.

Bauer, Bruce. *The Sextant Handbook: Adjustment, Repair, Use and History.* Camden: International Marine, 1992.

Beechey, Frederick W. *A Voyage of Discovery Towards the North Pole, Performed in His Majesty's Ships* Dorothea *and* Trent *Under Command of Captain Buchan R.N., 1818.* London: Richard Bentley, 1843.

Berton, Pierre. *The Arctic Grail. The Quest for the North West Passage and the North Pole, 1818–1909.* Toronto: McClelland and Stewart, 1988.

Biddlecombe, Capt. George. *The Art of Rigging Containing an Explanation of Terms and Phrases and the Progressive Method of Rigging Expressly Adapted for Sailing Ships.* Reprint. New York: Dover Publications, 1990.

Bockstoce, John. *Arctic Passages: A Unique Small-Boat Voyage in the Great Northern Waterway.* New York: Hearst Marine Books, 1991.

Bone, David W. *Capstan Bars.* New York: Harcourt, Brace and Company, 1932.

Braithwaite, John. *Supplement to Captain Sir John Ross's Narrative of a Second Voyage in the* Victory *in Search of a North-West Passage.* London: Chapman & Hall, 1835.

Cyriax, Richard J. *Sir John Franklin's Last Arctic Expedition. The Franklin Expedition, A Chapter in the History of the Royal Navy.* Facsimile Edition. Plaistow and Sutton Coldfield: Arctic Press, 1997.

Dodge, Ernest S. *The Polar Rosses. John and James Clark Ross and Their Explorations.* London: Faber and Faber, 1973.

Donnet, J. L. James. *Arctic Miscellanies: A Souvenir of the Late Polar Search by the Officers and Seamen of the Expedition.* Second edition. London: Colburn and Co., 1852.

Egede, Hans. *Description of Greenland. Shewing the Natural History, Situation, Boundaries and Face of the Country . . . Etc.* London: C. Hitch, 1745.

Fisher, Alexander. *Journal of a Voyage of Discovery, to the Arctic Regions, Performed Between the 4th of April and the 18th of November, 1818, in His Majesty's Ship Alexander.* London: Richard Phillips, n.d. (1819).

Fleming, Fergus. *Barrow's Boys.* New York: Atlantic Monthly Press, 1998.

Franklin, John. *Narrative of a Journey to the Shores of the Polar Sea, in the Years 1819, 20, 21, and 22.* London: John Murray, 1823.

Huish, Robert. *The Last Voyage of Capt. Sir John Ross, Knt. R. N. to the Arctic Regions; for the Discovery of a North West Passage; Performed in the Years*

*1829–30–31–32 and 33 . . . Transmitted by an Officer Attached to the Last Expedition.* London: John Saunders, 1835.

Johnson, Donald S. *Phantom Islands of the Atlantic: The Legends of Seven Lands That Never Were.* New York: Walker and Company, 1994.

Kane, Elisha Kent. *The U.S. Grinnell Expedition in Search of Sir John Franklin. A Personal Narrative.* New York: Harper & Brothers, 1854.

Kemp, Peter. *The Oxford Companion to Ships and the Sea.* Oxford: Oxford University Press, 1993.

Leslie, Sir John, Robert Jameson, and Hugh Murray. *Narrative of Discovery and Adventure in the Polar Seas and Regions: With Illustrations of their Climate, Geology, and Natural History; and an Account of the Whale Fishery.* Edinburgh: Oliver and Boyd, 1835.

Lloyd, Christopher. *Mr. Barrow of the Admiralty. A Life of Sir John Barrow, 1765–1848.* London: Collins, 1970.

Lyon, George F. *The Private Journal of Captain G. F. Lyon, of HMS* Hecla, *During the Recent Voyage of Discovery Under Captain Parry.* London: John Murray, 1824.

M'Clintock, F. L. *The Voyage of the 'Fox' in the Arctic Seas. A Narrative of the Discovery of the Fate of Sir John Franklin and His Companions.* London: John Murray, 1859.

Middleton, W. E. Knowles. *Invention of the Meteorological Instruments.* Baltimore: Johns Hopkins Press, 1969.

Mirsky, Jeannette. *To the North! The Story of Arctic Exploration from Earliest Times to the Present.* New York: Viking Press, 1934.

Nourse, Prof. J. E. *Narrative of the Second Arctic Expedition made by C. F. Hall.* Washington, D.C.: Government Printing Office, 1879.

Osborn, Sherard. *Stray Leaves from an Arctic Journal.* London: Longman, Brown, Green, and Longmans, 1852.

Parry, Ann. *Parry of the Arctic: The Life Story of Admiral Sir Edward Parry, 1790–1855.* London: Chatto and Windus, 1963.

Parry, William Edward. *Journal of a Voyage for the Discovery of a North-West Passage from the Atlantic to the Pacific; Performed in the Years 1819–20, in His Majesty's Ships* Hecla *and* Griper. London: John Murray, 1821.

Parry, William Edward. *Journal of a Third Voyage for the Discovery of a North-West Passage from the Atlantic to the Pacific; Performed in the Years 1824–25, In His Majesty's Ships* Hecla *and* Fury. London: John Murray, 1826.

Pielou, E. C. *A Naturalist's Guide to the Arctic.* Chicago: University of Chicago Press, 1994.

Porter, Roy. *London: A Social History.* Cambridge: Harvard University Press, 1994.

Rae, John. *Narrative of an Expedition to the Shores of the Arctic Sea in 1846 and 1847.* Facsimile Edition. Toronto: Canadiana House, 1970.

Ross, John. *A Voyage of Discovery, Made Under the Orders of the Admiralty, in His Majesty's Ships* Isabella *and* Alexander, *for the Purpose of Exploring Baffin's Bay, and Inquiring into the Probability of a North-West Passage.* London: John Murray, 1819.

Ross, John. *Narrative of a Second Voyage in Search of a North-West Passage, and of a Residence in the Arctic Regions During the Years 1829, 1830, 1831, 1832, 1833 . . . Including the Reports of Commander, Now Captain, James Clark Ross . . . and the Discovery of the Northern Magnetic Pole.* London: A. W. Webster, 1835.

Ross, John. *Appendix to the Narrative of a Second Voyage in Search of a North-West Passage, and of a Residence in the Arctic Regions During the Years 1829, 1830, 1831, 1832, 1833.* London: A. W. Webster, 1835.

Ross, John. *Explanation and Answer to Mr. John Braithwaite's Supplement to Captain John Ross's Narrative of a Second Voyage in the* Victory, *in Search of a North-West Passage.* London: A. W. Webster, 1835.

Ross, John. *Observations on a Work, Entitled, "Voyages of Discovery and Research Within the Arctic Regions," by Sir John Barrow, Bart. Being a Refutation of the*

*Numerous Misrepresentations Contained in the Volume.* London: William Blackwood and Sons, 1846.

Ross, M. J. *Polar Pioneers. John Ross and James Clark Ross.* Montreal: McGill-Queen's University Press, 1994.

Savage, Candace. *Aurora: The Mysterious Northern Lights.* San Francisco: Sierra Club Books, 1994.

Savours, Ann. *The Search for the North West Passage.* New York: St. Martin's Press, 1999.

Scoresby Jun., William. *An Account of the Arctic Regions, with a History and Description of the Northern Whale-Fishery.* Edinburgh: Archibald Constable and Co., 1820.

Sobel, Dava. *Longitude: The Story of a Lone Genius Who Solved the Greatest Problem of His Time.* New York: Walker and Company, 1995.

Stamp, Tom, and Cordelia Stamp. *William Scoresby: Arctic Scientist.* Whitby: Caedmon of Whitby Press, 1975.

Sutherland, Peter C. *Journal of a Voyage in Baffin's Bay and Barrow Straits, in the Years 1850–1851, Performed by H.M. Ships "Lady Franklin" and "Sophia."* London: Longman, Brown, Green, and Longmans, 1852.

Traill, Henry Duff. *The Life of Sir John Franklin, R. N.* London: John Murray, 1896.

Whall, W. B. *Ships, Sea Songs and Shanties.* Glasgow: James Brown and Son, 1910.

Woodward, Frances J. *Portrait of Jane: A Life of Lady Franklin.* London: Hodder & Stoughton, 1951.

# Index

# Index

# Index

# Index